Caetana Says No

Here are the true and dramatic stories of two nineteenth-century Brazilian women – one young and born a slave, the other old and from an illustrious planter family – and how each in her own way sought to have her way: The slave woman struggled to avoid an unwanted husband; the woman of privilege assumed a patriarch's role to endow a family of her former slaves with the means for a free life. But these women's stories cannot be told without also recalling how their decisions drew them ever more firmly into the orbits of the worldly and influential men who exercised power in their lives. These are stories with a twist: In this society of radically skewed power, Lauderdale Graham reveals that more choices existed for all sides than we first imagine. Through these small histories she casts new light on larger meanings of slave and free, female and male.

Sandra Lauderdale Graham has taught at LaTrobe University in Melbourne, Australia; at Mount Holyoke College; at the University of Texas at Austin; and as a Visiting Professor at the University of New Mexico. She is the author of *House and Street: The Domestic World of Servants and Masters in Nineteenth-Century Rio de Janeiro* and won the Conference on Latin American History Prize for an article on slave prostitutes in 1992. She now lives and writes in Santa Fe, New Mexico.

New Approaches to the Americas

Edited by Stuart Schwartz, *Yale University*

For Richard

and for the ones who come next

Marina
Thomas
Cole
Miles
Annie
June
Marshall

CAETANA SAYS NO

WOMEN'S STORIES FROM A
BRAZILIAN SLAVE SOCIETY

SANDRA LAUDERDALE GRAHAM

CAMBRIDGE
UNIVERSITY PRESS

CAMBRIDGE UNIVERSITY PRESS
Cambridge, New York, Melbourne, Madrid, Cape Town, Singapore, São Paulo, Delhi

Cambridge University Press
32 Avenue of the Americas, New York, NY 10013-2473, USA

www.cambridge.org
Information on this title: www.cambridge.org/9780521815321

First published 2002
Reprinted 2005, 2006, 2007

Printed in the United States of America

A catalog record for this publication is available from the British Library.

Library of Congress Cataloging in Publication Data

ISBN 978-0-521-81532-1 hardback
ISBN 978-0-521-89353-4 paperback

Contents

Maps, Illustrations, Charts, and Tables

TABLES

Abbreviations Used in
the Footnotes

ACM-BA	Arquivo da Cúria Metropoliana, Salvador, Bahia
AESP	Arquivo do Estado de São Paulo, São Paulo
AF-PSP	Arquivo do Forum, Paraibuna, São Paulo
AIHGB	Arquivo do Instituto Histórico e Geográfico Brasileiro
Almanak Laemmert	Almanak administrativo, mercantil e industrial da corte e provincia do Rio de Janeiro
ANRJ	Arquivo Nacional, Rio de Janeiro
APEB	Arquivo Público do Estado da Bahia, Salvador
BNRJ-SM	Biblioteca Nacional, Rio de Janeiro, Seção de Manuscritos
CDH-USS	Centro de Documentação Histórica, Universidade Severino Sombra, Vassouras
Codigo Philippino, 1870	Codigo Philippino; ou Ordenações e leis do reino de Portugal, recopilados por mandado d'el-rey D. Philippe I. 14 ed. segundo a primeira de 1603 e a nona de Coimbra de 1824. Addicionada com diversas notas ..., Candido Mendes de Almeida, comp. and ed.
Constituições primeiras, 1853	Constituições primeiras do Arcebispado da Bahia. Feitas e ordenadas pelo ... 5° Arcebispo do dito Arcebispado do Conselho de Sua Magestade: Propostas e aceitas em o synodo diocesano que o dito Senhor celebrou em 12 de junho do anno de 1707. Impressas em Lisboa no anno de 1719 e em Coimbra em 1720 ..., Sebastião Monteiro da, Vide, comp.
FW	Família Werneck

HAHR	*Hispanic American Historical Review*
Leis do Brasil	*Coleção das Leis do Brasil* (Brasil, Law, statutes, etc.)
Repertório das sesmarias	*Repertório das sesmarias concedidas pelos Capitães Generais da Capitania de São Paulo desde 1721 até 1821* São Paulo (state), Arquivo do Estado de São Paulo
RIHGB	*Revista do Instituto Histórico e Geográfico Brasileiro*
SAP	Seção de Arquivos Particulares, Arquivo Nacional
SJ	Seção Judiciária, Arquivo Público do Estado da Bahia
SM	Seção de Manuscritos, Arquivo do Estado de São Paulo
SPE	Seção do Poder Executivo, Arquivo Nacional
SPJ	Seção do Poder Judiciário, Arquivo Nacional

Note on Brazilian Spelling and Currency

In 1940 the Lisbon Academy of Sciences issued a set of rules to standardize Portuguese spelling; these rules were adopted in 1943 by the Brazilian Academy of Letters. Until that time the spelling of many words varied, especially proper names, and sometimes within a single document, for example, José and Joze. I have followed a convention among scholars of Brazil of using modern spelling in the text, but I have retained the original spelling in citing authors, titles, archival sources, and in quotes.

During the nineteenth century, the Brazilian unit of currency was the *mil-réis*, or 1,000 *réis*, written 1$000. A larger unit was the *conto*, equal to 1,000 mil-réis, or one million réis, and written 1:000$000. For convenience to the reader, I have rendered amounts of money into réis, using commas. In this way, one conto, 300 mil-réis, and 50 réis becomes 1,300,050 réis. During the central period of this book, from roughly 1830 to 1865, the value of 1,000 réis varied from a high in 1835 of 80 U.S. cents to a low of 46 cents in 1830. More often it varied between 51 cents and 58 cents; the average over the period was about 58 cents.

ACKNOWLEDGMENTS

Books have their own histories, and the history of this book goes back a long way. Research in Brazil is unavoidably costly and the time free to write precious; I am grateful for the small and large grants that have moved this book along. At the University of Texas, the History Department, the Institute of Latin American Studies, and the University Research Institute each contributed over a career to the research and writing that are a part of this and other projects. I enjoyed support from a Fulbright-Hays Faculty Research Fellowship for research in Rio de Janeiro and Salvador, and in 1998 and 1999 a fellowship from the American Council of Learned Societies combined with a Faculty Research Assignment from the University of Texas provided for a year of uninterrupted writing.

Work in Brazilian archives continues to be for me a deeply compelling pleasure, made possible by the day-to-day assistance of highly professional and congenial staffs. In Salvador, I especially thank the staff at the Arquivo Público do Estado da Bahia and their director, Anna Amélia Vieira Nascimento, herself an historian. As archivist for the Santa Casa de Misericórdia in Bahia, Neusa Esteves has expertly guided me through its rich and meticulously kept sources, and provided a breathtaking view of the lower city and the Bay of All Saints. I found Caetana's case at the Arquivo da Cúria on the Praça da Sé in Salvador, where Zenaide Braga Lima watched over its books of parish records and neat stacks of ecclesiastical court hearings and made folders of divorce and annulment cases available. She also brought delicious mangoes from her orchard. At the Instituto Histórico e Geográfico Brasileiro in Rio de Janeiro, years ago I read the 1847 edition of Fransico Peixoto de Lacerda Werneck's *Memória* bound in green leather lettered in gold; since then librarian

Maura Corrêa e Castro has always responded knowledgeably and generously to my many research questions. At the Arquivo Nacional in Rio de Janeiro, Isabel Falcão, Silvia Ninita de Moura Estevão, and Beatriz Moreira Monteiro enabled me to return to Werneck's letters, which I first consulted years ago on the other side of the Praça da República.

This book has taken me as far afield as Santo Antônio de Paraibuna, near the headwaters of the Paraíba River in São Paulo, to the Arquivo do Forum, where, with the kind and interested help of Sidney de Castro Britto, I learned more about Caetana, the family who owned her, and their connections to others in the county. To pursue Inácia and her family, I returned to Vassouras, where in 1975 I worked at the local notary office perched at a tiny table amidst the bundles of old papers, while the notary's daily business went noisily on around me. In the small space my presence made a crowd, which the notary patiently put up with. All that has changed, and historical materials are now catalogued, conserved, and comfortably read at the Centro de Documentação Histórica at the Universidade Severino Sombra in Vassouras, with Carlos Eugênio Libano Soares as director. I thank each of these archivists and librarians.

On precise matters that required special expertise, I consulted with colleagues who unfailingly responded quickly and in detail. I think especially of Hal Langfur, Linda Lewin, Muriel Nazzari, B. J. Barickman, and Hendrik Kraay. In Brazil, Laura de Mello e Souza clarified the meanings of crucial popular religious practices. And for years Alida Metcalf has been both colleague and friend, always willing to share her research and reflections.

I have been lucky in having colleagues willing to take time from their own work to consider mine. For their rigorous and clarifying comments on various drafts of these stories, I thank Jim Sidbury, Kevin Kenny, Eugenia Herbert, Robert Herbert, and members of the Santa Fe Seminar. Curt Schaafsma, besides instructing me about the Southwest, offered his time and the resources of his computer in a last-minute restoration of a photograph. Besides Inga Clendinnen's alert reading of both stories, I am especially grateful to both Inga and John Clendinnen, who at a crucial moment asked hard questions and generated a flurry of messages back and forth across the Pacific.

One of the special moments in preparing this book came when Gabriel and Claudia Fonseca invited Richard and me to visit their lovingly restored Monte Alegre in Pati do Alferes, Werneck's favorite fazenda and the place where he died in 1861. The grandson of Brazilian historian

Octávio Tarqüínio de Souza, Gabriel understood my wish to see the house was not so odd after all.

Over many years, I have thought off and on about the persons, events, and puzzles that make up these stories. This book began with a trip through the Paraíba Valley and to Vassouras in the late 1970s, when I formed a passion to bring the excitement of archival research and sources to undergraduate students. Inácia's will was one of a collection of documents that I gathered and translated, and students at the University of Texas, Mount Holyoke College, and the University of New Mexico used to reconstruct, unaided by historians' finished books, the ambivalent workings of a remote slave society. With other students I rehearsed, and we argued over, both their renderings and mine of Caetana's petition. They have gone on to other pursuits, but I hope some will read what I finally came up with, and find in these pages echoes of the pleasure and stimulation I took from our discussions. Long ago my friend Gilberto Ferrez provided copies of a series of nineteenth-century photographs from his grandfather's collection for my students to consult. I think he knew how much they and I valued what we learned from these documents.

Again, as always, I dedicate this book to Richard Graham, who has been essential in the pleasure of its making.

PROLOGUE

These stories begin with a marriage and a death. They tell of two women, one young and born a slave, the other old and from an illustrious family. By their origins these women mark the tangible extremes of wealth, influence, and power in nineteenth-century Brazilian life and culture. Yet, each in her own way sought to have her way: the slave woman to avoid an unwanted husband; the woman of privilege to endow a family of her former slaves with resources for a free life. Their attempts drew them ever more firmly into the relations of influence exercised by the men who had power in their lives: the planter and owner of the slave woman who ordered her marriage, and her uncle and godfather, a fellow slave; and another planter who managed his elderly aunt's affairs while she lived and who served as executor for her estate after she died. The women's stories cannot be told, then, without including their crucial ties to these worldly and important men. But even by making the stories as complete as possible, they end ambiguously. Or, rather, they have no endings. Whether the slave woman succeeded in living an unmarried life is uncertain, although later I tell you my ideas about that; and how the family of freed slaves ended up remains differently unresolved.

The broad setting is the Paraíba River Valley in southeastern Brazil during the early 1830s into the mid-1860s. From its headwaters in the Serra do Quebra Cangalha, the river at first flows southwest to a pass through the mountains, where it abruptly changes course as it descends into the valley and then continues in a northeasterly direction roughly paralleling the coast for most of its 500 miles. Fed on its northern bank by waters from the Serra da Mantiqueira and on its southern side by waters from the chain of mountains that follow the coast to form the Serra do Mar, the Paraíba empties into the Atlantic Ocean north of Campos. The river widens in the middle stretches of the valley, but despite its plentiful water supply, frequent rapids prevent it from being navigable except near the mouth and then only by small boats that draw little water. Summer rains fall from late spring through early autumn; sunny winter days are dry and the nights cool. Chains of low hills with elevations of between 300 and 1200 feet surround the region.[1]

Beginning in the late eighteenth century and early years of the nineteenth century, men with energy, ambition, and the capital to purchase slaves found these conditions ideal for growing a new crop: coffee. Encouraged by sweeping grants of thickly forested land from a Portuguese crown hungry for colonial profits, they cleared land and planted coffee up and down the Paraíba Valley. They transported their harvests by mule back over primitive roads across the escarpment to small coastal towns and then by boats to the noisy, crowded ports of Santos or Rio de Janeiro.

The coffee region that flanked the Paraíba, stretching from eastern São Paulo province and through the neighboring province of Rio de Janeiro, is the location for the two stories of this book. The central events occurred on two plantations, one in the county of Paraibuna, near the headwaters of the Paraíba, and the other several hundred miles downriver in the middle Paraíba Valley parish of Pati do Alferes. They are distinct stories without connection to each other except in the important sense that they belonged to – and I use them to illuminate – the same general culture, society, and economy. Although the main action of the first story is completed by the time the central events in the second begin, they can be read in either order, and each can stand alone. But I intend them as a contrasting pair to exemplify both the cohesive threads that bound this culture into a recognizable whole and the variations that demonstrated its perennial flexibility.

Neither story is handed down to us complete and neither is told by the women themselves. These are retrieved stories gathered and pieced together from sources originally recorded and stored for very different and particular reasons. The core documents are an ecclesiastical petition for annulment consisting of 200 handwritten pages and a last will and testament of eleven pages. From archives in both towns of Santo Antônio de Paraibuna and Vassouras, as well as from the National Archive and

---

[1] The indispensible geographical description of the greater Paraíba Valley and its tributaries and an assessment of conditions there for cultivating coffee is in C. F. van Delden Laërne, *Brazil and Java: Report on the Coffee-Culture in America, Asia, and Africa* (London: W. H. Allen, 1885), pp. 261–267.

the National Library in Rio de Janeiro, I have drawn on other wills, the post-mortem inventories that contain probate proceedings, a detailed listing of all property, together with records of any disputes ignited by its division, and the telling letters from a planter's copybook. A second tier of surrounding sources deepens and expands the contexts of the original stories: legal codes, both civil and ecclesiastical; a statistical profile of São Paulo province published in the 1830s; household census lists; a twenty-year span of a local directory (what they called an almanac); occasionally published commentary on local events; and one planter's manual of advice to his son on establishing and running a plantation. Correspondence between local government officials, to the provincial president, and finally to the minister of justice in the emperor's cabinet and back down again recorded the urgent responses to a failed slave uprising. Besides consulting contemporary maps and photographs, I have visited both settings on several occasions and, where I could, the plantation houses where the women and men I write so sketchily about once lived real and vivid lives.

There is a strong judicial slant to the principal sources that is both unavoidable and advantageous. Unavoidable because the imprint of Brazilian culture was deeply juridical and because Brazilians bothered to carefully authenticate and record all manner of transactions, while codified law regulated the transfer and disposal of family property and the church spoke firmly on how to become married or unmarried. Even ordinary Brazilians knew the necessity of a notary's seal and the importance of a priest's writings in the parish record books. Court records, each case its own compilation of documents stitched together with heavy thread, have the particular advantage of chronicling disputes that stretched over years and which refer backward in time to prior, precipitating events. So from a sequence of actions (the term for a legal case in Portuguese is *processo*), we glimpse something of the origins and consequences of action. Courts took testimony from relevant witnesses whoever they were – the lowborn and illiterate as well as the rich and influential – who in turn were apt to supply information on the intimate or the mundane that no other source can provide the historian.

Yet for all that such sources allow us to approach the private zones of choice and action that were so securely anchored in public understandings, and lucky as we are to have them, they are by their nature implacably silent on deeper, perplexing questions of motivation. Why Caetana rejected marriage or how she thought she could avoid being a wife did not concern ecclesiastical judges; Werneck did not explain the decisions he took regarding his aunt's former slaves, and no one in our hearing asked. We must content ourselves not with tidily persuasive conclusions, but with the uncertain process of piecing together historically grounded but more ambiguous possibilities, something closer to archaeology than full-blown biography. These are histories writ small about events seen close up, as close up as we are likely to get.

And because they are small and up close, they bring into focus surprising truths about the workings of a society and culture obscured in more encompassing and distanced views. It is not often that we can witness an inexperienced young slave woman oppose her master's order only then to flee her own family, or see an old woman assume a patriarch's role toward a family of slaves and then fail to carry it off. If in their own time and social place they were readily understood people, they nonetheless show us how unusual could be the small-scale relations of gender and slavery. These people and what they did are at once, borrowing Michael Wood's fine phrase, "ordinary and mysterious, mysterious in the way the ordinary often is."[2]

Santa Fe, New Mexico   Sandra Lauderdale Graham
December 2001

---

[2]   Michael Wood, *The Magician's Doubts: Nabokov and the Risks of Fiction* (London: Chatto and Windus, 1994), p. 30.

Map of Brazil

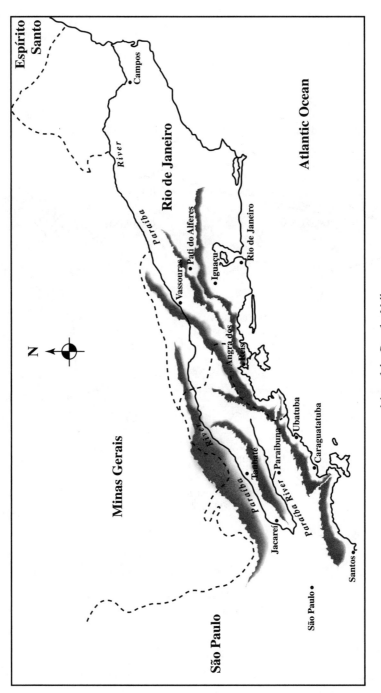

Map of the Paraíba Valley

CAETANA SAYS NO

PATRIARCHY CONFOUNDED

In the weeks preceding the wedding the usual Catholic preparations were made: Papers were signed, fees paid, banns posted. Then on a spring day in October 1835, on the plantation Rio Claro in the Province of São Paulo, a priest, who had journeyed from the nearby village of Santo Antônio de Paraibuna, prepared to celebrate mass in the plantation chapel. The benches arranged, he readied the altar with its candlesticks that stood four hands high, its missal, bell, and chalice, and placed the holy vestments over his own plain black cassock. Two witnesses stood ready, while the groom waited at the chapel door. The young bride, slow to dress in her best, at last presented herself for the ceremony. The mass said and the matrimonial blessing given, the priest left the plantation and returned home to the village.[1]

This pleasant but apparently unremarkable scene discloses a slave wedding, and with this fact it captures our attention. The bride, Caetana, perhaps seventeen years old, and the groom, Custódio, in his mid-twenties, were fellow slaves, or *parceiros*, a term that acknowledged them as companions belonging to a common master, the human property of

---

[1] Vigararia Geral do Bispado de São Paulo, Libello de Nullidade do Matrimônio, defendant, Custodio by his lawyer, São Paulo, 1836, Arquivo da Cúria Metropolitana, Salvador, Bahia (hereafter cited as ACM-BA), Libello de Divórcio e Justificação de Sevícias, 1839–1874, [pasta 8] (hereafter cited as Nullidade, 1836), fls. 11v, 62–62v, 64; Inventário, Captain Luiz Marianno de Tolosa, Santo Antônio de Paraibuna, São Paulo, 1853 (hereafter cited as Inventário, Luiz Marianno Tolosa, 1853), Arquivo do Forum, Paraibuna, São Paulo (hereafter cited as AF-PSP), Pacote 4, fl. 11v. I have retained the original spelling of personal and place names in quoting or citing manuscript sources; otherwise, I use modern spelling.

Captain Luís Mariano de Tolosa, owner of Rio Claro.[2] A slave marriage blessed by the church and made legally binding would seem an unusually gracious ending to a tale of slave love.

Far from it. As Caetana later told her dramatic story – and it remains dramatic even through the retelling by a scribe in the inevitably flattening language of court documents – she felt not only a "great repugnance for the state of matrimony," but she found *this* man particularly distasteful.[3]

It was their master who, one day, without consulting or even warning her, simply told her she was to marry. Despite his "emphatic tone" she summoned her courage to refuse. But in the end she obeyed, against her will and from fear of Tolosa's threats; after all, he was her master and "would do what he wanted." Once married, however, she knew what she must do: She would refuse her husband. This time her determination drew the ire of the other male with visible authority in her life, her uncle and godfather, who threatened to beat her if she did not submit to her husband as a wife should. With few choices left her, late at night Caetana ran from her uncle's house back to Tolosa himself. In her distress she managed finally to persuade him that she would never willingly accept the marriage. Tolosa relented and separated the couple.

And he did more. He launched a petition before an ecclesiastical court to annul the marriage. The legal process began in the distant city of São Paulo, far from the plantation and Caetana's direct experience. She was named as plaintiff, Custódio as the pro forma defendant, and two attorneys were appointed as *curadores*, or legal protectors, to act for them in court, the usual procedure in cases involving persons not regarded as legally adults – minor children, mentally defective persons, and slaves. The court duly noted that Captain Tolosa had given permission for the case to proceed, and by late summer, in February 1836, less than four months after the wedding, Caetana's petition was before the church court.[4]

---

[2]   Ages, especially slave ages, are often uncertain; when census and court records differed, I took the court records as more likely to be accurate; for Caetana's age, see Nullidade, 1836, fl. 46v. See *Diccionario da lingua portugueza*, Antonio de Moraes Silva, comp., 2 vols. (Rio de Janeiro: Editora-Empreza Litteraria Fluminense, 1891), vol. 1, p. 480: "O escravo chamava parceiros a seus companheiros na familia" – i.e., "the slave called his companions in the [master's extended] family *parceiros*."

[3]   Nullidade, 1836, fl. 11.

[4]   Ibid., 1836, fls. 11v, 47v, 24v. Church procedure for hearing such cases was established in Sebastião Monteiro da Vide, *Constituições primeiras do Arcebispado*

Annulment petitions appear infrequently in church records. Among the more than 700 cases housed in Salvador at the Curia Archive and in Rio de Janeiro at the National Archive, including appellate cases sent to the High Court at Bahia from other parts of the empire, most couples who wanted to end their marriages sought a "divorce," that is, separation. Only a scattering of persons asked for annulments, and of those who did, Caetana's is the only slave case I discovered.[5] When they did occur, annulments could be lengthy affairs. Caetana's petition was under consideration for nearly five years, from February 1836 when proceedings were initiated in São Paulo until October 1840 when ecclesiastical judges of the High Court in Bahia, having reviewed the appealed case, confirmed the lower court's decision.

The thick bundle of papers resulting from their ecclesiastical inquiry requires some assessment. What can be learned from legal texts is inviting because they contain drama, conflict, a story. There is exquisite detail supplied by nine witnesses, pages of formal allegations, attorneys' briefs, and judges' opinions recorded over that long time. We are lucky to have Caetana's case, and only because Tolosa relented and went to court do we know about it at all. But it is a retrieved story and the very mode of its recording – according to judicial language and procedure – means that it provides evidence slanted to answer certain questions and not others. We know actions and even sequences of actions, but most often motivations must be inferred. Church lawyers elicited testimony that bore on annulment, while we want to know why a young slave woman fought fiercely against being married. These sources cannot readily or directly reveal the interior life of the woman who engages our

---

da Bahia. *Feitas e ordenadas pelo ... 5° Arcebispo do dito Arcebispado do Conselho de Sua Magestade: Propostas e aceitas em o synodo diocesano que o dito Senhor celebrou em 12 de junho do anno de 1707. Impressas em Lisboa no anno de 1719 e em Coimbra em 1720....* (São Paulo: Typ. "2 de Dezembro," 1853), Liv. 1, Tit. 74, nos. 320–323 (hereafter cited as *Constituições primeiras*, 1853). The authority of the *Constituições primeiras*, 1853 was extended to independent Brazil by Decreto e Resolução, 3 November 1827, and recommended by Aviso, 25 June 1828; quoted in M. J. de Campos Porto, *Repertorio de legislação ecclesiastica desde 1500 até 1874* (Rio de Janeiro: Garnier, 1875), p. 191.

5   The complete name of the city, São Salvador da Bahia de Todos os Santos, or Holy Savior of the Bay of All Saints, is usually shortened to Salvador and used interchangeably with Bahia, which was, confusingly, also the name of the province and now of the state. Arquivo da Cúria Metropolitana, Salvador, Bahia; Arquivo Nacional, Rio de Janeiro, Seção do Poder Judiciário (hereafter cited as ANRJ-SPJ). In Salvador I identified 28 annulment cases, nearly half of which originated in Bahia; the others were appealed from all parts of the empire.

curiosity so many years after her time. Having found the appealed case
at the church archive in Bahia with the original included in its pages,
I returned to Paraibuna and the place where it all began to trace the
surrounding events. By adding local census lists, wills, and the property
inventories prepared for purposes of probate to the annulment record,
I can reconstruct lived contexts, sketch likely scenarios, and suggest
unfamiliar possibilities.

These same sources lead out from the immediate events of Caetana's
story to the multiple contexts in which it was embedded and shed light
on the fuller society of which Rio Claro was so small a part: village life;
conflict among planters; patterns of land ownership, debt, and inheritance; the institutions of civil authority; and church law. Occurrences
of slave marriages, uses of godparenthood, hierarchies of labor, distinctions in living conditions, the precariousness of slave family life and the
stability of it – all these are brought into new relief when viewed through
this slave woman's experience. We are able to consider the dealings of
male reputation and the uses of male authority, both civic and domestic; planter friendship; hoped-for female celibacy; and the rankings of
authority within a slave family.

And further, this remarkable and surely unique legal text enables us
to discover how events in one small realm of slave–master relations,
when seen close up, are instructively revealed to be more complex and
less arbitrary than we suppose. It would be easy to dismiss Tolosa as the
powerful master and Caetana as the helpless slave, but that gloss does
not work. He did order her to marry, and she knew she had to obey; but
she struggled, and he relented. A nearly model household of patriarchal,
slave-owning order became problematic when Caetana said, "No." Because of her the entire hierarchy of males – owner, uncle, husband, and
church – was thrown into turmoil. So it is a story with a twist: a regretful
master, a tough slave family, and an indifferent church. In this society
of radically skewed power, more choices existed for all sides than we first
imagine. Caetana's vision of liberty was not escape from bondage, but
simply an unmarried life. Her struggle was not directed against slavery
in any standard political sense, but was young female resistance against
male authority. It is not what we expect, but it is what happened.

SETTINGS

The settings for Caetana's story – fazenda, town, county – begin with the
property owned in the 1830s by Captain Tolosa and his wife, Dona Ana

Joaquina Moreira de Tolosa. About Tolosa's background we know next to nothing, only that he was a "Brazilian citizen," despite his Spanish-sounding name, and born in Taubaté, while Ana Joaquina was the daughter of the prominent Moreira da Costa family, also of Taubaté, the important regional center on the Paraíba River some ten leagues, or about forty miles, northwest of Paraibuna. Ana Joaquina almost certainly had inherited from her parents' vast lands, lands secured in the eighteenth century as a royal grant from Portugal's ruling sovereign by her father and a kinsman, probably a brother: lands a league across and three leagues deep located between the Paraitinga and Paraibuna Rivers. An inventory of the Tolosas' holdings drawn up in 1834 described a patchwork of lands measured not by a surveyor's coordinates but marked by references to neighbors such as the 424 *braças* of irregularly bounded lands bordering the royal land grant once made to a now-deceased priest, or the half league of land between lands belonging to a Dona Marciana and the widow Dona Maria Custódia. There was no need to record full names; contemporaries would recognize them. References to equally familiar features of the landscape such as "below the winter waterfall" (apparently dry during other seasons) or "beyond the Paraibuna River" located other plots. Another parcel was simply a "quantity of land" half a league deep, another was a "small portion of land where Antônia da Cunha lives." Landholdings were not contiguous, and no single number neatly summarized the area they covered, but knowing that at least four pieces of land each ran half a league or about two miles deep and a fifth measured nearly four miles square, we can say that Rio Claro's lands were extensive, if not vast. Well watered by the Paraibuna River, which in turn flowed into the Paraíba, these lands also included substantial tracts of "wilderness" or virgin forest.[6]

Like most properties in the district, Rio Claro's cultivated lands were devoted principally to coffee. While census reports for 1830 and 1835

[6] São Paulo (state), Arquivo do Estado de São Paulo (hereafter cited as AESP), *Repertório das sesmarias concedidas pelos Capitães Generais da Capitania de São Paulo desde 1721 até 1821* (São Paulo: Tip. do Globo, 1944; rpt., São Paulo: Secretaria de Estado da Cultura, 1994), 67 (hereafter cited as *Repertório das sesmarias*); Inventário, Anna Joaquina Moreira, Santo Antônio de Paraibuna, São Paulo, 1834 (hereafter cited as Inventário, Anna Joaquina Moreira, 1834), AF-PSP, Pacote 7, fls. 2, 15–17v; Land register, Antonio Tertuliano dos Santos, Santo Antônio de Paraibuna, São Paulo, 10 May 1856, Registro no. 241, AESP, Registro de Terras da Província de São Paulo, vol. 43, Paraibuna, 30/6/1854–30/5/1857, fl. 64 (hereafter cited as Registro de Terras, 1856).

indicate that Tolosa also grew substantial amounts of corn, beans, and rice, 1835 figures for exports from the nearest port show that only small amounts of these products (and some tobacco) went to market out- side the region, suggesting that planters used these crops mostly to feed themselves and their slaves, from time to time selling small surpluses locally. And like the many planters who also raised cattle, horses, or pigs, Tolosa slaughtered or sold livestock to others in the county.[7] Coffee, on the other hand, counted as the valued export. First planted in Brazil in 1727 in the Amazon region, coffee did not become commercially signi- ficant until the 1820s, when a handful of soon-powerful families settled the middle Paraíba River Valley and began to ship coffee through the port of Rio de Janeiro. About the same time, coffee appeared upriver in northern São Paulo province and in areas between the river valley and the coast. As early as 1814 a São Paulo official, Manuel da Cunha de Azeredo Souza Chichorro, the man who later appears as Tolosa's friend and Caetana's unsolicited ally, informed the captain-general that the counties of the captaincy "planted much coffee."[8] And the trees flour- ished. In the 1830s, when only one sugar mill owner could be counted among eighty-three big coffee planters and another 267 small-scale farm- ers who raised some coffee and cattle, coffee clearly provided the district's economic fulcrum.[9]

---

[7] Mappa dos Habitantes alistentes desta Segunda e Nova Com[panhi]a da Freguesia de S[anto] Antonio de Paraibuna distrito da Villa de Jacarehei, em apresentes com seus Nomes, Empregos, Naturalidades, Idades, Estados, Cores, Ocupasões, Cazoalidades que aconteserão em cada huma de Suas Respectivas familias desde a fatura da data do anno antesedente, AESP, Seção de Manuscritos (hereafter cited as SM), Maços de População, Jacarei, Santa Branca, Paraibuna, 1830– 1850, Maço 2, Parahybuna, 2ª Companhia, 1830, Caixa 86, Ordem 86, Fogo 89, Luiz Marianno de Toloza (hereafter cited as Mappa dos Habitantes, 1830); 1° Distrito de Santo Antonio pertencente ao Municipio de Parahybuna, 1835, AESP-SM, Maços de População, Jacarehy, Santa Branca, Parahybuna, Maço 2, Caixa 86, Ordem 86, 1830–1850 (hereafter cited as 1° Distrito de Santo Antonio de Parahybuna, 1835); Daniel Pedro Müller, *Ensaio d'um quadro estatístico da província de São Paulo: Ordenado pelas leis provinciais de 11 de abril de 1836 e 10 de março de 1837*, 3rd rpt. ed., intro. Honório de Sylos (São Paulo: Governo do Estado de São Paulo, 1978), pp. 124–129, 231–233.

[8] Affonso d'Escragnolle Taunay, *Pequena história do café no Brasil (1727–1937)* (Rio de Janeiro: Departamento Nacional do Café, 1945), pp. 31–39, 54, 44–45; the quote appears on p. 44.

[9] Müller, *Quadro estatístico*, pp. 241–242, 130; 1° Distrito de Santo Antonio de Parahybuna, 1835; and População da Freguezia de Santo Antônio de Parai- buna, Agosto de 1832, AESP-SM, Maços de População, Jacarehy, Santa Branca,

How rich had coffee made Tolosa? A rough measure of his wealth can be calculated following Daniel Pedro Müller's 1838 estimate that a vigorous coffee bush yielded two pounds of coffee per year. In 1834 approximately 30,000 coffee bushes grew at Rio Claro. Consistent with this estimate, in 1830 Tolosa marketed 2,000 *arrobas*, or about 63,400 pounds of coffee.[10] Tolosa's crop might seem paltry compared with the 1850s, when coffee in the middle Paraíba Valley was at its zenith and a single planter harvested coffee from several hundred thousand bushes, but measured against others at more or less the same time in this part of the valley, Tolosa was a major producer. As one among the county's eighty-three coffee fazendas, Rio Claro nevertheless accounted for nearly one-tenth of all the coffee sold from the county in 1830.[11] About forty years old when Caetana's case began, Tolosa must have begun to grow coffee as a relatively young man, putting him among the first generation of planters to stake their fortunes and their futures on coffee. The gamble paid off. In the 1830s, assuming an annual crop of at least 2,000 arrobas at an average top price of 3,200 *réis* per arroba, Tolosa could anticipate a

Parahybuna, Maço 2, Caixa 86, Ordem 86, 1830–1850 (hereafter cited as População da Freguezia de Santo Antônio de Paraibuna, 1832).

[10] Müller, *Quadro estatístico*, p. 27; Inventário, Anna Joaquina Moreira, 1834, fl. 17. Writing about the middle Paraíba Valley in 1885, C. F. van Delden Laërne, *Brazil and Java: Report on Coffee-Culture in America, Asia, and Africa* (London: W. H. Allen, 1885), pp. 328–329, shows that old trees produced on average less than one pound of coffee annually. Luiz Marianno de Toloza, Mappa dos habitantes, 1830, Fogo 89.

[11] Laërne, *Brazil and Java*, pp. 328–329; Müller, *Quadro estatístico*, pp. 125, 129–130; Taunay, *Pequena história do café*, p. 55; Lista Geral dos Habitantes, e Existentes, na 3ª Comp[anhi]a de Ordenança da Villa de Jacarehy com declaração de Seus Nomes, Empregos, Naturalidades, Idades, Estados, Cores, Ocupações e Cazual-idades que acontecerão em cada huma de Suas Respectivas Familias, desde a factura da Lista antecedente, 1829, Fogo 12, Claudio José Machado (hereafter cited as Lista Geral dos Habitantes, 3ª Companhia, 1829); Anno de 1829, Lista Geral dos Habitantes, e Existentes, na 6ª Comp[anhi]a de Ordenança da Villa de Jacarehy com declaração de Seus Nomes, Empregos, Naturalidades, Idades, Estados, Cores, Ocupações e Cazualidades que acontecerão em cada huma de Suas Respectivas Familias, desde a factura da Lista do anno antecedente, Fogo 1, Custodio Ferreira Braga (hereafter cited as Lista Geral dos Habitantes, 6ª Companhia, 1829); José Lobato de Moura e Silva, ibid., Fogo 23; 1828, Lista dos Habitantes, e Existentes, na 3ª Companhia, de Ordenança da Villa de Jacarehy com declararão de Seus Nomes, Empregos, Naturalidades, Idades, Estados, Cores, Ocupações e Cazualidades que acontecerão em cada huma de Suas Respectivas Familias, desde a factura das Listas [illegible], 1828, Fogo 37, Ignacio Bicudo de Gouveia (hereafter cited as Lista dos Habitantes, 1828).

yearly gross income at Rio Claro of 6,400,000 réis, or the equivalent of about $4,288 calculated in 1830s U.S. dollars, on which he then paid a 5 percent agricultural tax to the province and a 7 percent imperial export tax. It was a substantial income, enough to buy two houses in town or as many as ten prime male slaves. The estate Tolosa and his wife owned jointly had a net value in 1834 of more than 55 million réis, or in 1834 dollars about $43,450.[12] Among his fellow planters Tolosa was a solidly rich man in a prospering economy.

Ownership of Rio Claro is not a simple matter to reconstruct. As the 1834 inventory makes clear, Tolosa and his wife together owned only half the estate's largest parcels of land and half the coffee bushes, as well as half the cattle, mules and mule teams, pigs, sheep, and goats, and therefore half the profits. On the other hand, they owned outright the houses, work sheds for carpentry and blacksmithing, tools, corn cribs, and the mills for grinding corn and sugar – that is, the physical plant. The slaves listed in 1834 numbered somewhat more than half those counted in a census of the entire fazenda in 1830. Assuming that new slaves were bought or born in the intervening four years, their number suggests that Tolosa and Dona Ana Joaquina also owned half the slaves at Rio Claro.[13]

Who, then, was the other half-owner? Tolosa's household in 1830 included two resident priests, the Reverends Valerio de Alvarenga Ferreira and Manuel Inocêncio Muniz Barreto. About Father Manuel we know only that he continued to live at Rio Claro and was a friend to Father Valerio, who mentioned him in his will. Father Valerio, however, was important at Rio Claro as Tolosa's partner and joint owner of the fazenda. The transcript of Caetana's marriage certificate identified Caetana and Custódio as "slaves of the Reverend Valerio de Alvarenga Ferreira and Company," although throughout the pages of the annulment petition Tolosa appears as sole owner of both slaves. Certainly, Tolosa made the decisions. How the two men came to form a partnership is unknown, and

---

[12] Mappa dos habitantes, 1830, Fogo 89, Luiz Marianno de Toloza; Müller, *Quadro estatístico*, pp. 122, 210. I have converted Brazilian currency to U.S. equivalents at the time using Julian Smith Duncan, *Public and Private Operation of Railways in Brazil* (New York: Columbia University Press, 1932), p. 183. See the Note on Spelling and Currency. José Claudio Machado, Lista Geral dos Habitantes, 3ª Companhia, 1829, Fogo 12, in 1829 sold coffee on the Rio de Janeiro market for 3,300 réis per arroba, confirming Müller's estimate; Inventário, Anna Joaquina Moreria, 1834, fls. 11, 15–26v, 33v.

[13] Inventário, Anna Joaquina Moreira, 1834, fls. 15–26v.

no visible family tie connecting Father Valerio to either Tolosa or his wife (he was not a brother and coheir, for example) explains his financial involvement with Rio Claro. Perhaps the priest had backed Tolosa by investing in Rio Claro, or, conversely, perhaps he had the land and Tolosa the capital. In any case, sometime before 1847, when the priest made his will, they had dissolved their partnership, but continued to do business intermittently. The priest referred affectionately to Tolosa as "my good, constant, and loyal friend and partner," and "greatly trusting his integrity," appointed him executor of his estate. By the time the priest died in 1848, his stake in Rio Claro had been reduced to only half a sugarcane field, a quarter portion of some tea-producing land, and half the value of a lean-to and a stucco wall, while he owned substantial holdings in land and coffee and orange trees on three other fazendas, a warehouse, and houses in town. Without children, grandchildren, or living parents to receive his property as the law required, Father Valerio was free to appoint as his heirs the widow Gertrudes Teresa de Jesus (their relationship is never explained, although it likely had more to do with the priest's role as local patron than concubinage), and Tolosa. Tolosa's share was a tract of land at the fazenda Cedro, miles away from Rio Claro, with more than half a mile of frontage and "more or less" three miles deep, virgin land that one day would be further divided among his children.[14]

This pattern of dispersed and discontinuous landholdings – smaller parcels of land squeezed in among larger tracts with diverse owners – had wide-ranging social implications and is key to understanding land tenure in early nineteenth-century Brazil. Paraibuna fazendas were not miniature sovereign empires, but reflections of a community's complex interactions over time, by which inheritance and debt split up original land grants and allowed a creditor to intrude into another planter's lands. The law stipulating that all children inherit equally from their parents' estate conspired against a plantation remaining intact for long, and if each child received a share of both the more and the less valuable lands, then a fazenda would be even more quickly fragmented.[15] Of course,

---

[14] Mappa dos Habitantes, 1830, Fogo 89, Luiz Marianno de Toloza; Inventário, Padre Valerio de Alvarenga Ferreira, Santo Antônio de Paraibuna, São Paulo, 1848 (hereafter cited as Inventário, Padre Valerio de Alvarenga Ferreira, 1848), AF-PSP, Pacote 1, fls. 3, 5, 6v, 18v–20v; for the marriage certificate, see *Nullidade*, 1836, fls. 62–62v; for references to Tolosa, see Nullidade, 1836, fls. 1, 8, 51v, and passim.

[15] Candido Mendes de Almeida, comp. and ed., *Codigo Philippino; ou Ordenações e leis do reino de Portugal, recopilados por mandado d'el-rey D. Philippe I. 14 ed.*

heirs could forestall dividing valuable land into uselessly small sections by agreeing to administer a fazenda jointly, each receiving a portion of its product, and thereby retain the original boundaries. But only for a time. Eventually, their deaths would occasion further division to their heirs, and breaking up the land into ever smaller units became unavoidable.

Debt further fragmented the ownership of large holdings. Planters rich in land and slaves were frequently cash poor, finding it necessary to buy on credit luxuries from abroad, even basic food supplies to feed their laborers, and above all additional slaves. For all practical purposes, banks that lent to ordinary citizens did not exist in Brazil before the 1860s. The Banco Commercial e Agricola, established in 1857, operated principally to supply merchants with short-term commercial services and issued few mortgages to planters in its first years. This was instead an "economy of obligation" and credit a face-to-face matter that depended on trust and reputation. In Paraibuna in the 1830s and '40s, family members continued the long-standing practice of borrowing from each other or from other more solvent planters, while grown children secured loans against their future inheritances. Most planters dealt on credit with their commission agents, the men who managed the sale and export of their coffee in the major trading centers such as Rio de Janeiro, and who deducted what a planter owed in installments from his income. Loans were often carried for years at normally high interest rates, with land or slaves mortgaged for collateral, and when these private lenders foreclosed they were drawn into real estate transactions and the sale of land in order to recover their capital. If not settled during a planter's lifetime, debts were discounted from the value of the estate before the heirs received their shares. In this way property regularly passed out of the hands of a principal family to other, more distant relatives or to unrelated associates.[16]

segundo a primeira de 1603 e a nona de Coimbra de 1824. Addicionada com diversas notas ... (Rio de Janeiro: Typ. do Instituto Philomathico, 1870), Liv. 4, Tit. 96, 97 (hereafter cited as *Codigo Philippino*, 1870), describes inheritance law and division of property among heirs as practiced in Brazil after independence from Portugal; a similar division of large holdings into smaller ones occurred among Bahia sugar estates. See B. J. Barickman, *A Bahian Counterpoint: Sugar, Tobacco, Cassava, and Slavery in the Recôncavo, 1780–1860* (Stanford: Stanford University Press, 1998), pp. 105–108; Katia M. de Queirós Mattoso, *Bahia: A cidade do Salvador e seu mercado no século XIX* (São Paulo: Hucitec, 1978), pp. 40–44; Katia M. de Queirós Mattoso, *Bahia, século XIX: Uma província no império* (Rio de Janeiro: Nova Fronteira, 1992), pp. 462–463.

[16] On early rural banking in Brazil, see Stanley J. Stein, *Vassouras: A Brazilian Coffee County, 1850–1900* (Cambridge: Harvard University Press, 1957), esp.

These many transactions produced a complex and tightly connected, but nevertheless small, society in which kinship and commerce combined in contrary ways to serve as both its foundation and its undoing. Rio Claro was no exception. In 1834, with coffee production in the region at record levels, Tolosa and his wife owed nearly one-fifth the value of their holdings in debt, very likely incurred in the purchase of African slaves and the opening of new coffee fields.[17] Thirteen years later, if the priest's estate amounted to a considerable sum, so too did his debts, more than half the value of his estate, which, however, scarcely distinguished him from most of his neighbors. By the time of his death, Father Valerio was bound to Marcelino José de Carvalho, a landowner in his own right and heir to the largest fortune in Paraibuna (and probably a relative), by a sizable debt, and by another twice as large to a big moneylender based in Rio de Janeiro with lucrative business dealings all along the coast, Antônio Tertuliano dos Santos. The estate paid them both, not with cash but with lands from the fazenda Cedro (Santos almost certainly selling his portion), the same fazenda from which Tolosa also inherited land from the priest, a prime example of a larger holding carved into smaller tracts and going into the hands of multiple owners.[18]

Debt proved rancorous. Carvalho, discontented with the settlement, said the land was appraised at a price inflated four times its true value and sued the estate. He alleged the judge, the scribe of the court, and the appraisers were all "suspect," being "relatives, friends, or dependents" of the executor and heir, Tolosa. In cahoots they had paid favored lenders

---

pp. 17–20; Joseph E. Sweigart, *Coffee Factorage and the Emergence of a Brazilian Capital Market, 1850–1888* (New York: Garland Publishing, 1987), esp. pp. 125–127. Craig Muldrew uses the phrase for England at an earlier time, but the relationships he examines shed light on practices in early nineteenth-century Brazil, *The Economy of Obligation: The Culture of Credit and Social Relations in Early Modern England* (New York: St. Martin's Press, 1998), esp. pp. 2–4, 125, 148–172. As early as the 1820s residents in the major provincial capitals could invest money or store valuables for safe-keeping at savings banks called *caixas*; see, e.g., Inventário, José da Silva Barros, Salvador, Bahia, 1823, Arquivo Público do Estado da Bahia, Seção Judiciária (hereafter cited as APEB-SJ), 04/1826/2297/13, fls. 4, 5.

[17] Inventário, Anna Joaquina Moreira, 1834, fl. 33v.

[18] Inventário, Maria Custodia de Alvarenga, Santo Antônio de Paraibuna, São Paulo, 1846, AF-PSP, Pacote 7, fls. 1, 2, 25v–52, 65; Land register, Marcelino José de Carvalho, Santo Antônio de Paraibuna, São Paulo, 30 May 1856, Registro nos. 380, 381, 382, 383, 385, 387, AESP, Registro de Terras, vol. 43, Paraibuna, 30/6/1854–30/5/1857, fls. 100, 100v, 101, 101v, 102v; Inventário, Padre Valerio de Alvarenga Ferreira, 1848, fls. 27, 34v, 35v–36v, 44v.

with the most easily sold property, while to those "not in the good graces" of the dead priest, his executor and heirs, useless land was assigned, useless because, as was well known, being high in the mountains Cedro lands were subject to yearly frosts. Their motives were clear: If they had paid what the estate owed, very little would be left for them. Ignoring the point made by Tolosa's lawyer that in a small place ties of family and friendship were inevitable in almost any transaction, the judge dismissed the suit on legal grounds.[19] Those charged had spent time and money repudiating the accusations of a powerful man from a powerful family who thought himself cheated. Tolosa and Carvalho had probably clashed before. Neither was likely to forget this time, and in this face-to-face country town they would meet often.

Endless comings and goings further connected the surrounding fazendas to the village of Santo Antônio de Paraibuna, such that any neatly drawn distinction between urban and rural life is misleading. No local census counted the town's population separately, and the only figures are for the parish as a whole: 143 households and nearly 3,000 persons, of whom roughly a quarter were slaves. Nonetheless, certain services clustered in the village and certain business could be done only there. Besides 20 local merchants, the town counted on the skills of five carpenters, a brick or tile maker, six tailors, and six shoemakers, and by 1835 residents supported four blacksmiths, nine shopkeepers who paid rent for their shops, and some 20 women who lived from their sewing. Only four muleteers posted themselves for hire in town because, as the census taker noted in 1832, most planters kept their own; some 39 laborers could be hired on a daily basis. In the two general stores merchants likely stocked and sold farm implements, gunpowder, and salt, or bought hides, corn, or manioc locally for resale.[20] Even literacy seemed to belong more noticeably to the village. In addition to the handful whose professions depended on a sophisticated literacy, another 90 townspeople who could read and write lived with a "decent subsistence," and the single primary school taught 23 boys. (Although surely most of the big land owners and exporters had to be literate, the census did not report on planter literacy.) The village could not supply all needs, however. Anyone who wanted a pharmacist, weaver, goldsmith, cabinetmaker, or

[19] Inventário, Padre Valerio Alvarenga Ferreira, 1848, fls. 60–61, 76v, 89v, 91–91v, 97–97v.

[20] População da Freguezia de Santo Antônio de Paraibuna, 1832; 1º Distrito de Santo Antonio de Parahybuna, 1835.

notary had to travel to the neighboring town of Jacareí, some 28 miles away. Tolosa owned at least one house in town, which he perhaps rented out, but just as likely used himself when attending to the business of his several public offices.[21]

A series of overlapping jurisdictions – ecclesiastical, judicial, civil, and military – further tied fazendas such as Rio Claro to the town and eventually to levels of authority beyond its boundaries. Elevated in 1832 from parish to village and thus invested with a municipal council, making it a kind of county seat, Paraibuna assumed responsibility for maintaining public fountains, bridges, and the few inadequate roads that more often than not were thick with mud or choking dust. The traffic that trudged along them was usually persons on foot, mules, and horses; the creaking, fixed-axle ox carts came later. The council also inspected weights and measures, butcher shops, and other suppliers of "wet and dry foodstuffs," and levied fines on violators of its ordinances. The council conducted its business in borrowed chambers, however, for the only two public buildings in 1838 were the parish church and a building Müller dismissively described as "constructed of wood which serves as a jail." (He omitted to note, however, that in many places the council and the jail occupied the same building.) Five priests and the lay brotherhood of the Most Holy Sacrament looked after the souls of the 3,169 inhabitants – Caetana's marriage certificate was there in one of the parish church's big registry books – while civil justice was served by one municipal judge, a public prosecutor, and two justices of the peace.[22]

Tolosa stood out as a man of local authority. In the early 1830s, his fellow parishioners, those qualified by income to vote (the stipulated amount was minimal but had to derive from investment, not common wages), elected him justice of the peace. The post, created by the constitution in newly independent Brazil in 1824, its powers specified and extended three years later, was both a way to avoid clogging the courts with petty squabbles as well as a liberal counter to central authority

---

[21] Müller, *Quadro estatístico*, pp. 47, 263, 241; Inventário, Anna Joaquina Moreira, 1834, fl. 11.

[22] Helen Nader, *Liberty in Absolutist Spain: The Habsburg Sale of Towns, 1516–1700* (Baltimore: Johns Hopkins University Press, 1990), persuades that in Iberian culture the usually assumed distinctions between urban and rural are seen as too firmly fixed and misleading in their implication of exclusiveness by showing that their connections were many and institutionally rooted. Müller, *Quadro estatístico*, pp. 95–99, 46–47, 247, 253; Nullidade, 1836, fls. 62–62v.

deliberately set outside the channels of appointed positions and patronage through which the emperor gathered and distributed his power. Its
creation was a bid to make a local official responsive to local needs.
Untrained, but handsomely paid the same salary as a high-ranking magistrate with a degree in the law, the justice of the peace's responsibility to
conciliate quarreling, feuding, disorderly, brawling community members
before their conflicts reached the courts made him a widely known figure
in the county. He resolved doubts about the use of local resources, such
as access roads, river crossings, waters used in agriculture, pastures, and
small fishing dams, and mediated disputes over hunting rights, boundaries, fences, and the damages caused by slaves or domestic animals. He
saw to the conservation of forests. He dealt with threats to public order,
breaking up rowdy gatherings and, in case of riot, calling in the troops,
who could act only on his explicit order. He was charged with prevent-
ing and destroying runaway slave communities. He jailed drunks, put
vagrants and beggars to work, got prostitutes to make pledges of good
conduct, and divided his district into "blocks" of no more than twenty-
five families each in order to count and keep track of the population. He
kept a list of wanted criminals, made arrests, interrogated the accused,
assembled evidence, enforced municipal regulations, and protected the
property rights of orphaned children. He knew his neighbors and a good
deal about their affairs.

And as an official elected by a majority of them, he was scarcely
impartial. With extensive powers that put him at the center of local
disputes where passions ran high, the position itself could be a source of
controversy and tension. He also sat on the local board that determined
who was eligible to vote, often an openly contentious matter. It was
generally thought that a qualified man owed it to his community to
serve. Once elected, only serious and prolonged illness allowed a justice
of the peace to cut short his three-year term; if he accepted a second
term – the accumulated authority would have been a temptation for
many men – he could then decline to serve again in this powerful but
onerous post.[23] Tolosa was justice of the peace in the years just before

---

[23] Decreto, 15 October 1827, Brazil, Laws, statutes, etc., *Coleção das Leis do Brasil*,
Art. 2, 3, 4, 5, para. 1–6, 8–12, 14–15, 6, and 7 (hereafter cited as *Leis do Brasil*).
Thomas Flory, *Judge and Jury in Imperial Brazil, 1808–1871: Social Control and
Political Stability in the New State* (Austin: University of Texas Press, 1981), pp. 47–
66, interprets the position as inherently controversial, overlapping as it did with
existing judicial and police functions, and polarizing political views over the

Caetana's wedding, and she would have glimpsed his importance, the demands on his time. It was surely not easy for a young slave woman openly to oppose such a man.

Tolosa did his job well, the prestige lingered, and his reputation grew. By 1848, at the time the priest's estate was being settled, Tolosa had been appointed first alternate municipal judge for four years, a position that carried no remuneration, but which demonstrated he had attracted the attention and favor of those in the provincial government. There was no requirement of a law degree for alternate as there was for the judgeship; Tolosa was chosen as a local citizen who met the formula: "notable for his fortune, intelligence, and good conduct." When challenged by Carvalho over the handling of Father Valerio's estate, Tolosa had exempted himself as acting judge, passing responsibility not to the second alternate, his son-in-law and also an interested party, but to the third alternate.[24] With Tolosa's own authority secure, it now extended to the next generation of men in the family. But this was after Caetana's time.

Tolosa's career was further anchored in the small-scale military units designed to keep public order. Having worked his way up through the militia ranks first as a cavalry soldier, he was then promoted to second lieutenant in 1824, and eventually acquired the title of captain. Reformed in 1831, these "citizens' militias" were to be organized throughout the Empire in even the most remote county and smallest parish to "defend the Constitution, the Liberty, Independence, and Integrity of the Empire" and to "maintain obedience to the Laws, conserve or reestablish order and public tranquility."[25] Income excluded the poorest men, while status exempted the already privileged, unless they chose to serve as officers, for whom the guard was a compelling source of local power.[26] Guardsmen were not only assigned to respond to threats of sedition or put down slave insurrections but to provide men for the mundane

central government's authority. Roderick J. Barman, *Brazil: The Forging of a Nation, 1798–1852* (Stanford: Stanford University Press, 1988), pp. 145, 193, and 213, is less interested in local conflict, and instead sets the position in the larger context of national institution-building.

[24] Lei 261, 3 December 1841, *Leis do Brasil*, Cap. 2, Art. 19; Inventário, Padre Valerio Alvarenga Ferreira, 1848, fl. 76v.

[25] Lei, 18 August 1831, *Leis do Brasil*, Tit. 1, Art. 1, 2, and 10; for the reforms a year later, see Decreto, 25 October 1832, *Leis do Brasil*, Art. 4.

[26] Lei, 18 August 1831, *Leis do Brasil*, Tit. 3, Cap. 1, Art. 18; Decreto, 25 October 1832, *Leis do Brasil*, Art. 8.

duties of capturing criminals, conducting prisoners to trial, transporting valuables, patrolling the towns, guarding the jail, searching for runaway slaves, or restoring order after an election brawl. Although the officers who commanded the National Guard gained standing in the community by overseeing these common police duties, the guard itself was subordinate to the justice of the peace in each county, an on-the-ground demonstration of the supremacy of judicial over military authority.[27]

The notion of a citizens' army rested on the assumption that inherently disorderly men could be brought to obey the laws of the land only if they themselves were recruited to enforce those laws. "No one can deny," argued one deputy during parliamentary debates in 1831, "that citizens' safety is best guarded by those same citizens with an interest in its conservation."[28] But keeping order generated new worries that a delegation of power to the many would get out of hand. Lawmakers nervously warned that troops could not take up arms or act as a body without orders from their "chiefs," and officers were barred from distributing cartridges without authorization.

Moreover, as better-off men avoided serving, small farmers, merchants, and artisans – men who could ill afford time away from work – increasingly bore the weight of ensuring local order, as well as the costs.[29] Each recruit had to pay for his own uniform, arms, and horse if he aspired to the prestigious cavalry. For their efforts these citizen-soldiers were themselves closely watched. Breaches in discipline such as failing to be at one's post or being drunk or disorderly were punishable by fines or costly days in prison and a further loss of work and income.[30] Men such as Severino José Moreira hoped to avoid the guard altogether. A free man and unmarried, Moreira was drafted into the infantry. He had no illnesses or physical defects to disqualify him, but he was poor and lived "at the favor" of Father Valerio de Alvarenga and Company on land at Rio Claro. In 1834, at about the time of Caetana's wedding, his

---

[27] Lei, 18 August 1831, *Leis do Brasil*, Tit. 1, Art. 7, 8, 6, 14; Richard Graham, *Patronage and Politics in Nineteenth-Century Brazil* (Stanford: Stanford University Press, 1990), p. 63.

[28] Evaristo Ferreira da Veiga, 25 May 1831, Brazil, Congresso, Câmara dos Deputados, *Anais*, I, 1831, p. 93.

[29] Thomas Flory, *Judge and Jury*, p. 92.

[30] Lei, 18 August 1831, *Leis do Brasil*, Tit. 2, Cap. 5, Art. 66; Tit. 3, Cap. 9, Art. 80–106; and Tit. 4, Cap. 2, Arts. 113–116; Jeanne Berrance de Castro, *A milícia cidadã: A Guarda Nacional de 1831 a 1850* (São Paulo: Companhia Editora Nacional, 1977), pp. 24, 26.

petition to be excused from service was turned down, although he alone supported his mother, sister, and nephews with his labor.[31] If the guard was supposed to bind men of unequal social qualities into disciplined units, it functioned poorly.

Serving as justice of the peace, in 1832 Tolosa simultaneously assumed authority over Paraibuna's one infantry company with fifty-two soldiers and thirty cavalrymen, drawing Rio Claro ever more directly into the lines of power, obligations, patronage, and factions that stretched from town and county to province and empire.[32] In the same year Dona Ana Joaquina gave birth to their fifth child; she was seriously ill.[33] With the master often called away, Caetana had her hands full helping to care for an infant, other young children, and a sick mistress.

In this microcosm of an intentionally divided society, Tolosa stood at its apex. His career encapsulated the workings and inequalities of local power and reflected the general preoccupation with public order. Against this background the familiar and unending work of the fazenda went on at Rio Claro.

WORKERS

Especially in these early years, but even when machines became more readily available, labor throughout the Paraíba Valley was human labor and principally, although never exclusively, slave labor. Work routines followed the seasons only roughly. Planting was best done in the winter months of June and July, but could continue through spring and into summer during the late spring rains in November and December. The preparation of new fields for planting involved clearing dense forests. On steeper hillsides, trees could be partially cut, always beginning at the bottom and working uphill, and then felled as a "slayer" tree at the top was sent crashing down the slope, each tree toppling ones below it – a very precise skill. Only an experienced man could identify the ideal slayer tree, and the cutting could be deadly if trees fell too soon or in unanticipated directions. In later decades when slaves were scarce

[31] Severino Joze Moreira, Petition, Paraibuna, December 1834, Autos Civeis, Documentos Diversos, 1838–1887, AF-PSP.

[32] Cartas Patentes Confirmadas, 1824–1825, AESP, Patentes, sesmarias, e cartas imperiais, Lata 95, No. 453, Livro 295, fl. 91v; in 1832 Tolosa signed the local census as Juiz de Paz, see População da Freguezia de Santo Antônio de Paraibuna, 1832; Müller, *Quadro estatístico*, p. 222.

[33] Inventário, Anna Joaquina Moreira, 1834, fls. 2, 8v.

and more costly, planters hired free men for the felling, reserving their expensive slaves for safer work. In a rush to clear fields, planters burned the felled timber, relying on rain to extinguish smoldering fires, and planted around the remaining stumps.[34] Writing in the late 1840s, one planter raised his voice against the waste by urging his fellow planters to cut and remove logs to the paths where they could be gathered and used for building, as though this were not the general practice.[35] Either method required male strength.

At Rio Claro, as at most coffee and sugar plantations, field work was the domain of both men and women, who worked side by side, often with their children in tow. Skilled hands transferred tender young plants from seedling bed to field, each shoot being gently patted into its hole and the earth carefully diked to protect against its being uprooted by heavy rain. Tending the bushes, keeping the soil loosened at the foot of each growing bush, and weeding two or three times a year was ongoing work. Mature coffee bushes sent out their small pale pink or white flowers as many as three times a year, causing the fruit on some bushes to ripen to a rich red, while on others the berries were still green. Often both ripe and green berries grew on a single bush or branch. A good harvest ran from early winter into spring. Branches were stripped from the trunk out, fruit of all shades of ripeness falling to the ground and gathered into big straw sieves or baskets for later winnowing, time-consuming work for slaves that only later would be sped up with water-flowing sluices in which the fruit was separated from dirt and twigs, ripe from unripe berries. Slaves balanced loaded baskets on their heads or wore them strapped low against their backs, maximizing the body's efficiency. From the fields men and women carted coffee to a central compound where the berries were spread out on beaten earth, stone, or brick terraces to dry in the sun. They turned the berries using heavy wooden rakes, gathering them into mounds at night and covering each mound with a tarpaulin against the dew or rain, "a process that takes a great deal of time, and is very fatiguing for the slaves," according to one observer.[36] Hulling

---

[34] Müller, *Quadro estatístico*, p. 32; Laërne, *Brazil and Java*, pp. 288, 279.

[35] Francisco Peixoto de Lacerda Vernek, *Memoria sobre a fundação de huma fazenda na provincia do Rio de Janeiro, sua administração e épocas em que se devem fazer as plantações, suas colheitas, etc., etc.* (Rio de Janeiro: Laemmert, 1847), pp. 12–13.

[36] Laërne, *Brazil and Java*, pp. 285–288, 300–303, 310–316; G. M. O. Maloiy et al., "Energetic Cost of Carrying Loads: Have African Women Discovered an Economic Way?" *Nature* 319 (February 1986): 668–669; Marc Ferrez, "Two Slaves Picking Coffee, ca. 1885," (photograph), copy in my possession.

Figure 1. Slaves with their rakes, hoes, and baskets in hand being mustered for the day's work of picking and weeding coffee. Some are dressed in their best, posing for the photograph. The only woman in this group wears rings on her fingers, and the second man to her left stands jauntily, his white jacket unbuttoned and his hat set more for effect than work. Heading the group is a white administrator with his umbrella, and next to him is the black overseer, identified by his shoes as a freed man. He holds a ring of keys. (Marc Ferrez, c. 1885)

the dried coffee was the work of male slaves who oversaw the use of a water-driven wooden pestle to break the outer hull away from the coffee beans. Only when sorted and bagged was the coffee ready for shipment to market.

If most slaves worked most of the time at coffee, some also grew corn, beans, and rice, and raised cattle. Artisan slaves – carpenters, black-smiths, stone masons – constructed the buildings, roads, and bridges on a fazenda. House slaves cooked, cleaned, laundered and ironed clothes, carried water, emptied kitchen slops and night soil, and delivered mes-sages. A slave woman with milk from her own pregnancy might nurse her mistress's infant, or as a "dry nurse" take care of older children. Slave children had their own chores: sorting coffee, tending goats, husking beans, watering gardens, or looking after younger children. The number and variety of skilled slaves depended on the size and prosperity of the place, the diversity of its production, and the comforts a family chose to have. In later decades when coffee boomed and planters devoted land and field slaves almost exclusively to coffee, they bought not only luxury goods but even basic foodstuffs. But early planters like Tolosa typically relied more on their own production.[37]

A profile of the slaves at Rio Claro can be retrieved from census counts conducted throughout the region in the 1820s and early 1830s. By the time of Caetana's story, Rio Claro stood out as the largest single holding in the county, with 134 slaves. A widow and her son ranked second to Tolosa with half as many slaves, while Tolosa's neighbor and friend kept fifty-three slaves.[38] Given high infant death rates and a general preference to buy additional fully grown slaves rather than raise newborns to working age, the twenty-five slave children under ten years, nearly one-fifth of Rio Claro's slaves, suggest that Tolosa took more seriously than some planters the rearing of young slaves. Distinguishing adolescents from adults is more difficult because the census taker ignored slaves' actual ages, probably in the belief that only an approximate age mattered anyway, and grouped them into crude ten-year divisions. All thirty-one adolescents between the ages of ten and nineteen were assigned the age ten, while the seventy-eight adults became simply twenty, thirty, or forty years old. Although overall at Rio Claro males outnumbered females by about two to one, among adult slaves the imbalance was less pronounced, with women accounting for nearly half of the adult slaves. Caetana could find female company among the thirty-nine slaves on the fazenda who were young girls or women. The disproportionate number of adolescent boys, twenty-six compared with only five girls, half African and half creole, suggests that rather than rely on a natural increase among his slaves, Tolosa had expanded his labor force by purchasing young males who would soon be mature, working-age men.[39]

At Rio Claro, Caetana lived among nearly equal numbers of creoles – that is, Brazilian-born slaves – and Africans. She herself was a creole, born on the fazenda, who grew up speaking Portuguese with no recalled experience of a particular African village or tribal ways or the feared and terrible Atlantic crossing. All the young children on the fazenda were also creoles, while half the adolescents were Africans. On the

[37] Vernek, Memória, pp. 10–11.
[38] Mappa dos Habitantes, 1830, Fogo 89, Luiz Marianno de Toloza; ibid., Fogo 30, Maria Custodia de Alvarenga; 2° Distrito de Juiz de Paz da Vara de Santo Antônio de Paraibuna do Municipio da mesma, Quarteirão no. 2, AESP-SM, Maços de População, Jacarehy, Santa Branca, Parahybuna, 1835, Maço 2, Caixa 86, Ordem 86, Fogo 38, Manoel da Cunha de Azeredo Coutinho Souza Chichorro (hereafter cited as 2° Distrito de Santo Antônio de Paraibuna, 1835).
[39] Mappa dos Habitantes, 1830, Fogo 89, Luiz Marianno de Toloza.

other hand, African adults outnumbered creoles almost two to one, there being more African men than women and slightly fewer creole men than women. Among somewhat older slaves – men in their forties and women in their thirties – Africans were especially numerous.[40] After 1831, when the African trade in slaves to Brazil became illegal and ships suspected of transporting slaves north of the equator could be searched by British patrols and their human cargoes seized, planters like Tolosa had to decide whether to buy contraband slaves, often without papers to prove ownership, making future sale awkward but otherwise causing practically no risk to themselves, or to compete for the locally born slaves or Africans legally imported before 1831, who were still sold openly in Brazil. The contraband trade thrived until the early 1850s, when parliament bowed to intensifying British pressure, and planters, heavily burdened with debts to slave dealers, accepted a law that effectively ended the Atlantic trade by making criminals of all those who engaged in the shipping or sale of slaves from Africa.[41] Typically, men sold at somewhat higher prices than women, creole slaves being valued and trusted more than Africans.[42]

[40] Ibid.

[41] Leslie Bethell, *The Abolition of the Brazilian Slave Trade: Britain, Brazil and the Slave Trade Question, 1807–1869* (Cambridge: Cambridge University Press, 1970), esp. pp. 313–314, 339–341; Richard Graham, *Britain and the Onset of Modernization in Brazil, 1850–1914* (Cambridge: Cambridge University Press, 1968), pp. 164–166, argues for greater Brazilian initiative in ending the trade; Law 581, 4 September 1850, and Law 731, 5 June 1854, in Agostinho Marques Perdigão Malheiro, *A escravidão no Brasil: Ensaio histórico-jurídico-social*, 3 parts in 1 vol. (Rio de Janeiro: Typ. Nacional, 1866–1867), part 3, Appendices 3 and 4. The possible implication that planters' debts became uncollectible, giving them a direct interest in seeing the law passed, requires further research. On the contraband trade, see Flory, *Judge and Jury*, pp. 100–101; for a rarely documented example of a slaver going aground on the Brazilian coast and of slaves at the time sold illegally and without papers, later claiming their freedom, see Juizo Municipal e de Orfãos, Acção de Liberdade, plaintiff, Africana Maria and others, Espírito Santo, 1872, ANRJ-SPJ, Caixa 1645, N. 3865.

[42] Mary C. Karasch, *Slave Life in Rio de Janeiro, 1808–1850* (Princeton: Princeton University Press, 1987), pp. 43–44, finds little difference in prices for urban men and women in the first half of the century; Robert W. Slenes, "The Demography and Economics of Brazilian Slavery: 1850–1888," Ph.D. diss., Stanford University, 1976, pp. 252–261, shows a more substantial difference during the later period. Individual manumissions more often went to creole than African slaves; see João José Reis, *Slave Rebellion in Brazil: The Muslim Uprising of 1835 in Bahia*, trans. Arthur Brakel (Baltimore: Johns Hopkins University Press, 1993), pp. 142–143. Stuart B. Schwartz, "The Manumission of Slaves in Colonial Brazil: Bahia,

Table 1. *Rio Claro Slaves, 1830, According to Birthplace, Sex, and Age (in percentages)*

	Africans	Creoles	Totals
Women			
Children 1–9 years	0	7	7
Adolescents 10–20 years	1	3	4
Adults 20 years or older	16	10	26
Subtotals	17	20	37
	(n = 22)	(n = 27)	(n = 49)
Men			
Children 1–9 years	0	11	11
Adolescents 10–20 years	10	10	20
Adults 20 years or older	24	8	32
Subtotals	34	29	63
	(n = 46)	(n = 39)	(n = 85)
Totals	51	49	100[a]
	(n = 68)	(n = 66)	(n = 134)

Note: Absolute numbers are in parentheses.
[a] I have rounded percentages to the nearest whole number.
Source: Mappa dos Habitantes alistentes desta Segunda e Nova Com[panhi]a da Freguesia de S[anto] Antonio de Paraibuna distrito da Villa de Jacarehei, em apresentes com seus Nomes, Empregos, Naturalidades, Idades, Estados, Cores, Ocupasões, Cazoalidades que aconteserão em cada huma de Suas Respectivas familias desde a fatura da data do Anno antesedente, Arquivo do Estado de São Paulo, Seção de Manuscritos, Maços de População, Jacarei, Santa Branca, Parai-buna, 1830–1850, Maço 2, Parahybuna, 2ª Companhia, 1830, Caixa 86, Ordem 86, Fogo 89, Luiz Marianno de Toloza.

The details of individual work assignments remain uncertain because neither the census taker nor Tolosa bothered to record his slaves' specific occupations, usually not even placing them within the broad categories of field work, coffee processing (called "factory" work), domestic service, or skilled crafts. Slaves incapacitated by age or illness were not distinguished from healthy slaves. Most slaves at Rio Claro were only minimally identified by their first names and approximate ages; their ethnic origins were noted only as "African" or "creole" without saying where in Africa or Brazil they were born.

Nonetheless, distinctions in occupations and status dramatized a hierarchy among laborers. At least a partial accounting of those who

1684–1745," *Hispanic American Historical Review* (hereafter cited as *HAHR*) 54, no. 4 (November 1974): 603–635.

belonged to the worker elite at Rio Claro is possible from the court proceedings. We discover that not all those who worked for Tolosa were slaves. Although in 1830 the listing of residents at Rio Claro included only the two priests, family members, and slaves and no free workers or former slaves, among the small sample of workers who testified seven years later, two nonslaves appear. Luísa Jacinta played a prominent role in events as Caetana's aunt and godmother. Born a slave and since freed, she was married to Alexandre, and at more than fifty years old she was an aging woman. Having once enjoyed the status of house servant, she now "lives from agriculture" as a "dependent" at Rio Claro.[43] If "agriculture" meant common field work, it would have been a bitter demotion; far more likely, Luísa Jacinta had been superannuated and given her own small plot to farm.

On the other hand, the mulatto João Ribeiro da Silva had been born a free man. The record does not say when he left his birthplace, the southern town of Curitiba, or arrived in Paraibuna. He figured in Caetana's story as her brother-in-law, married to her sister, a free man who lived among slaves. At twenty-five years old he was in his prime, yet nothing in his testimony revealed the actual work he did, only that he "lives from his agriculture," the same blunt description also used for Tolosa. The court scribe further assigned him the equally ambiguous status of "dependent," suggesting that he farmed land at Rio Claro with Tolosa's permission.[44] He may well have served as Tolosa's foreman, directing slaves at their labor and seeing to it that Tolosa's instructions were carried out. No one else named in any of the sources was identified as foreman, and yet, as coffee production at Rio Claro expanded, the number of slaves increased, and Tolosa took on other obligations, he may have wanted someone to assume a foreman's duties. Of the persons known to us, Silva was the most likely to be chosen. The role would have cast him as intermediary at once answerable to Tolosa for the work performed and a conveyor of grievances from the slaves, including his own kin, to the master, a position potentially as influential as it could be uncomfortable. No foreman at Rio Claro would have had much final say in running things, however, for Tolosa appears as the fully in charge owner-manager.

In practical terms the slave Alexandre, husband to Luísa Jacinta and uncle-godfather to Caetana, outranked Silva. If necessary, Tolosa

---

[43] Nullidade, 1836, fls. 41v–42.
[44] Ibid., fls. 39–41v.

could oversee his work force alone as he apparently had in the past, but Alexandre was indispensable. As *armador da tropa* he captained the mule teams that carried Rio Claro's coffee to the tiny coastal settlement of Caraguatatuba for shipment on to a larger port. In Caraguatatuba, Tolosa owned a warehouse for storing coffee, kept canoes, and moored the two substantial two-masted boats, the *Good Voyage* and the *Santo Antônio*, in which he owned shares.[45] It is not clear whether his boats sailed directly to the nearer port of Santos or all the way to Rio de Janeiro, or transferred the coffee to larger boats somewhere en route, probably at Ubatuba or Angra dos Reis. In any case, moving the coffee off the fazenda 32 miles over the perilously steep escarpment to the coast took acquired know-how, especially in driving rain or in spring when thick fog settled in the higher valleys. The dangers can be gauged from the rough-cut paving stones used to bank the sharpest turns and probably set there by slaves, still visible when I traveled a deeply rutted dirt road on the escarpment in the late 1970s. Without an expert muleteer to guide animals and slaves, no coffee reached market and no goods from Rio de Janeiro could be packed in from the coast to the fazenda. The trips also meant that Alexandre, entrusted with the wealth of the fazenda and the well-being of his team, was his own master for days at a time. He was unquestionably a deeply trusted man, a man of influence on the Tolosa fazenda.

Both Custódio and Caetana were members of the fazenda's slave elite. We recognize them by their non-field work as ranked among the more capable, trained, and favored slaves of the plantation. Custódio was described as a master tailor, implying he was not self-taught, but had been apprenticed at his craft. He may have cut and sewn the standard rough cotton clothes allotted slaves, or directed their making, but more likely that work fell to one of the women. Less likely, but not implausibly, Tolosa might have hired out his services as tailor to others in the district. But tailoring was a valued skill and Custódio probably tailored clothes for the men of the family: the priests, Tolosa, and his sons. At another point in the record, however, a passing reference to Custódio as a house slave, his precise tasks unspecified, suggests that tailoring did not occupy all his time.[46]

Caetana served in the Casa Grande as a *mucama*, or personal maid, to the women of the family.[47] She would have been one among several

[45] Ibid., fls. 53v–55; Inventário, Anna Joaquina Moreira, 1834, fls. 16v–17.
[46] Nullidade, 1836, fls. 49, 52.
[47] Ibid., 1836, fl. 47v.

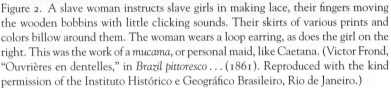

Figure 2. A slave woman instructs slave girls in making lace, their fingers moving the wooden bobbins with little clicking sounds. Their skirts of various prints and colors billow around them. The woman wears a loop earring, as does the girl on the right. This was the work of a *mucama*, or personal maid, like Caetana. (Victor Frond, "Ouvrières en dentelles," in *Brazil pittoresco* . . . (1861). Reproduced with the kind permission of the Instituto Histórico e Geográfico Brasileiro, Rio de Janeiro.)

house servants who cooked, cleaned, and laundered, but as the most trusted of them she routinely would have entered the family's private quarters. Indoor work was understood as privileged, less strenuous than the long hours spent in the field at heavy work, in the sun's direct heat or the dank chill of winter. A mucama could expect finer clothes, perhaps a more varied or ample diet gleaned from the family's table, earlier attention to illnesses, and the small, sought-after protections a proper mistress or master was supposed to provide. Such favors nonetheless came at a price: an elevated expectation of obedience and loyal service, and near-constant surveillance by an ever-watchful mistress.

Historian Stuart Schwartz has chided recent ethnographers of slave culture for seeking to understand the patterns of family, community, and religion at the "cost" of missing the centrality of work in shaping slave lives, a practice he called "ethnographic fantasy."[48] It would be misleading to set "work" and "culture" in opposition, as if work were

---

[48] Stuart B. Schwartz, *Slaves, Peasants, Rebels: Reconsidering Brazilian Slavery* (Urbana: University of Illinois Press, 1992), p. 39.

somehow separate from the assumptions, understandings, and responses by which slave women and men made all aspects of their lives intelligible. But however pervasive, demanding, even brutal the work, however thoroughly it permeated slave experience and set the outline of a slave's identity in their own eyes as well as in the eyes of both fellow slaves and owners, in the record of this case the actual routines of work are not much described or remarked on. Work remains in the background, taken for granted, a point of departure. For both slaves and owner it is other concerns that come into relief here.

FAMILY

A slave wedding is not something we expect. The standard account portrays slaves as denied the opportunity to marry or to conduct family life. More than a century before the events of this story, in 1707, a Catholic synod issued from the Brazilian capital of Salvador da Bahia a compilation of diocesan laws known as the *Constituições primeiras*. These laws were intended to be both consistent with canon law and the Council of Trent and apply to the special circumstances of Brazil. The synod thought it necessary to state that slaves could marry "with captive or free persons," and their masters should not impede them by either threats or punishment. The law further admonished masters not to sell a married slave to a place so distant that the spouse would be prevented from following. But at the same time, the *Constituições primeiras* also reassured masters that a slave remained a slave even if married to a free or freed person, and was obligated to continue serving the master even if that meant separation from husband or wife. In the domain of private and personal authority binding master and slave, the church could not enforce marriage among slaves, but only encourage masters to acquiesce, while conceding that marriages should occur at a "suitable time and place" – that is, with the master's permission.[49] The expected response

---

[49] See *Constituições primeiras*, 1853, Liv. 1, Tit. 71, no. 303. In this regard both Brazilian and Spanish law differed from Roman Law, on which they were largely based, which did not recognize marriage between free and slave persons. See *Las siete partidas*, trans. and notes Samuel Parsons Scott (Chicago: Commerce Clearing House, 1931), Part IV, Tit. V, Law I and n. 1; and Part IV, Tit. XXII, Law V, n. 1. Writing at about the time of the *Constituições primeiras*, the Italian Jesuit André João Antonil scathingly criticized slaveowners for the poor treatment of their slaves, and not least their blatant failure to encourage and

of a master is encapsulated in the terse two-word denial delivered by one master in 1876 to his slave's request to marry: "Time inappropriate."[50] The *Constituições primeiras* convey the clear understanding that typically slaves sought to marry, while masters denied permission and had to be entreated to fulfill their Christian duty.

Despite the church's urgings to marry, its own requirements often impeded the possibility. As formally set out by the Council of Trent in 1563 and routinely practiced in nineteenth-century Catholic Brazil, the necessary proofs of parentage and eligibility were daunting for the poor generally and especially for slaves, and cumbersome for their owners. The church required proof that neither partner had married previously, which in turn required that the priest in any parish in which either partner had lived as an adult for longer than six months had to supply a written statement attesting the supplicant to be single. Securing such a document was a time-consuming and expensive business involving literacy and social skills few slaves were allowed to acquire. Proof of identity and eligibility, the posting of banns, fees for the priest to say mass – all depended on a master's committed effort as well as contributions from his pocket.[51]

The surprise is that so many owners did accede to their slaves' wishes to marry. While we must rely on fragmentary evidence drawn from widely scattered times and places, wherever records exist we discover slave families blessed by church marriages. Once owned by Jesuits, the fazenda Santa Cruz had belonged to the Crown since 1759, when the Jesuits were expelled from Brazil and their property confiscated. In 1791 Crown administrators prepared an inventory of Santa Cruz's extensive holdings, including the 1,342 resident slaves (another five had fled). Slaves were counted as members of family groupings: couples, parents and their children, grandparents and grandchildren, single parents (both women and men) and their children, brothers and sisters. Nearly

honor marriage among them; *Cultura e opulência do Brasil* (1711; rpt., São Paulo: Melhoramentos, 1976), p. 90.

[50] Registro de Casamento, 1876, Paroquia de Santa Rita, Rio de Janeiro, Liv. 7, fl. 114v.

[51] Canon Law established the qualifications and procedures to marry in *Constituições primeiras*, 1853, Liv. 1, Tit. 64, nos. 269, 270, 272, and Tit. 65, 66; marriages by African-born slaves contracted in Africa were simply ignored, Liv. 1, Tit. 71, no. 304. On fees being excessive for the poor, see Sandra Lauderdale Graham, *House and Street: The Domestic World of Servants and Masters in Nineteenth-Century Rio de Janeiro* (Cambridge: Cambridge University Press, 1988), p. 73.

two-thirds of adult women and men were married, and more than 77 percent of all slaves lived in families of one kind or another, while single men and women and groups of men made up the remainder. The inventory implies slaves were not only counted but lived as families, in the jumble of irregularly sized huts on one side of the church square, as portrayed in an 1844 drawing. The slaves had probably been summoned to their huts, where the the census taker listed them in households.[52]

It would be easy to dismiss Santa Cruz as exceptional, first as a Jesuit, then as a Crown property not subject to divisions of inheritance and the separations inheritance usually meant for slaves, were it not that married slaves can be found almost as readily on privately owned estates. They appear in the numerous local household census rolls for towns in São Paulo province taken at the end of the eighteenth century and in the early decades of the nineteenth; slave marriages were recorded by parish churches; and sometimes the inventory of property drawn up on the occasion of an owner's death noted married slaves or, more rarely, other family connections. In Itú, a town in the sugar-growing hinterland of São Paulo city, an 1822 household list counted four sugar mills with 137 slaves. Although once-married and now widowed slaves were identified and spouses were paired, children were often listed separately, dooming our efforts to confidently link parents and children. A conservative estimate nevertheless suggests that at least eighty-one slaves, or roughly 59 percent of all slaves, on these sugar mills lived as families, while 53 percent of all slaves over the age of sixteen years were married. In the same sugar zone, but more remote in time, in the 1740s, as many as 83 percent of slaves on the three principal estates of Santana de Parnaíba lived in families, an even greater percentage than on the seemingly exceptional fazenda Santa Cruz. In 1829 at the largest sugar estate in Guaratinguetá, in the upper Paraíba Valley, slightly more than half of the 135 adult slaves were married.[53] Santa Cruz was perhaps

[52] Inventario dos escravos pertencentes a Real Fazenda de Santa Crus...em 12 de junho de 1791, ANRJ, Cód. 808, vol. 4, fls. 164v–183v; Richard Graham, "Slave Families on a Rural Estate in Colonial Brazil," *Journal of Social History* 9, no. 3 (Spring 1976): 383, 386. The drawing appears in *The Brazil of Eduard Hildebrandt*, ed. Gilberto Ferrez (Rio de Janeiro: Distribuidora Record, 1991), pp. 68–69.

[53] Mappa dos Habitantes da Villa de Itú em o anno de 1822, AESP-SM, Maços de População de Itú, Lata 78, 1822 e 1829, Fogos 1–4; Alida C. Metcalf, *Family and Frontier in Colonial Brazil: Santana de Parnaíba, 1580–1822* (Berkeley: University of California Press, 1992), pp. 169–170; Mappa dos habitantes existentes na 1ª

distinguished more by the meticulousness of its records than the fact of its slave families.

The pattern was repeated in the newly forming coffee regions. A summary made in 1828 of married or widowed persons in the district adjacent to Paraibuna discloses figures that further revise the earlier view of few slave marriages: 40 percent of all slave women and 24 percent of the men were married. Slaves, who numbered 21 percent of the total population, accounted for as many as 18 percent of the new marriages contracted that year. Of course, rates of marriage varied from one fazenda to another. In Paraibuna, 90 percent of the adult slaves owned by Tolosa's neighbor, the widow Dona Maria Custódia de Alvarenga, were married, including all the women slaves twenty years or older and 87 percent of the men. And younger men and women, still in late adolescence at the time of the census, might marry at some later time. Of the thirty-seven adult slaves Claudio José Machado owned, only 32 percent were married in 1829, while ten of the twelve adult slaves, or 83 percent, on Inácio Bicudo de Gouveia's small fazenda were married. Somewhat more than half of the sixty adult slaves, 56 percent, belonging to coffee planter Custódio Ferreira Braga, his wife, and their administrator were married. By comparison, marriage rates among whites and colored persons were nearly equal: 71 percent of whites were married, while among blacks and mulattos, both free persons and former slaves, the figure was 68 percent.[54]

At the fazenda of Tolosa's friend and neighbor, Chichorro, a count of the household made in 1835 recorded information lacking for other fazendas. The census taker noted that slaves had reported their own, precise ages. Equally unusual, the fifty-three slaves were listed in family groups: Eleven families can be identified, most with children, including a widowed African man living with his two young children. Nine men were unmarried, most of them Africans. The younger men might yet marry, but it is doubtful that Jacinto, forty-eight years old, João Congo,

Companhia das Ordenanças da Villa de Guaratinguetá, 1829, AESP-SM, Maços de População de Guaratinguetá, Fogo 1.

54 Mappa Geral [illegible] da Villa de Jacarehy do Anno de 1828, AESP-SM, Maços de População, Jacarehy, Santa Branca, Parahybuna, 1830–1850, Maço 2, Caixa 86, Ordem 86; Mappa dos Habitantes, 1830, Fogo 30, Maria Custodia de Alvarenga; Lista Geral do Habitantes, 3ª Companhia, 1829, Fogo 12, Claudio José Machado; Lista dos Habitantes, 1828, Fogo 37, Ignacio Bicudo de Gouveia; Lista Geral dos Habitantes, 6ª Companhia, 1829, Fogo 1, Custodio Ferreira Braga.

fifty years, or Antônio, fifty-two years, ever would. Cipriana, an African and the only unmarried adult woman, at thirty-five years was probably also past marrying age. The pattern was almost strictly African wife and husband and locally born children, reflecting the strong presence of imported African slaves among adults in an expanding economy. There were no families in which both husband and wife were creole slaves, and only one mixed marriage in which the husband, Domêncio, was African and the young wife, Benedita, creole. There was only one African child, the boy Lauriano, eight years old, among twelve other children, suggesting that parents had not brought children with them from Africa or that their African-born children had been sold separately or had died. The next generation of marriages would be among creoles. Unexceptionally for Paraibuna, nearly two-thirds of the slaves on Chichorro's fazenda were married.[55]

Slave marriages were not so unusual, although earlier historians have led us to think so. In his 1957 study of Vassouras, Stanley Stein ignored the question of slave marriages and referred in passing to "mated slaves" or slaves who "co-habited."[56] Among recent historians who profoundly revise our understanding of family life among slaves, the work of Robert Slenes is notable and convincing, especially as presented in his 1999 book, *Na senzala, uma flor*, the fruit of long and meticulous research and provocative interpretation. We can now say that in the rural regions so far studied, it is common to discover that between a quarter and a third of adult slaves married, and in some places many more.[57]

---

[55] 2° Distrito de Santo Antônio de Paraibuna, 1835, fogo 38, Manoel da Cunha de Azeredo Coutinho Souza Chichorro.

[56] See Stein, *Vassouras*, esp. pp. 43–44, 155, 170–171; Karasch, *Slave Life in Rio de Janeiro*, pp. 287–298; Florestan Fernandes, *The Negro in Brazilian Society*, trans. Jacqueline D. Skiles, A. Brunel, and Arthur Rothwell (New York: Columbia University Press, 1969), esp. pp. 72–130.

[57] Robert W. Slenes, *Na senzala, uma flor: Esperanças e recordações na formação da família escrava, Brasil sudeste, século XIX* (Rio de Janeiro: Nova Fronteira, 1999), and for percentages of slaves married across time and regions, see pp. 69–130, 263–266. See also his earlier work: Robert W. Slenes, "Senhores e subalternos no oeste paulista," in *História da vida privada no Brasil*, ed. Fernando A. Novais, vol. 2: *Império: A corte e a modernidade nacional*, org. Luiz Felipe de Alencastro (São Paulo: Companhia das Letras, 1997), pp. 273–275; Slenes, "Escravidão e família: Padrões de casamento e estabilidade familiar numa comunidade escrava (Campinas, século XIX)," *Estudos Econômicos* 17, no. 2 (May–August 1987): 217–227; and Slenes, "The Demography and Economics of Brazilian Slavery," pp. 445–467, esp. 451–453. Percentages for the areas Slenes reports on are

The question becomes not why so few slave marriages, but why so many? Whether masters benefited from a tighter rein on married slaves who, with precious family to protect, were less inclined to flight or rebelliousness and more inclined toward the securities of compliant service is arguable. Almost certainly, fewer women than men fled plantations. Mothers who refused to leave children behind could not move through difficult terrain or readily hide out with young, noisy, and needful children in tow. And if there was always a fear of reprisals against the kin who remained behind, the chance to visit kin on another plantation was reason enough to be absent for a night or a Sunday whenever possible. Women and sometimes entire families figured in the *quilombos*, or fugitive settlements, that runaways formed in the hills and forests outside the villages and towns with which they often traded. On the south coast of Bahia in the early 1800s, a young woman fled the sugar plantation where she was owned, traveled miles further down the coast to find her slave "partner," was then threatened with being returned to her owner by a bush captain, and finally was vigorously defended by her partner. They remained together at the quilombo where she later gave birth to their child.[58]

If some Brazilian owners counted on family ties to bind their slaves to the fazenda, others just as quickly encountered the constraints that having married slaves could impose. Although no law prevented a sale that would separate husband and wife or parents from their children until as late as 1869, the church had long ruled against sales that impeded slave marriages. But then, the church could be ignored. Perhaps more convincing, masters knew their attempts to break up families could be seriously disruptive, provoking not only disaffection but threats, flight, and possibly violence; eventually, concessions might be needed to restore even the uneasy balance of normal slave–master relations.[59]

generally lower than those derived from Paraibuna census lists. For Rio de Janeiro province in the colonial period, the central work is Sheila de Castro Faria, *A colônia em movimento: Fortuna e família no cotidiano colonial* (Rio de Janeiro: Nova Fronteira, 1998).

[58] On *quilombos* the best works are João José Reis and Flávio dos Santos Gomes, eds., *Liberdade por um fio: História dos quilombos no Brasil* (São Paulo: Companhia das Letras, 1996); see, esp., João José Reis, "Escravos e coiteiros no quilombo do Oitizeiro, Bahia, 1806," p. 354; and Flávio dos Santos Gomes, *Histórias de quilombolas: Mocambos e comunidade de senzalas no Rio de Janeiro, século XIX* (Rio de Janeiro: Arquivo Nacional, 1995).

[59] Lei 1695, 15 September 1869, *Leis do Brasil*, Art. 2, and Lei 2040, 28 September 1871, Art. 4, para. 7; *Constituições primeiras*, Liv. 1, Tit. 71, no. 303; Agostinho

Slenes's view that slaveowners deliberately encouraged their slaves to marry in order to control them overstates the case. Writing about "relations of power" between masters and their slaves in western São Paulo province and especially the region surrounding Campinas, Slenes describes a "slave owning class, dominant and frequently arbitrary, but above all astute: a class that wields force and favor to snare the slave in the trap of his own hopes." Masters acted, he says, "with the intention of turning slaves into dependents and hostages to their own solidarities and domestic projects."[60] This is strong language that amounts to saying slaveowners acted from a deliberately formed strategy of persistent manipulation. And as explanation for slave families it is unconvincing, not because slaveowners were not astute or ruthless, but because their collectively agreed-upon policy has not been demonstrated. That family allegiances had the outcome of further binding slaves may sometimes have been the case, but outcome does not prove intention, and detailed, persuasive evidence for their intentionality is so far lacking.

Less ambitious and more mundane explanations suffice. An alternative interpretation is not a doting master, but a simpler speculation that Brazilians generally found family a useful way of ordering society, their own slaves included. A preoccupation with people who roamed from place to place and getting them to settle down is a theme much commented on by both secular colonial officials and churchmen, and appears in Brazilian canon law as a general recommendation for encouraging the poor to honor their marriage vows and live in stable families.[61] Planters likely shared their worries, finding marriage for their slaves convenient both because it meshed with the Catholic culture that permeated all of Brazilian social life, relieving them of a need to invent and enforce an alternative, and because married slaves were measurably more content.

At Rio Claro married slaves were overwhelmingly the rule. In 1830, nearly 98 percent of all adult slaves were married, including all thirty-four women and all but two of the forty-four slave men.[62] Did two resident

---

Marques Perdigão Malheiro, A escravidão no Brasil: Ensaio histórico-jurídico-social, 3 parts in 2 vols. (Petrópolis: Vozes, 1976), Part 1, Art. III, Par. 30; Stuart B. Schwartz, Sugar Plantations in the Formation of Brazilian Society: Bahia, 1550–1835 (Cambridge: Cambridge University Press, 1985), p. 390; Lauderdale Graham, House and Street, pp. 81–82.

[60] Slenes, "Senhores e subalternos," pp. 234, 236, 273–275.

[61] Constituições primeiras, 1853, Liv. 2, Tit. 70, nos. 299–302; see also Liv. 2, Tit. 38, no. 154, on vagabonds and the requirement that they should confess yearly, by implication as members of a fixed parish.

[62] Mappa dos Habitantes, 1830, Fogo 89, Luiz Marianno de Toloza.

Table 2. *Marital Status of Adult Slaves at Rio Claro, 1830 (in percentages)*

	Africans		Creoles		
	Women	Men	Women	Men	Totals
Single					
20 years and older		3		9	2.5
Married[a]					
20 years and older	100	97	87	91	
Younger than 20 years[b]			13		97.5
Totals	100	100	100	100	100
	($n = 21$)	($n = 33$)	($n = 15$)	($n = 11$)	($n = 80$)

[a] No adults were identified as widowed.

[b] Although two women were younger than 20 years and therefore not adults by my defini-tion, they were married and so I have included them. Because there is no way to distinguish young adults between, say, 16 and 20 years, young adult men at Rio Claro are almost certainly undercounted.

Note: Absolute numbers are in parentheses.

Source: Mappa dos Habitantes alistentes desta Segunda e Nova Com[panhi]a da Freguesia de S[anto] Antonio de Paraibuna distrito da Villa de Jacarehei, em apresentes com seus Nomes, Empregos, Naturalidades, Idades, Estados, Cores, Ocupasões, Cazoalidades que aconteserão em cada huma de Suas Respectivas familias desde a fatura da data do Anno antesedente, Arquivo do Estado de São Paulo, Seção de Manuscritos, Maços de População, Jacarei, Santa Branca, Paraibuna, 1830–1850, Maço 2, Parahybuna, 2ª Companhia, 1830, Caixa 86, Ordem 86, Fogo 89, Luiz Marianno de Toloza.

priests at Rio Claro fix this fazenda as more scrupulous than some, a place where the sacrament of marriage was a requirement as much as a favor? If so, marriage nevertheless became more than a formality. Caetana lived among her own blood kin: mother, sister, and uncle. And this core family then expanded to include her sister's husband, the free mulatto João Ribeiro da Silva, and her uncle's wife, the former slave Luísa Jacinta. An uncle of Custódio's was alluded to. There may have been others – nieces or nephews, cousins, even other siblings – who did not testify and so are unknown to us.[63] Having family mattered in the slave variant of this culture that located and validated a person's identity within the family. Those who lacked family ties lacked full social membership and remained more vulnerable to the wear and tear of daily hardships than those encircled by the protecting presence of family. Caetana could claim such belonging.

What marks Caetana's case as special was not the presence of kin but the opportunity for us to discern a further network of kin usually not

[63] Nullidade, 1836, fls. 12, 39, 40, 41v, 53v.

visible in the minimally recorded ties of marriage and parentage found in most documents. The search for blood or marriage-related kin is typically hampered by the usual naming practice by which owners assigned their slaves only first names.[64] A sister such as Caetana's, married and living in her own household but listed by her first name, would be lost to us because records rarely preserved the crisscrossing kinship relations of siblings, uncles, aunts, cousins, nieces, nephews, grandparents, and certainly not ties with in-laws. As it was, the court's scribe never identified the sister by any name at all. Their mother, Pulicena, referred to by her name only once, remains a shadowy figure; Caetana's father is entirely lost to us. Dead, sold to another plantation, a runaway? The record does not say; he was never referred to. Nor do we learn whether Caetana's uncle was brother to her mother or to her father, a fact that may have counted in their responses to each other but which remains unavailable to us.

Caetana's sister and uncle open up our understanding of slave families by introducing nonslaves into the circle of kin. Caetana's brother-in-law, a free mulatto and never a slave himself, had married a slave woman, Caetana's sister; Caetana's uncle married a slave woman who at some subsequent time had gained her freedom, while he remained a slave. There is no reason to assume that this family was unique; surely, other families similarly cut across the legal conditions of slave, free, and freed, if we can recover the relationships.

Historians have suggested that the frequency of slave marriages depended more on regional demographic patterns among slaves than on church rules or a master's compliance. They argue that persistent imbalances in the numbers of male and female slaves – usually more men than women caused by the greater availability of men in the African trade, the women being too valuable to sell – jeopardized the possibility of slaves forming families and explain the presumed low rates of marriage among slaves.[65] On reflection it seems a strangely naive argument that assumes

---

[64] Slaves' names for themselves are another matter; see Reis, *Slave Rebellion in Brazil*, pp. 154–156, for an example of slaves retaining African names. Such names were probably not known and certainly not recorded in official documents by their owners; surnames, even when known, are often perplexing for historians, because they follow no fixed pattern. Maria Luiza Marcílio notes how childrens' names within a single family might vary; see *A cidade de São Paulo: Povoamento e população, 1750–1850* (São Paulo: Pioneira, 1974), pp. 70–76.

[65] Schwartz, *Sugar Plantations*, pp. 383–384; Stein, *Vassouras*, pp. 155–156; Metcalf, *Family and Frontier*, pp. 160–162.

the man's point of view, not the woman's: Evidently, slave women could choose from an ample field of available men. And in any event a slave woman's choices were not necessarily limited to slave men, as Caetana's sister's marriage to a free man reminds us. A scarcity of potential slave spouses may be the reason slave men remained single or took nonslave partners, but not why slave women did.

In Paraibuna, the rush to purchase new slaves reduced men's chances to find wives on their home fazendas. Such was the case on José Lobato de Moura e Silva's Paraibuna fazenda in 1829. Of the sixty-six slaves he and his son owned, fifty-two were adults twenty years or older, and all but two were Africans. They were sharply skewed by gender: forty-two men and only ten women. All ten women but only seven men were married, suggesting that three women had married off the fazenda. A disproportionate number of thirty-five young male slaves would remain without wives unless they, too, found partners on neighboring fazendas or married free women, an unlikely outcome given the general surplus of men. It was a women's market.[66]

On this score a crisis was brewing at Rio Claro. The sex imbalance so pronounced in colonial society, and which apparently began to even out during the nineteenth century among a population of increasingly creole slaves,[67] was still evident at Rio Claro in the 1830s. The twenty-six younger African males who soon might want partners would not find them on the fazenda, and Tolosa's preference that his slaves should marry would become unenforceable. While Caetana might have chosen any of several young slave men as her husband, Custódio was one of the many contenders for the other one or two young women available as wives.[68] For Custódio, who acknowledged that he wanted to marry, rivalries must have run high. Being a favored slave and already in his twenties evidently gave Custódio an edge over the others in Tolosa's decision to see Caetana married.

Whether slave families lived housed as families, with all the large and small comforts and irritations of proximate living and with whatever domestic autonomy such housing afforded, is something historians are beginning to discover. Historian Stanley Stein in his study of middle

---

[66] Lista Geral dos Habitantes, 6ª Companhia, 1829, Fogo 23, José Lobato de Moura e Silva.

[67] Stein, *Vassouras*, p. 78; Mieko Nishida, "Manumission and Ethnicity in Urban Slavery: Salvador, Brazil, 1808–1888," *HAHR* 73, no. 3 (August 1993): 375.

[68] Mappa dos Habitantes, 1830, Fogo 89, Luiz Marianno de Toloza.

Paraíba Valley coffee society in the second half of the nineteenth century emphasizes the "windowless cubicles of the mated slaves" and the equally stark dormitories that housed single women separately from the men. The author of a manual addressed to planters in the 1830s advised that even married slaves should live apart, being allowed to meet briefly at night.[69] By contrast, a wealthy and respected Paraíba Valley coffee planter advocated housing slave families together. Writing in 1847, he described suitable slave quarters as being arranged in a single row and divided into rooms 24 hands (or roughly 18 feet) square, with a wide veranda running the full length of the building. "Each room," he noted, "should house four single blacks, or if they are married, only husband, wife and children."[70] These standard long, low whitewashed quarters were commonly built in the shape of a quadrangle on larger fazendas, part of the central compound of work buildings. The arrangement was described by one planter as "loathed" by slaves, while for planters it had the advantage of enabling casual, daily surveillance.[71] An inventory of individual living units on a northeastern sugar estate in 1850 noted a "new house with tile roof in which the overseer lives," an old tiled-roof house for the sugar packer, as well as fifty-five thatched "houses," probably better characterized as huts, similar to the seventy-one "thatched houses that serve[d] as slave quarters" among the other stone and mortar buildings on one of the many sugar estates belonging to Antônio Pedroso de Albuquerque in the 1870s and 1880s.[72]

But for married slaves, in both the Campinas region of western São Paulo and in the province of Rio de Janeiro, marriage was qualification for access to land: a field or garden, called a *roça*, where slaves raised their

[69] Stein, *Vassouras*, pp. 43–44; C. A. Taunay, *Manual do agricultor Brazileiro, obra indispensavel a todo o senhor de engenho, fazendeiro e lavrador*, 2nd ed. (Rio de Janeiro, 1839), p. 171, cited in Stein, *Vassouras*, p. 155.

[70] Vernek, *Memoria*, pp. 9–10.

[71] Letter from Conselheiro Paula Souza to César Zama, 19 March 1888, in *A Provincia de São Paulo*, 8 April 1888, p. 1, cols. 1–3; Marc Ferrez, "Brazilian Coffee Fazenda . . . before 1890," three photographs in my possession. For a published example, see Marc Ferrez, "Coffee Plantation: Plantation House, Terraces for Drying Coffee, and Slave Quarters, c. 1882," in Gilberto Ferrez, *Photography in Brazil, 1840–1900*, trans. Stella de Sá Rego (Albuquerque: University of New Mexico Press, 1984), pp. 66–67.

[72] Inventário, Bento de Araújo Lopes Villasboas, Baron of Maragogipe, 1850, APEB-SJ, Inventários e Testamentos, 01/95/136/01, fl. 50v; Juizo de Direito da Vara Civel, Divórcio, defendant, Antonio Pedroso de Albuquerque, Salvador, Bahia, 1882, APEB-SJ, 05/157/06, fl. 86.

Figure 3. At this coffee fazenda the slave quarters enclose a central patio, possibly a second drying terrace. Some quarters have both a door and a window, and some a fireplace and chimney. Coffee beans raked into mounds dry on the lower terrace. In the background stand denuded hills where coffee bushes once grew, and before that dense virgin forest. (Marc Ferrez, c. 1885)

own crops of corn, beans, potatoes, coffee, and sugarcane. Crops meant a more plentiful or varied diet, or cash from their sale could be spent on small luxuries, saved against harder times, or accumulated toward the buying of freedom. And with land, these slaves were further privileged in sometimes having housing – and sleeping and eating spaces, Slenes emphasizes – separate both from the collective slave quarters and from a master's watchful gaze. They gained their own hearth and the possibility of preparing food according to their own tastes and spiritual prescriptions, and eating it with chosen kin, away from the work gangs.[73]

[73] Slenes, *Na senzala, uma flor*, pp. 149–151, 187–197, 201, and 237–253, explores not only the practical, but also the spiritual, implications of having hearth and fire, and the possible African meanings of both domestic space and food. Hebe Maria Mattos de Castro, *Das cores do silêncio: Os significados da liberdade do sudeste escravista, Brasil século XIX* (Rio de Janeiro: Arquivo Nacional, 1995), further argues that having a slave wife was the bridge for male slaves from the collective, masculine world of the slave quarters to a familial and more personalized life (pp. 151, 153).

Figure 4. A scene of slave domesticity. Small-scale slave quarters with three units, with fences on either side for penning domestic animals and probably a small garden nearby, are set apart from the central working plant of the fazenda. Laundry is spread to dry on the bushes, and three women work at chores, while a man looks on. (Victor Frond, "Cases à Nègres," in *Brazil pittoresco* ... (1861). Reproduced with the kind permission of the Instituto Histórico e Geográfico Brasileiro, Rio de Janeiro.)

Caetana's case provides only a handful of clues – but provocative ones – about her family's housing. João Ribeiro da Silva, Caetana's brother-in-law, recalled a conversation that took place in the "house" of Caetana's mother – not room or slave quarters, but *casa*, or house, suggesting not only a separate dwelling but perhaps one that by long occupancy was recognized as belonging to Caetana's mother.[74] It seems implausible that only in the telling did a "windowless cubicle" become transformed into a house. The case further reveals that once married, Caetana and Custódio went to live in her aunt and uncle's house. With this admittedly slight evidence, it seems that at least some of Tolosa's slaves lived in individual, if roughly constructed, huts or houses. Their houses probably came attached to one or more family garden plots, where her aunt and brother-in-law farmed. Their own housing, rather than the collective quarters assigned other slaves, was a reward reserved for privileged slaves such as Caetana's family.[75]

[74] Nullidade, 1836, fls. 39–39v.
[75] Hebe Maria Mattos de Castro, "Laços de família e direitos no final da escravidão," in *História da vida privada no Brasil*, ed. Fernando A. Novais, vol. 2: *Império:*

About the furnishings of slave quarters we know little, except that the principal piece of furniture was a bed. Stein offers a meager inventory that included a bed or cot made of "boards supported on two saw horses, covered with a mat of woven grass."[76] A bed raised off the ground was rare; a woven mat spread directly on a beaten earth or brick floor would have been usual. Following the wedding, Caetana refused to let Custódio "into the bed despite his pleadings," according to Custódio.[77] The literalness of the language – "into the bed" – suggests that "bed" was not a euphemism for sexual relations, but simply the telling of what happened, but whether "bed" meant floor mat or raised cot, we never learn.

Field slaves locked in collective quarters at night and house servants kept in cramped rooms near the kitchen are a prevalent image of Brazilian slave life, one confirmed by a São Paulo planter who removed the locks on the slave quarters at his fazenda when free workers replaced slaves there in the late 1880s. Travelers to Brazil described slaves, especially single men and women, sleeping in locked rooms or dormitories and the routine of the nightly lockup, although the effectiveness of the locks, given the poor constructions of slave quarters generally and the number of runaways, can be questioned.[78]

But in slave times who held the keys? A French cotton merchant who visited the sugar-producing northern province of Pernambuco in 1816 gives us pause by reporting that at Salgado estate slave quarters each had a door that the slaves "were very careful to lock," and when "barred inside they opened them with great reluctance."[79] From a criminal case in 1878, historian Hebe Maria Mattos de Castro describes slave quarters on a modest sugar farm in Rio de Janeiro province. The slave woman

---

A corte e a modernidade nacional, org. Luiz Felipe de Alencastro (São Paulo: Companhia das Letras, 1997), p. 361, tells of Pedrinho, a carpenter, mule-driver, and field hand on a fazenda in the province of Minas Gerais who lived with his wife in a house where he had his own field and a horse.

[76] Stein, *Vassouras*, p. 44.

[77] Nullidade, 1836, fl. 50v.

[78] Stein, *Vassouras*, p. 169; Warren Dean, *Rio Claro: A Brazilian Plantation System, 1820–1920* (Stanford: Stanford University Press, 1976), p. 45; Letter from Conselheiro Paula Souza to César Zama, 19 March 1888, in *A Provincia de São Paulo*, 8 April 1888, p. 1, cols. 1–3; Slenes, *Na senzala, uma flor*, pp. 160, 165, 176; Castro, "Laços de família," pp. 351–352, provides two explicit examples of male and female slaves being locked in their quarters.

[79] L[ouis] F[rançois] de Tollenare, *Notas dominicais, tomadas durante uma viagem em Portugal e no Brasil em 1816, 1817 e 1818* (Salvador, Bahia: Editora Progresso, 1956), p. 79.

Justina lived in a room next to the kitchen with her three children, while her adolescent son and two other slaves slept in the kitchen. She kept the key to her room and could lock it. Or an overseer might keep the keys as when one overseer ran to unlock quarters from which he had heard shouts.[80] If any slaves at Rio Claro were locked up for the night, Caetana was not one of them. Late at night she ran unrestrained from her aunt and uncle's house to find her master, whose own house was apparently not locked either.

If we generally think of slaves' lives as precarious and unpredictable, the stability of Caetana's domestic life seems striking. *Escrava da casa*, or "slave of the house," was a stock phrase in the vocabulary of Brazilian slave owners to describe those slaves – either women or men, but more typically women – born and raised in their master's household. It suggested years of familiarity, gradually accumulated trust, and eventually (but never certainly) the rewards due a favored slave. Born on Rio Claro and always slaves of Tolosa, Caetana and her sister were slaves of the house who had not faced the dread of being sold to a strange place or an unknown master. In 1835, two generations of Caetana's family lived on the fazenda, and if, as is likely, the sister bore children, the line would extend to three. Although free, João Ribeiro chose marriage to Caetana's sister at the cost of tying himself to a slave, whose children would be born slaves, and through her to the potentially arbitrary will of her owner as well as to the site of his fazenda, just as Luísa Jacinta stayed with her slave husband Alexandre despite her acquired freedom. In the calculation of affection against the real or imagined advantages of mobility, family ties held firm. Their willingness to stay at Rio Claro with Tolosa as the local patron suggests they thought they had a reasonable deal with him.

But slaves could not depend on such stability. All slave life was lived against the possibility of sale and removal to an unfamiliar place. Caetana learned that disobedience could suddenly erode the fragile trust holding her social world in place, for Tolosa could withdraw his favor as surely as he bestowed it. When he came to arrange the papers and Caetana again refused the marriage, he threatened to "put her out of the house." His dark threat hinted at a punishing withdrawal of trust and demotion to rough field work, possibly even sale.[81] With those few words, Caetana's seemingly secure place as a slave of the house

---

[80] Both examples are described by Castro, "Laços de família," pp. 347, 351.
[81] Nullidade, 1836, fl. 48.

was rendered precarious. She was made to understand what was always implied: Only by complying with his will could she retain her privileged position. It was a bleak lesson in the workings of a master's power, one she heeded.

Punishment might be postponed, reduced, or withdrawn, but in the long run another force was at work that could not be avoided. Inevitably, a master's death cast a long shadow of uncertainty over all slaves' lives. A death meant property, including slaves, passed to the heirs, and in Brazil, where children inherited equally, unless only one heir survived, it meant that property was divided. Brazilian law, a continuation of Portuguese law, specified that two-thirds of a person's or a couple's joint property be divided equally among the children or grandchildren or, in the event there were no descendant heirs, property reverted to parents or grandparents. A person could dispose of the other one-third of his or her property as he or she chose – she was said to have testamentary freedom over this one-third; and if there were no necessary heirs, a person could direct the entire estate to a chosen heir. The value of all gifts, loans, and dowries made to the children before the parents' deaths had to be returned to the estate for the final accounting, and, if a child had already received more than his or her final share of the estate, then he or she owed the difference to the estate. The result was that, inevitably, an owner's death caused the slaves to be divided among the heirs, along with the other property.[82]

How was it at Rio Claro? An approximate answer can be pieced together by comparing slaves listed in the 1830 county census with those who appeared in later probate records. Of the 134 slaves at Rio Claro in 1830, at most twenty-one were still there in 1853, and of those, only fifteen had names distinctive enough to be identified confidently.[83] Some had surely died, the record of their deaths lost, if any were kept, their names simply not appearing in later documents. Others were sold and scattered.

Some were freed. In her will, in the standard language of such documents, Dona Ana Joaquina promised freedom at her death to seven

---

[82] On inheritance law and property division, see *Codigo Philippino*, 1870, Liv. 4, Tit. 96; Lei 1695, 15 September 1869, *Leis do Brasil*, Art. 2, and Lei 2040, 28 September 1871, Art. 4, para. 7; Metcalf, *Family and Frontier*, pp. 153–154, 175–182, emphasizes the separation of slave families through the process of inheritance, some going to heirs, some sold to cover debts.

[83] Mappa dos Habitantes, 1830, Fogo 89, Luiz Marianno de Toloza; Inventário, Luiz Marianno de Tolosa, 1853, fls. 6–11v.

slaves "for the good services and loyalty with which they served me."
Among these, place names taken as last names identified José Nagô and
Ana Rebolla as Africans, captured, transported in the slave trade, and at
some time bought by the Tolosas. Maria Nova, Bueno, José Carioca, and
Cipriano may have been Brazilian-born; Creole Bonifácio certainly was.
Except for Ana Rebolla, who was in her thirties, we do not know their
ages or how they might have been related to each other or to others on
the fazenda. Perhaps the order of their listing indicated two families.[84]
They were likely house servants whom their mistress had come to favor over the field slaves she might scarcely have known. Did freedom,
however longed for, also stir new anxieties, where to go and how to find
work? In 1832, the county population included few freed slaves: thirty-
two women and twenty-five men, compared with 776 slave women and
men.[85] How would they live marked as former slaves when most laborers were slaves, and planters were inclined to believe black men and
women worked only under the lash? How deep were their ties to Rio
Claro? Whom did they leave behind? Did Caetana, who would have
worked with them, find her place in the household altered by their
absence? Were there new duties? Was support from older, more experienced slaves missing? Had they been told of their conditional freedom,
waited, and hoped for it? If Dona Ana Joaquina had lived to be an old
woman, she might have outlived them and they would never have known
their freedom, or they might have grown old themselves, more fearful
of freedom's changes than welcoming. Alexandre, a creole and probably
born on Rio Claro, was lucky enough to be freed through the priest's
will when he was a young man of twenty-two, with a life still ahead
of him.[86]

Not all slaves who left Rio Claro left with their freedom papers. Dona
Ana Joaquina gave the slaves Francisco Guedes and Victoria as gifts to
her goddaughter and to the girl's mother; Rosa was bequeathed to her
mistress's relative or friend, Antônia de Poia, or to her daughter, whoever
lived longer. Perhaps these three thought themselves well off, perhaps
not; how much had their preferences influenced their mistress's choices?
Sometime around 1846, Abel, a creole who belonged to the priest, fled
the fazenda after at least sixteen years there, when he was already in his
late forties or early fifties and getting old. The priest's death probably

[84] Inventário, Anna Joaquina Moreira, 1834, fls. 2–2v.
[85] População da Freguezia de Santo Antônio de Paraibuna, 1832, fl. 3.
[86] Inventário, Padre Valerio Alvarenga Ferreira, 1848, fl. 3v.

affected him little, if he heard of it at all, except to make his capture a little less likely.[87]

In the usual course of settling an estate after the deaths of both spouses, property was assigned to the necessary heirs by the legally appointed "apportioner" whose job it was to calculate equal shares, based on the appraisers' estimates. For Tolosa's five children, grown and married by the time of his death in 1853, the property included land, buildings, and slaves, as well as cattle and work animals, assorted silver, furniture, kitchen utensils (all metal objects had value), and chapel furnishings. The ten slaves already given to them were taken into account, and each received additional slaves. Many were older slaves, nearly half of them already living at Rio Claro in the early 1830s, some as children. Teodora and Fortunato, both between ten and nineteen years old in 1830, would have known Ana Francisca, Tolosa's younger daughter and now their owner, since she was born. The slave Faustino and João Baptista, Tolosa's youngest son, had grown up together, being about the same age. And so it was with another son, Joaquim Mariano, and the slaves Felicidade and Tomé, all of whom were about the same age. The transfer to familiar owners might not have been seriously disturbing, except that only one son appears to have remained a planter in Paraibuna, while the others had either moved to town or out of the region altogether and would sell or remove slaves – who had lived and worked together for more than twenty years – from known surroundings and known colleagues.[88]

Among those who faced such partings from fellow slaves, six slaves nonetheless remained as married couples: the African Manuel Monjollo and his wife, Rita, both of whom must have been very old by 1853, judging by the low value assigned them by the appraiser; the carpenter Jerônimo and his wife, Josefa, who had been children at Rio Claro; and Domingues Vieira and his wife, Felicidade, also at Rio Claro since she was a child. Three of Tolosa's children each received one of the couples. The sources do not say what became of any children they had.[89]

Slave marriages were not always respected at Rio Claro, however. The debts owed by a master at his death might be devastating for his slaves. In 1848 ten slave couples were named in the inventory of Father Valerio's

[87] Inventário, Anna Joaquina Moreira, 1834, fl. 3; Inventário, Padre Valerio Alvarenga Ferreira, 1848, fl. 29v.
[88] Mappa dos Habitantes, 1830, Fogo 89, Luiz Marianno de Toloza; Inventário, Luiz Marianno de Tolosa, 1853, fls. 3–3v, 5v–19, 68–80.
[89] Luiz Marianno de Toloza, Mappa dos Habitantes, 1830, Fogo 89; Inventário, Luiz Marianno de Tolosa, 1853, fls. 68–80.

property, half of whom had lived at Rio Claro for at least eighteen years. While nearly half the slaves went to the priest's chosen heir, the widow Gertrudes, the others, including three couples, were assigned to various creditors, dispersed as payment for loans. Joaquina was used to pay part of the priest's debt to Tolosa with probably minor changes in her life until a few years later, when Tolosa transferred her to a third owner to settle another debt, and she was taken to a fazenda in another part of the county. When the priest died, Inés and Jonas, married and living at Rio Claro since at least 1830, were separated and paid to different creditors. Their grief must have been unspeakable.[90] Slave families blessed by their owners in an earlier era became helplessly vulnerable at their deaths. In the end, Rio Claro's remarkable stability proved to be no more than temporary.

Godparents

Family alliances fixed by blood and marriage were further extended by the practices of Catholic culture through the voluntary ties of ritual godparenthood. Selection of a godfather and godmother to sponsor a child at baptism knitted families into wider networks of patronage with ongoing exchanges of favors and deference. Godparents bore the serious and church-sanctioned duty to guide a child's spiritual well-being; they could be called upon to correct erring parents or substitute for those who, through death, illness, or absence, could not fulfill their duties. Not content that a child should receive only material care, the church provided spiritual parents from baptism, when the soul became capable of eternal salvation in the presence of God. Because godparents might well be called upon to replace real parents, their choosing was a delicate matter and produced an intricate pattern of ritual kinship that buttressed and mirrored the interlaced understandings of sacred and secular hierarchical order.

Reflection on the practices of Brazilian godparenthood among slaves begins with Stuart Schwartz's work on the Bahian sugar zone, which, although describing a geographically distant region and a different economy at an earlier time, remains one of the more detailed studies available. Noting Catholic doctrine, Gudeman and Schwartz emphasized the

[90] Mappa dos Habitantes, 1830, Fogo 89, Luiz Marianno de Toloza; Inventário, Padre Valerio Alvarenga, 1848, fls. 6v, 14–17v, 36v–41, 44v; Inventário, Luiz Marianno de Tolosa, 1853, fls. 11, 64v–65.

spiritual equality the sacrament of baptism bestowed on blessed souls and found it incompatible with relations in the mundane world. In the setting of a slave society of exaggerated and forced inequalities, they argued, the commercial relationship that connected master and slave was utterly at odds with and threatened by the equality presumed to follow from ritual kinship. They saw there an explanation for a persistent pattern: Across four parishes in the 1780s, no slaves had their masters as godparents.[91]

The pattern was echoed in other places and at other times. On sugar estates in colonial São Paulo, Alida Metcalf discovered only one master who urgently and exceptionally took the role of both priest and godfather to baptize a dying slave baby. Neither later in Bahia nor in nineteenth-century western São Paulo coffee fields did any slaveowners act as godparents for their own slaves, and in only two instances in the nineteenth century did slaveowners in the southern city of Curitiba sponsor their own slaves at baptism. Kathleen Higgins similarly found that slaves in the mining district of Sabará in eighteenth-century Minas Gerais did not have their owners as godparents.[92]

But if the pattern is consistent and beyond dispute, the explanation is more difficult. As eligibility for eternal salvation, baptism established equality of the baptized only before God, not before either Pope or Caesar. Catholic theology celebrates an elaborate hierarchy extending downward from the Holy Trinity to the angels, who themselves are ranged in ranked divisions, to the saints, then to the church similarly ordered from pope, archbishop, bishop, and priest, and finally to the lay faithful. Like other Catholics, Brazilians learned to pray to the Blessed Virgin Mary and the saints to intercede for them in their appeals for God's grace. By extension, supplication and intercession provided a religious grounding for the tough but flexible network of secular patronage

---

[91] Stephen Gudeman and Stuart B. Schwartz, "Cleansing Original Sin: Godparenthood and the Baptism of Slaves in Eighteenth-Century Bahia," in *Kinship Ideology and Practice in Latin America*, ed. Raymond T. Smith (Chapel Hill: University of North Carolina Press, 1984), pp. 35–58, and summarized in Schwartz, *Sugar Plantations*, pp. 406–412.

[92] Metcalf, *Family and Frontier*, pp. 188–189; Schwartz, *Slaves, Peasants, and Rebels*, pp. 137–160, esp. pp. 152–153 on Bahia and pp. 147–150 on Curitiba; Slenes, "Senhores e subalternos," p. 271; Kathleen J. Higgins, *"Licentious Liberty" in a Brazilian Gold-Mining Region: Slavery, Gender, and Social Control in Eighteenth-Century Sabará, Minas Gerais* (University Park: Pennsylvania State University Press, 1999), pp. 138–143.

relations that webbed an otherwise divided and potentially brittle society. In secular life, too, supplication and intercession connected visibly unequal persons, and by cutting across their social differences served not to dispel but to affirm them. Far from being incompatible with slavery, ritual kinship repeated the unequal paternal relationship and its analogous master–slave relationship.

Why, then, the striking abstinence? According to Gudeman and Schwartz, no master could assume sacred responsibility for a slave and simultaneously claim his right to "discipline, sell, or endlessly work" the slave without either compromising his own religious obligations or severely constraining his intention to profit from his slave.[93] They are bolstered in their view by an early nineteenth-century traveler to Brazil, Henry Koster, an Englishman long resident in Portugal and fluent in Portuguese, who claimed he had "never heard of the master in Brazil being likewise the god-father . . . for such is the connection . . . that the master would never think of ordering the slave to be chastised."[94] Yet nothing in the code of Luso-Brazilian paternalism, in either its religious or civil forms, constrained the head of a household against corporal punishment of those, including family members, over whom he exercised domestic authority. On the contrary, the *Código Filipino*, promulgated in 1603 and the basis for civil law in Brazil until 1916, expressly permitted him the right to physically "castigate" his family, dependents, and slaves. While on the question of work the church directed masters to refrain from working their slaves on Sundays and holy days, it acknowledged in the next breath that cane already cut urgently required milling, even on Sundays, thereby relieving planters of any conflict they might have felt between religious duty and their economic interests.[95] It is doubtful, then, that on this count there would have been reason for a master to avoid serving as godparent. Unquestionably, however, a master who sold his godchild, severing all contact and no longer able to guard the child's spiritual well-being, did repudiate his sacred duty. So although no institutional authority formally restricted owners from serving as godparents, and no ideology of equality diluted a master's authority over his slaves,

---

[93] The quote is from Schwartz, *Sugar Plantations*, p. 407; for a more elaborated discussion of the same point, see Gudeman and Schwartz, "Cleansing Original Sin," pp. 41–43.

[94] Henry Koster, *Travels in Brazil*, 2 vols. (Philadelphia: M. Carey and Son, 1817), vol. 1, p. 196 n.

[95] *Codigo Philippino*, 1870, Liv. 5, Tit. 36, para. 1; *Constituições primeiras*, 1853, Liv. 2, Tit. 12, nos. 371, 372, 378.

a perception of competing interests and a preference to distance themselves from their slaves seemingly did dissuade a master from taking on
the role of godparent.

But what if we focus instead on the slaves; who, then, did slaves
choose as godparents? Typically, other free persons. On both the Bahian
and the São Paulo colonial sugar estates for which we have information,
a majority of slaves with godparents – two-thirds or more – chose persons
from the lower ranks of free society, often single women or men, usually
lighter-skinned than they, and frequently farmers who worked their lands
themselves, or at best small-scale planters with a few slaves of their own.
Sometimes these free godparents were former slaves, about 10 percent of
the time in the Bahian example.[96] In Curitiba over the long span of 200
years and in early eighteenth-century Sabará, slaves generally chose
free persons as godparents, and especially free men as godfathers.[97] Slaves
stood to benefit from vertical relationships with persons who were not
far removed from them socially, but who nonetheless could bestow some
favors, and who in turn gained by having clients who visibly confirmed
their status. Even when slave clients belonged to another fazenda, they
owed deference and could be counted on for obedient work when hired
from a larger estate during the harvest, and, if one day they were freed,
the men could pledge their votes in support of a godfather's aspirations
for local power.

Slaves also chose other slaves as godparents. Notably, as many as
a third of the slaves in the Bahian and São Paulo examples preferred
other slaves, usually from their own slave quarters, sometimes from other
fazendas, but rarely from outside the parish, a reflection of the boundaries of their acquaintanceship and experience. Adult slaves in Bahia
in 1835 clearly preferred other slaves as both godfathers and godmoth-
ers. Rather than compete for free godparents, these slaves kept among
themselves. By serving as godparents slaves gained their own dependent and loyal followers among fellow slaves, duplicating in the slave
quarters patterns of patronage usually thought to include slaves only
as the recipients of favors, not as patrons. Here slaves became patrons.
Ties that connected some slaves excluded others, further marking a hierarchy among slaves. Robert Slenes describes two slave families on a

---

[96] Metcalf, *Family and Frontier*, pp. 188–189; Schwartz, *Sugar Plantations*, pp. 408–
409.
[97] Schwartz, *Slaves, Peasants, and Rebels*, pp. 148–149; Higgins, *"Licentious Liberty,"*
p. 138.

Campinas fazenda in the 1870s, each with three generations present, as the "founding" families of the slave quarters, holding the majority of non-field work occupations and providing most of the godparents, especially for "recently arrived" slaves who had not yet forged local family ties. Domestic and skilled slaves were especially sought out by others as having the influence to be effective intermediaries or the material resources to assure a family's well-being.[98] The benefits were reciprocal. By choosing slave godparents, slaves elevated some fellow slaves to positions of strength or reinforced a slave's already acclaimed status in the slave quarters.

In Caetana's family a double relationship was formed: slave kin as godparents for a slave baby. Alexandre and Luísa Jacinta, who was in her thirties at the time of Caetana's baptism and almost certainly then still a slave, were both Caetana's uncle and aunt and her godfather and godmother, as well as being fellow slaves at Rio Claro. Present in Caetana's life since birth, they remained a forceful presence in her life seventeen years later. Both were creoles: Alexandre born in Taubaté, north from Tolosa's fazenda and a rugged journey across the Serra do Quebra Cangalha near the Paraíba River, Luísa Jacinta from Vila Nova de São Luís near Guaratuba Bay on the southernmost coast of the province, a district that grew coffee and some cane. We do not learn how or when they came to belong to Tolosa, only that at some past time they married, perhaps at Rio Claro.[99] As a house servant eventually freed and the fazenda's muleteer, Luísa Jactina and Alexandre became influential slaves at Rio Claro. And as both blood and ritual kin they were unavoidably drawn into Caetana's affairs.

Slaves were not mistaken to see advantage in slave godparents. Consider the significance of Caetana's relationship. To be sure, missing are ties to free sponsors with whatever tangible benefits they could confer: protective or supportive intervention with a slave's master, perhaps even

---

[98] Metcalf, *Family and Frontier*, pp. 188–189; Schwartz, *Sugar Plantations*, pp. 408–409, and *Slaves, Peasants, and Rebels*, pp. 153–154; Slenes, "Senhores e subalternos," pp. 265 and 270, also points out that in Campinas slave godparents most often belonged to another owner. On slaves sponsoring other adult slaves more than children, see Schwartz, *Sugar Plantations*, p. 411. Elizabeth Johnson, "Slavery and the Benedictine Order in Late Colonial São Paulo," Master's thesis, University of Texas at Austin, 1996, describes the rankings of slaves over several generations demonstrated in godparenting networks (pp. 44–84).

[99] José Saturnino da Costa Pereira, *Diccionario topographico do Imperio do Brasil* (Rio de Janeiro: Typ. P. Gueffier, 1834), pp. 239, 66; Nullidade, 1836, fl. 41v.

manumission.[100] Yet, another slave, especially from the same fazenda, could prove more accessible and reliable, someone inclined to hold both godchild and parents in higher regard and respond more quickly or generously to some need. Well-regarded slaves such as Alexandre and Luísa Jacinta might prove more effective than free but poor sponsors who themselves barely survived on the edges of respectable white society. Rather than extend their reach into the uncertain ranks of the free poor, Caetana's family formed a bond that consolidated and affirmed existing ties and emphasized the position of some slaves over others on the fazenda.

Godparenthood encompassed not only the relationship between godparents and godchild, but also the important tie between godparents and the child's parents who became *compadres*. Understood in the exchange, as in all patronage relationships, was not only the downward granting of favors but a reciprocal upward pledge of service, deference, obedience, loyalty. Koster caught the sense of it when he described the commandant of a remote district who had knowingly built a clan by sponsoring one child of each of ten men, who then became linked to him as compadres. It was a bond, Koster continued, "which permits the poor man to speak to his superior with a kind of endearing familiarity, and unites them. . . . "[101] The same desire for a connection that could ease the tension of tangible and persistent inequalities also operated inside the slave quarters. Slaves, too, built new alliances among fellow slaves or strengthened existing ones. The promotion of some slaves as godparents demonstrated slaves' own strategies for finding a way through difficult daily problems. An alert borrowing of godparent ties for mutual, slave advantage.

CAPTAIN TOLOSA

Why had Tolosa initially wanted the marriage, and why did he later change course? The answer is not simple to discover. Caetana's work as a mucama drew her into the Tolosa family's intimate daily life and into the private quarters and bedrooms of the Casa Grande, service as personal maid to the young, unmarried daughters being her particular responsibility. To be a house slave, a "trusted person" – in Portuguese the

---

[100] Schwartz, *Sugar Plantations*, pp. 406–412; Metcalf, *Family and Frontier*, pp. 188–190; Karasch, *Slave Life in Rio de Janeiro*, p. 257.

[101] Koster, *Travels in Brazil*, vol. 2, p. 316.

phrase is *pessoa de confiança* – was a privileged position and understood as such; Caetana was following in her godmother's footsteps. But privilege bore its costs. Although Caetana witnessed the affairs of the Casa Grande at closer range than most other Rio Claro slaves, the family nevertheless recognized her as an outsider in their midst. Because daily present in their lives, this slave woman was seen to have the power to influence the daughters whose dresses she laundered and hair she combed, whose meals and outings she supervised. And if not closely supervised herself, went the standard view, she could bring them harm: bodily disease, slovenly habits, moral corruption. Hers was an ambivalent position that uneasily mixed trust with suspicion.[102]

And Tolosa viewed her with ambivalence. No more willing than any other householder of his class to dispense with the services of a mucama, he took steps to protect his household. It is here that we discover his reason for urgently pressing on Caetana a marriage she found repugnant. Caetana supplied the details that Tolosa no more than alluded to in his testimony. At a second interview to which her master called her, he told her "in milder but no less insistent words" he had decided she would marry because "by no means did he wish to have in his house, and even less in its interior, single slave women to serve his daughters." And because she was employed in this service as a mucama, he continued, "she would have to decide to marry with her fellow slave, Custódio."[103] Tolosa presented himself, then, as a responsible father protective of the well-being of his impressionable young daughters. Female sexuality was hardly being denied, for implicitly he acknowledged the sexuality of both the slave woman and his daughters. In his view the nubile Caetana was in danger of becoming an immoral influence by the example of her inevitable sexual conduct. As a married woman, her sexuality appropriately contained, she would become a respectable servant. Against regard for Tolosa's daughters, Caetana's wishes were dismissed. His decision acknowledged the complex intersection between slave and master families: Because of the master's daughters, a slave woman must marry.

A plausible explanation, but nonetheless slightly odd. Surely, the wife and mother would attend to these interior matters? But this was no longer so at Rio Claro. Three years earlier, ill and "in danger of death," Dona Ana Joaquina Moreira de Tolosa prudently dictated her will

---

[102] Elsewhere I have examined the ambivalent situation of the *mucama* in city households; see Lauderdale Graham, *House and Street*, esp. pp. 117–125.

[103] Nullidade, 1836, fls. 11, 47v.

(although being illiterate, someone else signed for her). She died in April 1834. Her death made Tolosa, then about forty, a widower responsible for their five children. The girls whose protection worried him so greatly were Maria do Carmo, twelve years old, and Ana Francisca, aged two years.[104] Without a wife to guide their upbringing and oversee the domestic life of his household, and with no sister, cousin, or aunt to substitute for her in these duties, Tolosa would have to rely more than ever on his house slave. Therefore she must marry.

The matter does not end here: What of the males of the household? Tolosa's three sons, João Baptista, eleven years old when his mother died, the thirteen-year-old Francisco, and the eldest, Joaquim, of fourteen years, were never mentioned with regard to Caetana.[105] The omission is notable. Brazilian boys are said to have taken their early sexual pleasure with slave women (who may or may not have consented in what were inherently highly coercive situations). Did Tolosa intend to protect Caetana, however imperfectly, from his sexually experimenting sons by providing her with a husband? (Surely, she would have known that a relationship with a son, too young and too lacking in authority to offer her anything in exchange, would only increase her vulnerability?)[106]

Then there is the further question of Tolosa's own relationship to Caetana. Did he wish to avoid the whisperings that might follow him if he lived as a widower in a household where an unmarried slave woman supervised his female children and where no older female relative was in charge? In the climate of Brazilian slave relations a husband for Caetana would be a naive and generally unpersuasive solution, not one adopted by slaveowners who found no need to disguise relations with their slave women, and for the more brutal among them the presence of a husband was no deterrent. Brazilian men often recognized the children born to them by slave women, as did Elias Baptista de Mello. A slaveowner in the coffee region downriver from Paraibuna, in 1878 he recognized as his "legitimate heirs and successors," along with the legitimate children he had had with his deceased wife, the two children born to the free *mulata* Florinda and a second mulatta, Paula, whom he freed in his will. Did a concern for respectability lead him to add that he had fathered

[104] Inventário, Anna Joaquina Moreira, 1834, fls. 1, 2, 8v.

[105] Ibid., fl. 8v.

[106] Trevor Burnard, "'Do Thou in Gentle Phibia Smile': Scenes from an Interracial Marriage, Jamaica, 1754–1786," paper presented at the Race and Slavery Seminar, Department of History, University of Texas at Austin, spring 1997.

these children after becoming widowed, or was he especially concerned with establishing the legality of naming them as heirs?[107] If Tolosa had wanted Caetana for himself, a slave husband could hardly explain any mulatto children she bore, his presence might hinder Tolosa's access to her, and neither neighbors nor family would be taken in. A sham husband would not be convincing, convenient, nor required. Different masters sought different levels of social respectability, and behaved accordingly. Tolosa chose to act with greater circumspection and decorum.

Nor is there any evidence Tolosa did desire Caetana. He later formed a close relationship with a free woman, Sabina Leonor de França, but how much later is not recorded, nor her precise status or color, only that their relationship endured and was acknowledged by Tolosa's grown children. Although Tolosa and Sabina never married, he provided for her with gifts: four slaves, registered in 1849 at the notary office in Jacareí; three years later a house in the village "opposite the patio of the parish church" and another on the rua de Cima; and eventually a pair of silver candlesticks, a silver tray, and scissors. (The children disputed the silver, and Sabina paid the estate for the candlesticks.) He instructed in his will that at Sabina's death the property should pass to her children, their heirs, or, if no heirs survived, to the local church Nossa Senhora do Rosário, but on no account could it be used to cover debts. In this way Tolosa shielded Sabina from potentially unscrupulous creditors, while by not marrying again he preserved the bulk of his property for his own children. It was the fairest arrangement he could devise and, according to an old friend who acted as witness to the transaction, something he had thought about for a long time.[108] Although the evidence is admittedly only suggestive, Tolosa had apparently directed his sexual energies and affection away from his fazenda.

---

[107] Inventário, Elias Baptista de Mello, 8 October 1878, Inventários Antigos, Pacote 5B, Cartório do Primeiro Ofício, Vassouras, Rio de Janeiro. A child born of an adulterous, or spurious, relationship could never inherit; see *Codigo Philippino, 1870*, Liv. 4, Tit. 92 and Tit. 93, esp. the notes pp. 943–944; and also Linda Lewin, "Natural and Spurious Children in Brazilian Inheritance Law from Colony to Empire: A Methodological Essay," *The Americas* 48, no. 3 (January 1992), esp. p. 363.

[108] Inventário, Luiz Marianno de Tolosa, 1853, fls. 25–28, 32–33v, 38, 61. The gifts would have come from the one-third of his estate that he could freely dispose of and could not exceed one-third without his children later having the right to insist that the excess be returned to the estate. See *Codigo Philippino, 1870*, Liv. 4, Tit. 96 and 97.

If in 1835 worry about his daughters allowed no compromise, why then did Tolosa suddenly reverse his position, giving Caetana refuge and permission to sleep alone? When she fled her godparents' house, crying and adamantly refusing to allow Custódio into her bed, Tolosa finally understood, he said, that he had indeed coerced the marriage. Was he just a changeable fool persuaded by a girl's tears? Why did he take the dramatic and unusual further step of petitioning for an annulment on her behalf? We might say that being neither a cruel nor an arrogant man he had acted according to the prescriptions of his time and, being more conscientious than some and taking marriage more seriously, regretted what he had done. Perhaps. Yet there was something more to it.

Tolosa's friend from a neighboring fazenda, Manuel da Cunha de Azeredo Coutinho Souza Chichorro – the string of surnames announced his prominence – came to Rio Claro to hear mass, as he was accustomed to do, on the same Saturday night Caetana escaped to the Casa Grande. Chichorro testified that he had already retired for the night when "Captain Luiz" came to him "greatly distressed," telling him that he had "made Caetana marry" and of Caetana's determination to suffer physical punishment rather than accept her imposed husband. What surprises us is Tolosa's lack of indifference once the ceremony was performed. He could have turned away, but instead he listened and sought his friend's counsel. According to Chichorro, it was he who urged Tolosa to separate the couple for the night.[109] So the crisis was averted.

We see two powerful men finally attentive to the deep distress of a young and vulnerable slave woman. We also see how even a master's authority could be constrained. Although Tolosa could order his slave to marry – he had demonstrated that already – to require her to live as a wife was an intolerable intrusion into the private domain, as he gradually came to acknowledge. In the face of her initial opposition, he had threatened her with physical punishment – a costly resort that revealed he feared losing control over his slave. Legitimacy of the master's rule in a slave regime is necessarily a precarious matter. In the absence of an explicit ideology built on race, which Brazilian planters never felt obliged to elaborate, slave owners justified their power through conduct that custom gradually established as appropriate. His later support of the slave woman allowed Tolosa to present himself as a just man deserving of both his slaves' loyalty and the respect of his neighboring planters.

[109] Nullidade, 1836, fls. 45–46.

Elsewhere I have commented on situations in which other slaveowners, women as well as men, were compelled by their peers to conform to the rules of acceptable slaveowner conduct, sometimes at the cost of both reputation and property.[110] In this Tolosa was not exceptional, and he was, after all, a man with a considerable local reputation to protect.

In the immediate management of his fazenda Tolosa had deflected the dissension that could rend this family of his most valued slaves and would likely stir discontent among the rest. But he could do so because of the discreet intervention of a prestigious outsider with no direct stake in the outcome.

In the copious lexicon of Brazilian kinship terms, godfather meant not only lifelong, baptismal godfather, but in its more ample meaning referred to a temporary sponsor, someone who acted as mediator or intercessor. This meaning carried no connotation of long-term commitment or general concern for the sponsored's well-being, certainly no religious obligation, and such interventions were not limited to slaves. A temporary godfather mediated in a specific situation in which power was visibly and decidedly unequal and usually at the appeal of those with less power. The author of a recent study of slaves and masters in the downriver coffee county of Vassouras, based on the proceedings of criminal cases that involved slaves, interprets the role of sponsor as an informal substitute for official justice. In these cases the sponsor was usually a person of prominence with the authority and reputation to intervene convincingly on the slave's behalf and typically against the excessive or arbitrary violence of an overseer: an occasion when the customary expectations of tolerable conduct had been violated. The evidence demonstrates the considerable chances slaves took to solicit a sponsor – walking miles at night after the curfew and without permission to leave the fazenda, risking arrest – and are a measure of the

---

[110] See Lauderdale Graham, *House and Street*, pp. 104–107, 172–173 n. 63; Sandra Lauderdale Graham, "Slavery's Impasse: Slave Prostitutes, Small-Time Mistresses, and the Brazilian Law of 1871," *Comparative Studies in Society and History* 33, no. 4 (October 1991): esp. pp. 675–676, 685, 686–688, 693–694. On this I differ with Hebe Maria Mattos de Castro, who argues that the informal, then formal regulation of planters' power emerged only in the 1850s with the end of the African trade and the transfer of slaves across plantations and regions within Brazil. See "Laços de família," esp. pp. 355–360; and my reply, "A cultura do patriarcado rural às vésperas do império," paper presented at the Colóquio Internacional, "De Cabral a Pedro I," Fundação Calouste Gulbenkian, Lisbon, Portugal, 29–31 March 2000.

slave's perceived sense of urgency, danger, and the rightness of their action.[111]

In this way a slave sought redress against abuse without provoking a too-costly confrontation between an owner and his overseer that would either compromise the owner's authority or more likely leave the slave in the hands of an exposed and angered overseer. An influential outsider – planter or merchant in the district – with reason to want relations to remain even-tempered might agree to intervene even for slaves not personally known to him. The owner had reason to accept such a sponsor's mediation as a way to avoid taking the word of either overseer or slave against the other. In the end, a sponsor's presence could calm a dangerously tense moment and restore a sense of justice – and contribute to a slave regime's flexibility to endure.

Chichorro easily met the requirement of eminence. Born in Rio de Janeiro, he had studied law at Coimbra University in Portugal, held high-ranking positions in the colonial government, was named *fidalgo cavalheiro da casa imperial* and Commander of the Order of Christ, and was the recipient of extensive royal lands in the parish of Paraibuna and in the neighboring district of Jacareí. Having been a loyal advocate of Brazil's first emperor, Dom Pedro I, he was later honored by his son Pedro II as a founding member of the prestigious Instituto Histórico e Geográfico Brasileiro. Once a local judge, by 1835 Chichorro had retired from his post in the northern province of Pernambuco as a high court magistrate in one of the empire's four appellate courts. A married man in his middle years, he lived from his investments on a neighboring fazenda.[112]

Events at Rio Claro departed significantly, however, from the Vassouras pattern. There is no evidence that Caetana went beyond Rio Claro to seek Chichorro's intervention. Nor did Chichorro come to the fazenda that night intending to play the mediator. It was after he had heard mass and retired for the night that Tolosa woke him to "pour out"

---

[111] Bryan McCann, "Slavery Negotiated: Mediators on the Middle Ground, the Paraíba Valley, Brazil, 1835–1888," Master's thesis, University of New Mexico at Albuquerque, 1994, pp. 10–29. Maria Helena Pereira Toledo Machado similarly finds powerful neighbors acting as intermediaries between another planter's slaves and their overseer. See *Crime e escravidão: Trabalho, luta e resistência nas lavouras paulistas, 1830–1888* (São Paulo: Brasiliense, 1987), pp. 72–75.

[112] Augusto Victorino Alves Sacramento Blake, *Diccionario bibliographico brazileiro*, 7 vols. (1900; rpt., Rio de Janeiro: Conselho Federal de Cultura, 1970), vol. 6, pp. 55–56; *Repertório das sesmarias*, 370–371; Nullidade, 1836, fl. 45.

what was on his mind.[113] Tolosa's action was an admission of the sorry stalemate he had reached with his slave, for only a troubled man would disturb his friend's rest.

Some details of that night remain obscure. Where was Caetana while the two men talked? Left waiting in the kitchen of the Casa Grande? Sent back to her mother's? We know she did not return to her uncle's house. Yet, according to Chichorro, his advice was decisive, so only after he and Tolosa met was Caetana given a place to stay. In this instance, not slave but master had invited a third party into the negotiations, thereby extending the social boundaries of the fazenda, and further qualifying any assumption of the master–slave relationship as a strictly private matter. As intermediary one planter enabled another to reverse his stand without losing face and at the same time bind a frightened and relieved slave ever more tightly. Although there is nothing to say Chichorro actually urged annulment, Tolosa was surely encouraged by his advice and, as a former judge familiar with the law and court procedure, Chichorro could suggest how to proceed. With or without his friend's professional advice, Tolosa committed himself to pursue a petition in ecclesiastical court. And we are led to see a moment in the intimate workings of planter culture.

CAETANA

Caetana's refusal to marry falls into two phases. In the first she fought Tolosa's orders to take a husband. Whatever backing from family she might have hoped for, what she got initially was the ambiguous participation of her godmother. Having failed himself to gain Caetana's consent to wed, Tolosa needed someone else to try. Playing on the special relationship between goddaughter and godmother with its overlapping nuances of intimacy, authority, and deference, Tolosa enlisted Luísa Jacinta. What discussions occurred between Tolosa and Luísa Jacinta are not recorded. Whether she thought the marriage a good one for her niece, all we know is that she agreed to "talk personally" with her. Caetana, too, had called on her aunt when earlier she wanted someone to repeat to Tolosa what she had already told him.[114] Trusted by both parties, Luísa Jacinta was the ideal go-between.

The outcome hardly satisfied Caetana, however. Caetana recorded that despite her godmother's "thousand entreaties to accept the projected

[113] Nullidade, 1836, fl. 45.
[114] Ibid., fls. 39v, 41v.

union," she had replied sharply that she would not be "reduced to this," and her godmother should report this to her master "on whose part she said she had come." Whether the godmother delivered this tart message, Caetana said she never found out. Luísa Jacinta said clearly she had done as Caetana asked, but her master "showed little interest." Tolosa's actions at first convey the easy confidence of one accustomed to obedience, yet when Caetana refused to be persuaded he resorted to applying pressure indirectly through the aunt-godmother. Her efforts also rebuffed, Tolosa resolutely set the date for the wedding without Caetana's consent.[115]

Later, Caetana was to say that compliance with her master's decision had been unavoidable. By contrast, Tolosa emphasized his readiness to negotiate. He "gave her," he said, "ample liberty to choose one of the other unmarried slaves who served the house." (It is worth noting that the men had even less choice in the matter than Caetana.) She discounted the offer, understanding it was all the same: She would have to marry one man or another. He was her master, she said, and "as such would do what he wanted." In the words of her lawyer, Caetana, being no more than a slave, was "reduced to the hard necessity of obeying solely from fear of grave punishment and lasting harm" – even if "he was incapable of practicing such . . . bitter treatment, as she later became convinced." Yet, if Caetana understood from the start that she must and would give in, why did she risk anger and punishment by repeatedly refusing to comply, each time more adamantly? As the opposing lawyer for the church pointed out, Caetana's alleged fear of Tolosa hardly deterred her from resisting his orders.[116] If in the days before the wedding nothing he did encouraged her to believe he would be dissuaded, she nevertheless held out until the last moment. Something gave her courage. What exchanges between Tolosa and his slaves had she witnessed at Rio Claro in the past, or experienced herself, that led her to press for an indulgent response from him now? The sources are too narrowly cast to provide an answer. All we can say is that, finally acknowledging that Tolosa's instructions brooked no disobedience and she could not prevent the wedding, she appeared. As she stood beside Custódio at the altar, their right hands joined, hearing the priest's words, did she already have in mind a plan to refuse her husband?[117]

[115] Ibid., fls. 43, 11v and 47v.
[116] Ibid., fls. 52, 11v, 12, 100–100v.
[117] *Constituições primeiras*, 1853, Liv. 1, Tit. 68, no. 287.

The wedding over, Caetana's struggle quickly shifted to her husband and family. She left her mother's house to live with Custódio at her godparents' house, where she returned each night after the working day at the Casa Grande. For three nights she refused to "allow Custódio to touch her" or "put himself into her bed," despite his insistence. Custódio complained about Caetana to his mother-in-law with the hope she might persuade Caetana on his behalf, and he candidly reported to her and Caetana's brother-in-law that "certainly she did not by any means want to consummate the marriage." It could not continue, he announced. We never discover how long Caetana expected to hold off her husband, because by the fourth night she faced a crisis. Her uncle, Alexandre, away from the fazenda with the mule teams on the wedding day, returned two days later, and found her and Custódio living in his house. By the fourth day he was dismayed, he said, that she continued to refuse Custódio "even after he, her uncle and godfather" pleaded with her. Alexandre himself told how he had summoned her that day to warn her that he "would flog her if she did not submit to her husband." Both Custódio and Caetana's brother-in-law confirmed hearing his threat. Caetana said her uncle would "oblige her" to fulfill the marriage.[118] Time was running out.

There is no suggestion in the documents that the uncle acted on instructions from Tolosa, neither ones explicitly delivered nor ones simply understood. Although Tolosa could readily remove Alexandre (and the rest of the family) from his privileged position, doing so would cost him his most valued and trusted slave on whom he relied for the shipment of his coffee. Alexandre was not a man easily replaced, and therefore not a man to be hastily threatened. And anyway, what would Tolosa care if the marriage remained pro forma as long as Caetana appeared as a properly married woman? It was her uncle's own assertion of patriarchal authority that suddenly shifted Caetana's battle to bewildering new ground where she faced not the orders of a master, but the differently oppressive exhortation from kin and a fellow slave – her equal in slavery, but a man with convincing domestic and familial authority.

Her uncle's unyielding stand is initially perplexing. He felt provoked by Caetana's continued defiance of his authority. That much is clear. Perhaps he thought she should be brought into line: patriarchy at its untroubled work of controlling an unruly female by threatened violence. But why did he insist at all that the marriage should proceed? Why not

[118] Nullidade, 1836, fls. 12, 43v, 50v, 41, 53v, 54v, 41v, and 48v.

back her? Perhaps he shared Tolosa's fear of unyoked female sexuality, or perhaps he felt a special friendship for Custódio and willingly took the male side. He would have taken for granted a husband's sexual rights in marriage, an assumption sanctioned as much by popular sentiment as by the church.[119] Caetana's chosen denial of her husband as her sexual partner must have shocked not only him, but also her uncle and the others in her family. Seen from the outside it was an unthinkable, preposterous affront that this officially married girl refused her obvious role. Exasperation more than malice perhaps explains her uncle's angry explosion.

An additional account of violence threatened against Caetana appears in the formally presented articles that open the case. The statement reads that on the fourth day, Caetana received word that Custódio (helped by an unnamed relative) proposed to inflict "violence, lashes, and torment" in order to force her to the marriage bed.[120] If made, such a threat escalated the violence already announced by her uncle Alexandre. In her own testimony, however, Caetana referred to no such danger from Custódio. And because no witness corroborated hearing such words, we can ask whether Caetana's lawyer exaggerated a less menacing warning in an attempt to provide a legally permissible reason for Caetana to have abandoned her husband, one that cast Custódio as an offending husband and Caetana as the sympathetic victim. I have relied instead on the accumulated statements from witnesses as the more persuasive.

On that night, desperate, with no one among kin to turn to and certainly no male slave with the age, authority, or inclination to challenge her godfather, Caetana fled. She ran to the one place where she could go, the Casa Grande. Crying, she begged her owner to undo what he had caused to be done. In a reversal of expected outcomes, Caetana escaped her uncle's threats because her owner intervened and provided refuge. From those who might have been expected to help her, she got an ambiguous silence. Aunt, mother, and sister said and did nothing, while the men of her family closed ranks against her.[121] In the tight space between acquiescence and defiance – the only space left her – Caetana struggled for her independence. And in a single protecting gesture Tolosa affirmed his authority over his slave, her husband, and her uncle.

---

[119] The church's dictum of mutual sexual obligation was explicit, concerned as it was with generation; see *Constituições primeiras*, *1853*, Liv. 1, Tit. 67, no. 12.
[120] Nullidade, 1836, fl. 12.
[121] Ibid., 1836, fls. 12, 39v.

These are the events as they can be recovered from the sources. But what of Caetana? Where did she draw her determination, the unflinching conviction she was right to defy all pressures to marry, first from her owner, then from her family? How did a young slave woman who had grown up among slave families – all of the slave women at Rio Claro were married, including two who were not yet twenty years old, making thirty-eight slave couples and their children – come to think of herself as someone who could remain without a husband? Seventeen years old, she must have understood her time was coming. What gave her the idea she might choose not to marry?

Among the free population not all women married, nor hoped to marry. There is no way to know how many of the ninety-three single women listed in the Paraibuna census as "more than thirty years old" in 1832, in fact, lived in consensual relationships with men, how many among them were condemned to spinsterhood for being disagreeable or so wretchedly poor no man would have them, or how many committedly chose a single life. Caetana might have heard their stories at Rio Claro or from their slaves; she might have seen such women if occasionally one or another visited the fazenda. A woman who lived singly and reputably ("honestly" was the word contemporaries used), even if poor, was regarded publicly with respect.[122] Perhaps some such woman was a model for Caetana as she formed her desire for a single life.

A long tradition of convents and retreat houses in Brazil provided women with the example of an unmarried and chaste life. Since 1677 when the first convent was founded in Salvador, Bahia, women had been able to take vows of holy orders locally, without returning to Portugal. A religious life was available only to women of means, however, whose families sponsored them with substantial dowries that benefited the order: supporting the convent, enabling it to invest in real estate and with the resulting income acting as banker to many of the same families whose daughters, sisters, or aunts lived within the convent walls. If before consummating a marriage, either spouse decided instead to enter the religious life, even against the will of the other spouse, the marriage could be fully dissolved and the other spouse released to marry again.[123]

---

[122] População da Freguezia de Santo Antonio de Paraibuna, 1832, fl. 2; Marcílio, A Cidade de São Paulo, see pp. 106, 123, for the number of unmarried women at the end of the eighteenth century. Dona Inácia, the subject of the second story in this book, although not poor, was such a woman.

[123] Susan Soeiro, "The Social and Economic Role of the Convent: Women and Nuns in Colonial Bahia, 1677–1800," HAHR 54, no. 2 (May 1974): 209–232;

A second tier of retreat houses provided a secular alternative for women who wanted protection, often temporary, from the perceived dangers of the outside world. Although frequently overseen by nuns, retreat houses were supported by lay charitable institutions such as the Santa Casa de Misericórdia to shelter women whose honor was temporarily at risk – a husband away in Europe for months; a young woman orphaned and not yet married; a woman who wanted out of her marriage but had no grounds for ecclesiastical separation, or perhaps no wish for the public scandal that would ensue. If admitted, she paid her own keep: room, board, and clothing.[124] Either solution was reserved for women who could pay.

It was scarcely a choice a slave woman could make. Yet in either setting a woman might be accompanied by a slave servant (sometimes more than one) who prepared special meals, attended to her clothes, and ran errands. A nun at the Desterro convent in Salvador grew rich baking sweets in the convent kitchen, then sending her slave out on the streets to sell them for a nice profit.[125] Caetana might have been encouraged to imagine herself in such a life by her mistress's interest in Santa Thereza, the older and more prosperous of two retreat houses in the city of São Paulo in the 1830s. Dona Ana Joaquina maintained sufficiently close ties with Santa Thereza – through either a sister, cousin, or aunt, she did not say which – that at her death she left a generous bequest to the twenty-nine sisters and their sixteen slaves.[126] Caetana would have heard talk from her mistress about the place, its nuns and the recluses who lived there; she perhaps paid special attention to any mention of their slave servants.

As a slave, of course, Caetana could not profess the vows of a cloistered religious life, but she could desire chastity and an unmarried life in the

Kathryn Bliss, *Colonial Habits: Convents and the Spiritual Economy of Cuzco, Peru* (Durham: Duke University Press, 1999); *Constituições primeiras*, 1853, Tit. 72, nos. 305–306.

[124] On the founding and operation of one of the early retreat houses, see A. J. R. Russell-Wood, *Fidalgos and Philanthropists: The Santa Casa da Misericórdia of Bahia, 1550–1755* (Berkeley: University of California Press, 1968), pp. 320–336; for an example of a woman seeking to escape her marriage, see Francisca Izabel Santa Anna, 1810, Livro 4° de Termos de Recolhidas, 1808–1834, Arquivo da Santa Casa da Misericórdia, Salvador, Bahia, Gal. 3ª, 1182, fl. 162, and the probate of their common property, Inventário, Antonio José de Andrade, 1820, APEB-SJ, Capital, 04/1747/2217/06.

[125] Soeiro, "The Social and Economic Role of the Convent," p. 231.

[126] Inventário, Anna Joaquina Moreira, 1834, fl. 31; Müller, *Quadro estatístico*, p. 252.

secular world. Tolosa testified that Caetana not only refused Custódio but any husband, not wanting to marry anybody.[127] She had not rejected Custódio capriciously or even from modesty, but from a conviction against marriage itself. Was she trying to choose a celibate life, as convincingly as a slave woman could?

In the end we cannot know confidently Caetana's private reasons for refusing marriage. What we do know convincingly is how she struggled against the male authority of her owner and her uncle. Her story demonstrates that patriarchy was not solely the right of a white master, but was claimed as well by a slave man.

Annulment Denied

As established by the Council of Trent in 1563, annulment could be sought only if the marriage had not been consummated and: one or the other partner was impotent and incapable of producing children; one partner was already married or belatedly decided to forgo marriage for the religious life of a priest, nun, or monk; or the partners were related by either blood or marriage within the prohibited degrees of consanguinity or affinity. Once granted, annulment declared the marriage had never occurred and both spouses became free to marry as if for the first time. What the nineteenth-century Brazilian church referred to as *divórcio*, meaning only the separation of "bed and board" without the right to remarry, differed importantly from annulment, and was the required course if the marriage had been consummated. Couples could "divorce" only if one partner had abandoned the marriage, committed adultery, or harmed the other spouse so severely as to endanger her or his life. The church also required that there be a guilty and an innocent party; so if both husband and wife had committed adultery and were mutually guilty, the church refused to separate them and they were condemned to remain with each other. Only at the death of one spouse could the other marry again. The Council of Trent affirmed marriage as a holy sacrament and source of grace and, therefore, indissoluble. Both partners must profess the sacred vows before a priest and witnesses, in the light of day, and in a church "with doors open" to anybody who could give reason why the marriage should not proceed – just as Caetana and Custódio had been married.[128]

---

[127] Nullidade, 1836, fls. 46v–47.

[128] The most comprehensive history of divorce law, including annulment and separation, is Roderick Phillips, *Putting Asunder: A History of Divorce in Western Society*

This already extraordinary case was made additionally so by being framed to address not the concerns of the usual opposing two parties of a legal dispute but a triple set of interests: those of petitioner, owner, and church. The seven articles that comprised the opening petition, outlining the sequence of events and the argument Caetana's side would make, read as allegations directed against Tolosa, who was said to have imposed the marriage by ignoring Caetana's refusals and intimidating her, her eventual compliance being "forced consent." But of course Tolosa was not formally accused and did not appear in the proceedings as the defendant, only as another witness. He was spared the indignity of having to defend himself in court against a slave's charges not by a deliberately contrived move, because none was necessary, but conveniently, as a matter of procedure. As a rule the church did not allow one spouse to seek annulment without according the other an opportunity to respond in defense of the marriage. In this way Custódio, as the husband, inevitably became the defendant. And although Custódio was not charged and did not hold Caetana to the marriage, his presence in the case had the consequence of both protecting Tolosa and providing the opening for the church to name a "Defender of Matrimony" to argue for the indissolubility of the marriage.[129]

From here on presentation of Caetana's case unfolds as carefully scripted to persuade an ecclesiastical court in her favor. Her petition did not seek a separation or "ecclesiastical divorce," which presumed an injured and a guilty party, and Caetana had no charge to make against Custódio. Rather, she petitioned for an annulment. But on what grounds? Nonconsummation, although a necessary requirement for annulment to be considered at all, was not sufficient grounds to grant annulment, especially when one of the spouses had chosen to refuse to consummate their union, as Caetana had. None of the permissible grounds – kinship within a certain degree, impotence, bigamy, or religious vows – fit Caetana's situation.

But there was a further requirement for establishing the validity of any marriage: Both partners must freely consent, for only in such a

(Cambridge: Cambridge University Press, 1988), esp. pp. 4–8, 26, and 34–36; for Canon Law as it applied in Brazil regarding the sacrament of marriage, see *Constituições primeiras*, 1853, Liv. 1, Tit. 62–74; on annulment and separation, see Liv. 1, Tit. 72, nos. 305–317; that marriage be celebrated in church, with witnesses and doors open, see *Codigo Philippino*, 1870, Liv. 1, Tit. 68, nos. 289, 293; that marriage must be performed in open church was substantiated in civil law, see *Codigo Philippino*, 1870, Liv. 4, Tit. 46, n. 3.
[129] Nullidade, 1836, fl. 69v.

state was a person worthy to receive the grace the sacrament bestowed. If either married out of "force or fear," the marriage was invalid and could be annulled.[130] That Caetana had married against her will, on the insistence of her owner and from fear of punishment, became the central argument of her petition. If successful, annulment presented the ideal solution: Caetana released from marriage, Custódio allowed to marry again, and calm restored to Tolosa's fazenda.

In the unusual but not impossible circumstance of a slave petitioning an ecclesiastical court, the court record duly explained the several ex-ceptions to standard procedure.[131] Not only had the slave's owner given permission for the case to proceed, but the usual order to "deposit" the wife was waived. In separation cases involving charges of physical cru-elty, the court routinely removed the wife from the conjugal household into the custody of a supposedly respectable and responsible relative, guardian, or sometimes to a convent, confining her for her safety.[132] In this case there was no charge of an abusive husband, and Caetana was already under the care of her owner; to deposit her would be to remove a slave from her owner's dominion, something the court preferred not to do, and which in this instance was unnecessary. The court was prepared, however, to oblige Tolosa, as her master, to confer "all protection against whatever excesses her husband might dare to want to practice." For the duration of the proceedings Caetana would live apart from her husband,

---

[130] Lack of consent was the principal argument on which the case was built; see Nullidade, 1836, fls. 3v–4; Constituições primeiras, Liv. 1, Tit. 67, no. 285, no. 7, Tit. 68, no. 287; see also Phillips, Putting Asunder, pp. 8, 26–28, 34–35.

[131] Slaves, of course, did not have direct access to either ecclesiastical or civil courts, but could present their cases only through an intermediary who acted on their behalf once persuaded the grievance was legitimate; for Peruvian slave women who also challenged "forced," abusive, or unwanted marriages in ecclesiastical court, see Christine Hünefeldt, Paying the Price of Freedom: Family and Labor among Lima's Slaves, 1800–1854 (Berkeley: University of California Press, 1994), pp. 159–165.

[132] Not at issue here, but confinement further prevented a woman from having sexual contact with her husband or a lover and was thus a precaution against pregnancy and a possible heir whose father might be disputed and thus entangle any di-vision of property. Not all women appreciated being protected and sometimes tried to escape or avoid surveillance. Sometimes the depositor was accused of negligence; see, e.g., Juizo Ecclesiastico, Remoção de Deposito, Amaro José de Mesquita vs. Livia de Purificação, Rio de Janeiro, 1859, ACM-BA, Processos de Divórcio, [Pasta 60], esp. fls. 2, 14, 20–21v, 34; and Juizo do Vigario Geral, Maria Diniz da Silva Alçamin vs. Cicero Emiliano de Alçamin, Salvador, Bahia, 1859, ACM-BA, Processos de Divórcio, [Pasta 55], fls. 2, 3v–4, 15–18v, 22–23v, 39.

the marriage effectively suspended pending the court's decision. Tolosa was further required, and agreed "by his signature," not to sell either slave during the deliberations because the lawyers wanted to question them. If he found it necessary to sell or move either of them to some distant place, then he must first notify the opposing lawyer. The ecclesiastical court imposed no other limitation on his authority. Because "the master . . . was far from showing any hostility toward" his slaves, the court confirmed his freedom to exercise his rights as their owner in all other ways.[133]

The lower court judge, representing the Bishopric of São Paulo, agreed to hear nine witnesses, four of them slaves. Caetana's lawyer justified the unusual procedure of presenting evidence from slaves – in this case, "house slaves" – by the fact that they were the persons most likely to have information about the alleged facts. Domestic matters were usually difficult to prove, he said, but could be clearly substantiated by witnesses such as these, who not only lived within the larger household of the fazenda but who themselves had no interest at stake and hence no reason for making false statements. The court accepted his reasoning. Contrary to Brazilian civil law, which denied slaves a voice in court except in special cases, as when the slave's status qua slave was at issue, and criminal law, which permitted slave testimony in cases alleging, for example, extreme violence, both Caetana and Custódio, as the principal parties in the dispute, were allowed to testify: "Caetana put her right hand on the Bible and swore to tell the truth." The court regarded another two slaves, Alexandre and Margarida, a mulatta who was close enough to events to confirm others' statements but who otherwise does not appear in the story, as "informants" rather than witnesses.[134]

Legal proceedings did not move swiftly. On 24 April 1837, more than a year after Caetana's petition was first filed and accepted, the taking of written depositions from witnesses finally began. The venue was not a courtroom, but Captain Tolosa's house at Rio Claro, where a scribe had arrived two days earlier. It was respectfully noted that Senhor Chichorro had been called to appear at nine o'clock in the morning "to respond to the allegations of the case."[135] Overseeing the proceedings was the Reverend Antônio Moreira de Siqueira, described as a "resident

---

[133] Nullidade, 1836, fls. 5v, 5.
[134] Ibid., fls. 65–65v, 47, 53v, 55; on civil law, see *Codigo Philippino*, 1870, Liv. 3, Tit. 56, para. 3; and on criminal procedural law, see José Roberto da Cunha Salles, *Fôro penal: Theoria e pratica do processo criminal brasileiro* (Rio de Janeiro: Garnier, 1882), Art. 207, para. 2, and the commentary, esp. pp. 307, 309–310.
[135] Nullidade, 1836, fls. 32, 36v, 37v.

in the neighborhood of the village of Santo Antônio de Paraibuna of this Diocese," the same priest who had married Caetana. Later he was to contribute his own testimony. The others who testified were Caetana, Custódio, Alexandre, Luísa Jacinta, João Ribeiro da Silva, Margarida, and Captain Tolosa.

Apart from the priest, all witnesses, both slave and free persons, testified to knowing that Caetana did not want to marry and that a marriage with Custódio was especially distasteful to her; they bore out her claims of repeated refusals made to her master, as well as her uncle's subsequent threats ordering consummation. Beyond that general characterization, the testimony from three witnesses bears comment.

Chichorro, who was not a witness to events until after the wedding, carefully established that he subsequently talked with both Caetana and Custódio, who confirmed what he had heard from Tolosa – that is, he testified not on hearsay but from direct evidence. Nor could he be said to have intervened in the marriage, for, as he put it, he had urged that the couple should be separated for the night, "leaving reconciliation for another day," although after later talking with Caetana he acknowledged reconciliation was impossible.[136]

Custódio's testimony posed a different problem. He had to explain that he married willingly but without imposing marriage on Caetana, while also acknowledging she did not want him. He said he felt "no hatred for her," adding that whether or not she was willing to marry he knew certainly that she did not want to marry him, for she had "told him [so] . . . publicly in front of the other slaves," a humiliation that must have stung both at the moment and again in the telling. He could not say what persuaded her to appear at the last minute because he was already at the church door, but when she later refused to let him into their bed he understood the marriage had not been by her choice. He also declared he did not want to hold her to the contract, "seeing that she was forced into the marriage."[137]

Captain Tolosa's was the most delicately managed testimony. The petition made no sense unless he confirmed the allegations were true, but how, then, to excuse himself? His early threats of punishment were made in error, wrote the lawyer, when he mistakenly attributed her refusal to the "simple reason of embarrassment," a young woman's reluctance to assume an adult sexual role. Caetana's eventual compliance

---

[136] Ibid., fl. 46.
[137] Ibid., fls. 49v, 50, 50v.

was explained as a "demonstration of respect and a recognition of her wretched condition as a slave [rather] than a choice freely given . . . as [her master] perhaps mistakenly believed." Attributed to Caetana, this neatly worded defense is more credibly the invention of an adroit lawyer than a slave woman's spontaneous responses. I think we have to see minor collusion in these testimonies despite an official disclaimer that not "even a shadow of . . . influence" was exerted.[138] Certainly, in each of these statements we read the language of legal counsel.

The priest's testimony provided the pivotal account of the ceremony. Written in his own hand and not by the scribe, Father Antônio Moreira de Siqueira laconically described arriving at Rio Claro to confess Caetana and Custódio without knowing, he said, that they were to marry. The next day Tolosa presented him with a letter from the Bishop authorizing him to marry them. He reported that at the time of the ceremony he questioned them in the "customary way," and they replied affirmatively: Each wanted to marry the other. Having fulfilled his instructions to "receive and bless them in matrimony," he left the fazenda. He said he knew nothing regarding the other allegations, which he learned of only when he came to oversee the taking of testimony.[139]

The opposing lawyer, the "defender of matrimony," could find no reason in canon law for annulment: As the certificate of marriage attested and the priest confirmed, Caetana had consented by the fact of her presence at the chapel. More energetic and artful than Caetana's lawyer, he appealed to reputation. The plaintiff's statement that she had acquiesced from "fear of punishment and ill-treatment" could be "neither proved nor presumed," he argued, "knowing the character of her master," who, being "excessively humane, would never be capable of coercing her into a marriage against her will." And as she was a slave, and therefore lacked all honor or reputation, her allegations should be disqualified. "Nor can I perceive the motive for so great a reluctance for marriage, inappropriate for one in her servile condition to which no sentiments of honor attach." And so, he went on, her continued resistance to her owner's orders (a poor translation of the more precise original *ordens dominicais*) could only lead him to suppose that she refused to consummate the marriage for "very different reasons," which could not justify annulment. (He omitted to specify what those reasons were.) "No doubt," he added, "this is the first time a slave woman refuses the

---

[138] Ibid., fls. 12, 11v, 12v.
[139] Ibid., fls. 64–64v.

marriage bed," alluding to a prevalent view of slave women as lascivious. "Certainly the history of Ecclesiastical Tribunals offers no similar example." The marriage, he concluded, met the solemnities prescribed by the Council of Trent, the essential one being mutual consent given before a priest.[140]

The ecclesiastical judge decided against Caetana. Although he conceded that a "reverential fear" could have influenced her to contract a marriage despite her repugnance, he found the evidence for threatened abuse insufficient. (By implication, he also doubted the strength of her determination against marrying.) Accordingly, two years after proceedings began, in June 1838, father Lourenço Justiniano Ferreira, Vicar General of the Bishopric of São Paulo, ruled that a legally contracted marriage could not be annulled and sent Caetana "to go live with her husband."[141]

That consequence was postponed, however, for within two days an appeal was initiated and accepted: The case proceeded to the Superior Tribunal da Relação Metropolitana, the High Court in the northeastern city of Salvador, Bahia.[142] At this juncture things moved with unusual speed. There would not have been time in two days for a messenger to ride from the seat of the bishopric to Rio Claro and deliver the decision to Tolosa, receive his written reply, return to São Paulo, and for the court to authorize an appeal. And only if annulment had been granted would an appeal have been automatic, allowing the other spouse an opportunity to defend the marriage one last time. Tolosa must have arranged in advance for an appeal, should one become necessary. His commitment to Caetana's cause became even clearer.

Once before the High Court in Bahia the appeals lawyer acting on Caetana's behalf moved the argument to new ground. He began cautiously enough, reminding the judges of the "evils that will result from a union null in its origins by the lack of free consent," such a union being an "offense against Human and Divine Law and Religion." The

[140] Ibid., fls. 66–66v. Robert W. Slenes, "Black Homes, White Homilies: Perceptions of the Slave Family and of Slave Women in Nineteenth-Century Brazil," in More Than Chattel: Black Women and Slavery in the Americas, ed. David Barry Gaspar and Darlene Clark Hine (Bloomington: Indiana University Press, 1996), pp. 126–146, traces the characterization of Brazilian slave women as promiscuous, first made by contemporary writers and then perpetuated by historians; see, esp., pp. 126–127.
[141] Nullidade, 1836, fls. 70v, 71.
[142] Ibid., fls. 70, 72v–73.

sacrament had no meaning in the absence of consent, which "expresses in words the sentiments of the heart." Then declining to offer either evidence or argument regarding consent, he pointed out that Captain Tolosa himself, "a person beyond suspicion" who gained nothing in unmarrying two slaves he himself had obliged to marry, wanted the marriage annulled. Rather than asking how coercion might have been imposed, he introduced the thorny question of whether a slave's compliance could count as consent freely given. Consider, he wrote, the "wretched condition of a slave." He argued it was evident that the same degree of fear did not apply for a slave as for a free person: ". . . the probability of facing punishment and ill-treatment differs greatly when it is on the part of a slave, so much so that coercion could produce the effect of extracting a forced 'yes.' . . . The truth is that a master's 'I want and I order' is more than sufficient to coerce the slave. All one has to do is reflect a little on the relations that exist between [slave and master]."[143] Slaves could be tried for crimes that were understood to transcend the authority of a particular owner – violent acts, for example, especially murder or rebellion. Yet at the same time, as persons legally reduced to the status of property, slaves were denied the right to exercise their will. The appeals lawyer sought to center the argument on whether consent to marry had been freely given – a condition required by the church for a marriage to be valid, yet a condition rendered impossible and irrelevant by the civil understandings of slave status, and which could undermine every slave marriage in Brazil.

His strategy failed. In Bahia the court appointed José Joaquim da Fonseca Lima to act as "Defender of Matrimony." A young priest twenty-three years old in 1838, Lima later advanced to a moderately distinguished career under the patronage of his "devoted friend," Archbishop Dom Romualdo, serving variously as parish priest, teacher of ecclesiastical history and law, president of the council for public instruction, inspector of several parishes, provincial legislator, and administrator of the São Raimundo retreat house for women, among other positions. When his patron the Archbishop died about 1860, Lima went to Rio de Janeiro, where he became canon of the imperial chapel. In both places he

[143] Ibid., fls. 90–90v. The tension inherent in reducing some persons to slaves and thereby denying them moral responsibility is one of the themes of David Brion Davis, *The Problem of Slavery in Western Culture* (Ithaca: Cornell University Press, 1966). The Brazilian jurist Agostinho Marques Perdigão Malheiro discussed the ambiguous status of slaves in *A escravidão no Brasil*, esp. Part I.

became known as a talented orator invited to deliver sermons, speeches, and funeral orations.[144] In 1838, however, his career not yet assured, success in a slave woman's case mattered for him.

The defender of matrimony sidestepped the unanswerable question of a slave's consent, preferring to ask a different, safer question. How, he wanted to know, could the master "have inculcated a fear so unjust and grave when he spoke to his slave in a tone so positive that she had the courage to tell him that she did not want the marriage"? This fear was all the more doubtful because he was "a good and kind man," indeed, so kind that when she did not want to consummate the marriage, he protected her, and still protects her. Are we to believe, he asked, that in these important matters he would coerce her? And he persisted: How can it be said that the slave was "compelled by fear" when she displayed not the least fear in refusing to consummate the marriage, thus disobeying the same master who had committed himself to its celebration? Surely, it was strategy, and not a lack of imagination, that prevented the attorney from acknowledging that in marrying she was obeying an order from her owner whose power she knew she could not avoid, while her refusal to be bedded by her husband was a matter between slave equals.[145]

Father Lima piously recommended that "the sentence be confirmed, thus carrying out customary justice." Presided over by the Very Reverend João Nepomuceno Moreira de Pinho, Knight of the Order of Christ, ordained Vicar of the Parish of Pilar and a judge of the High Court, the five ecclesiastical justices spoke in one voice to uphold the lower court's ruling, and, in October 1840, exactly five long years after the ceremony, "by Holy Mother Church and in all peace and charity," they judged the marriage indissoluble. Confidently, they signed themselves with the Latin coda: "Justice Be Done."[146]

The record does not say when the news finally reached Rio Claro, or whether it surprised the waiting Caetana. The small notoriety that this unprecedented case had achieved almost certainly remained unknown to her. The drawn-out legal process with its pages of written depositions, lawyers' briefs, and judge's review, recopied by a scribe, and bundled on to the appellate court where the process was repeated – all this happened in places far from the fazenda and Caetana's experience, and being

[144] Sacramento Blake, *Diccionario bibliographico brazileiro*, vol. 4, pp. 480–483.
[145] Nullidade, 1836, fls. 100–100v.
[146] Ibid., fls. 100v–102v.

illiterate she could not have read them anyway. Only the two or three days of testimony gathering by the visiting scribe at the fazenda would have been real for her. She never heard the voices or saw the faces of the succession of important and ambitious men who argued and judged her case.

In every culture, law and legal process, however much they differ in degree of sophistication, in the assumptions they make, or in the details of their prescriptions, are meant to bring a resolution to the conflict and enable people to resume the usual conduct of their lives. The judges in Caetana's case offered no possibility of compromise, and so no resolution, not even as with divorce that of allowing a couple to live apart without dissolving the marriage. Yet, I suspect but cannot prove that in the end Caetana evaded the marriage. After all, her owner had initiated and pursued annulment proceedings in her name; owner, neighbor, husband, family, and unrelated fellow slaves had all said publicly that she married against her will; Custódio had verbally released her from the marriage; and for nearly five years she had lived separately from him without consummating the marriage. Given all that – and especially given her determined opposition – it is difficult to imagine Caetana dutifully assuming a wifely role. Surely, the marriage was in fact canceled.

As the case wound slowly through the legal bureaucracy, Caetana herself disappears from our sight. Rather than return her to her husband as the court ordered, it was in Tolosa's power to sell, rent, or give her away, a fate dreaded by slaves but for Caetana perhaps a solution. In 1853 when Tolosa died, Caetana would have been in her mid-thirties. By then Tolosa had sold Rio Claro. Settlement with the new owner, the Rio de Janeiro merchant Antônio Tertuliano dos Santos, to whom Tolosa owed money, occurred sometime earlier. Tolosa evidently struck a deal with Santos to remain at the fazenda, although whether he did so or lived in town with his mistress is unclear. The furniture, kitchen utensils, chapel objects, and livestock still belonged to him. Along with Rio Claro's lands, Santos had acquired eighty-four slaves, all unnamed. Was Caetana one of them? If so, then she might have gone on living at Rio Claro, although her name does not appear in Santos's own postmortem inventory in 1857. Tolosa kept the other forty-seven slaves, who are named. Among them was Custódio, then a man of forty-two years, one of a handful of nine skilled and expensively appraised slaves whom Tolosa had already distributed among his children. Although slave couples were carefully noted in the list of property, there is no mention of Custódio's having a wife. Caetana was not named.[147]

Epilogue

Caetana's story has the capacity to surprise us, refining our understandings of the expected workings of a slave regime in this small but densely webbed community. We glimpse the joyless occasion of a slave wedding and find more slave families blessed by church marriages than previously supposed; we watch once-protected families rendered vulnerable by a master's death, the dismantling of his fazenda household, and the sales and separations of slaves caught in the inevitable processes of inheritance. Exemplified in this one slave family, distinctions in ethnic origins and work skills further reflect the favors and privileges of a hierarchy among slaves. Slaves duplicated among themselves the unequal reciprocities of superior and dependent, old and young, male and female. Through the Catholic practices of godparenthood they reproduced in the slave quarters an expression of the flexible but durable bonds of patronage that connected Brazilians across status, racial, and gender differences. We see how a master's political and economic authority extended beyond the domestic boundaries of his own fazenda into a larger network of hierarchically arranged offices and responsibilities, underscoring his accountability; and we see how debt and death could bring wealth, reputation, and seemingly stable domestic life to ruin.

A young slave woman faced pressure, disapproval, even physical violence, and by her determination confounded the usual patriarchal orderings in a complex and nearly ideal household. A master bent on enforcing

---

[147] Inventário, Luiz Marianno de Tolosa, 1853, fls. 2v, 3, 5v–19, 21, 70v–80. Santos registered his ownership at the time of a general land registry conducted throughout Brazil beginning in 1855. See Registro de Terras, 1856, fls. 64–64v; Inventário, Antonio Tertuliano dos Santos, Rio de Janeiro, [1872], ANRJ-SPJ, 3J, Caixa 3873, No. 2573, fl. 70v. There is confusion about moneys owed: Probate records show that a debt was paid to Santos from the priest's fazenda Cedro lands, while Tolosa's son claimed that his father paid the priest's debt to Santos from his own property. Were there two debts, the second paid by Tolosa, who accepted responsibility for a debt contracted by the priest when they were still business partners? According to Santos's records, Tolosa defaulted on an equally large debt, yet Tolosa's records show no such outstanding debt. See Inventário, Luiz Mariano de Tolosa, 1853, fl. 48; Inventário [official copy], Antonio Tertuliano dos Santos, Rio de Janeiro, 1857, ANRJ-SPJ, 3J, Gal. A, Caixa 1136, No. 21, fls. 57–58.

his order then reversed himself to intervene on her behalf, displacing the uncle from his patriarchal role within the slave family; two men were stopped from inflicting on a slave/niece the physical punishment that was their right. An older man with visibly more than local eminence invited to adjudicate by the uncertain master guided his friend's decision to support his slave – a seldom witnessed moment in the informal, private, and usually unrecorded workings of planter relations – by invoking the still greater power of the church to release her officially and finally from the unwanted marriage. By twice denying the petition, ecclesiastical judges speaking for Holy Mother Church refused not only a slave woman but her patron, a prominent planter, and by extension his even more illustrious planter friend and former High Court judge. Yet in the confounding are revealed the great cohesive strands of patriarchy and patronage that bound Brazilian social life. This is a decidedly Brazilian slice of slave relations.

While in this destabilizing light the practices of slavery appear less arbitrary and more complex than we suppose, the sources are slanted away from the regions of deep motivation we want to know about and which remain inaccessible. In the end this woman escapes us, her tale unfinished not because the documents run out – a record of her flight, sale, or death might yet be found – but because, although I can reconstruct possible influences on her choices, her resolute refusal of a married life remains an authentic mystery. One truth is certain: Caetana said "No."

Luís Mariano de Tolosa's Household, 1830

District of Rio Claro, [1830], Corporal's Squadron

List of the Inhabitants of this Second and New Company of the Parish of Santo Antônio da
Paraibuna, district of the Town of Jacareí, shown with their Names, Employment,
Birthplaces, Ages, Marital Status, Colors, Occupations, [and] Incidental events that
occurred in each one of Their Respective Families since the Accounting on this date in the
previous Year. (Household 89)

Name	Birthplace	Age	Marital status[a]	Color[b]	
Reverend Sr. Valerio de Alvarenga Ferreira	Taubaté	56		W	
Reverend Sr. Manuel Inocêncio	Taubaté	34		W	Farmer
Captain Luís Mariano de Tolosa	Taubaté	36	M	W	Corn *alqueires*[c] 1,000
Dona Ana					Beans „ 100
Joaquina Moreira	Taubaté	36	M	W	Rice „ 80
Children					Coffee harvest
Joaquim	Taubaté	7	S	W	*arrobas*[c] 2,000
Francisco	Born here	6	S	W	
João	Born here	5	S	W	
Maria	Born here	4	S	W	
Slaves [men and boys]					
José	African	40	M	B	
Miguel	African	40	M	B	
Antônio	African	40	M	B	
Romano	Creole	40	M	B	
Miguel	Creole	40	M	B	
Antônio	African	40	M	B	
Antônio	African	40	M	B	
José	African	40	M	B	
José	African	40	M	B	
Christovão	African	40	M	B	
Manuel	African	40	M	B	
José	African	40	M	B	
Domingos	African	40	M	B	
Lourenço	African	40	M	B	
Simano	African	40	M	B	
João	African	40	M	B	
David	African	30	M	B	
Domingos	African	30	M	B	
João	African	30	M	B	
Miguel	African	30	M	B	
Bruno	African	30	M	B	
João	African	30	M	B	
Feliciano	African	30	M	B	

Name	Birthplace	Age	Marital status[a]	Color[b]
Bernardino	Creole	30	M	B
Domingos	African	30	M	B
José	African	30	M	B
Luís	African	30	M	B
Adão	African	30	M	B
Jonas	Creole	30	M	B
André	Creole	30	M	B
Antônio	African	30	M	B
José	African	30	M	B
Faustino	African	30	M	B
Inácio	African	30	M	B
Antônio	African	30	M	B
Alexandre	Creole	30	M	B
Abel	Creole	30	M	B
Domingos	Creole	30	M	B
Francisco	African	30	M	B
Juliano	Creole	30	M	B
Mateus	African	30	M	B
Leandro	African	30	S	B
Cláudio	Creole	10	S	B
Fernando	African	10	S	B
Isidoro	African	10	S	B
Gerônimo	African	10	S	B
Tobias	Creole	10	S	B
Felipe	African	10	S	B
Geraldo	Creole	20	S	B
Sorcato	Creole	10	S	B
Joaquim	African	10	S	B
Martinho	African	10	S	B
Tomás	Creole	10	S	B
João	Creole	10	S	B
Pedro	Creole	10	S	B
Gerônimo	Creole	10	S	B
Custódio	Creole	10	S	B
Amaro	Creole	10	S	B
Francisco	African	10	S	B
Felix	Creole	10	S	B
Faustino	Creole	10	S	B
Pedro	Creole	10	S	B
Tomé	Creole	10	S	B
Modesto	Creole	10	S	B
Gabriel	African	10	S	B
Severino	African	10	S	B

(continued)

List of the Inhabitants . . . (*continued*)

Name	Birthplace	Age	Marital status[a]	Color[b]
Patrício	African	10	S	B
Fortunato	African	10	S	B
Felisberto	African	10	S	B
Jacinto	African	10	S	B
Rufino	Creole	9	S	B
Brás	Creole	9	S	B
Baltesar	Creole	9	S	B
Fidelis	Creole	9	S	B
Mateus	Creole	8	S	B
Ambrósio	Creole	7	S	B
Vitoriano	Creole	6	S	B
Bento	Creole	6	S	B
Alexandre	Creole	4	S	B
Silverio	Creole	4	S	B
Jacob	Creole	4	S	B
Gerônimo	Creole	4	S	B
Boaventura	Creole	1	S	B
Rafael	Creole	1	S	B
Felizardo	Creole	1	S	B
Slaves [women and girls]				
Joana	African	30	M	B
Clara	African	30	M	B
Feliciana	African	30	M	B
Felipa	African	30	M	B
Matildes	African	30	M	B
Joana	African	30	M	B
Ana	African	30	M	B
Maria	African	30	M	B
Cipriana	African	30	M	B
Maria	African	30	M	B
Rita	African	30	M	B
Brigida	African	30	M	B
Maria	Creole	30	M	B
Rita	African	30	M	B
Maria	Creole	30	M	B
Catarina	African	30	M	B
Joana	Creole	30	M	B
Maria	African	30	M	B
Joaquina	African	30	M	B
Liberata	African	30	M	B
Felizarda	Creole	30	M	B
Romana	African	30	M	B
Benedita	Creole	30	M	B

Name	Birthplace	Age	Marital status[a]	Color[b]
Francisca	Creole	30	M	B
Luísa	Creole	30	M	B
[Iudi?]	Creole	30	M	B
Inés	Creole	30	M	B
Gertrudes	Creole	30	M	B
Catarina	Creole	20	M	B
Lucrécia	African	20	M	B
Dominga	Creole	20	M	B
Efigênia	African	20	M	B
Joana	African	20	M	B
Maria	African	20	M	B
Isabel	Creole	10	M	B
Teodora	Creole	10	M	B
Virenia	Creole	10	S	B
Claudiana	African	10	S	B
Isabel	Creole	10	S	B
Paulina	Creole	9	S	B
Josefa	Creole	9	S	B
Barbara	Creole	9	S	B
Caetana	Creole	9	S	B
Custódia	Creole	8	S	B
Felicidade	Creole	8	S	B
Maria	Creole	7	S	M
Ismênia	Creole	7	S	M
Manuela	Creole	1	S	B
Arcângela	Creole	1	S	B

[a] Marital status: Married (M); single (S); no widowed men or women appear in the list.
[b] Color: White (W); black (B); mulatto (M).
[c] An *alqueire* is a measure of volume equivalent to 14.3 quarts; an *arroba* is equivalent to 31.7 pounds.
Source: Mappa dos Habitantes alistentes desta Segunda e Nova Com[panhi]a da Freguesia de S[anto] Antonio de Paraibuna distrito da Villa de Jacarehei, em apresentes com seus Nomes, Empregos, Naturalidades, Idades, Estados, Cores, Ocupasões, Cazoalidades que acontecerão em cada huma de Suas Respectivas familias desde a fatura da data do Anno antesedente, Arquivo do Estado de São Paulo, Seção de Manuscritos, Maços de População, Jacarei, Santa Branca, Paraibuna, 1830–1850, Maço 2, Parahybuna, 2ª Companhia, 1830, Caixa 86, Ordem 86, Fogo 89, Luiz Marianno de Toloza.

Manuel da Cunha de Azeredo Coutinho Souza Chichorro's Household, 1835

[List of the Inhabitants of the] Second District of the Justice of the Peace of the Jurisdiction of Santo Antônio da Paraibuna, in the County of the same name, in the year 1835, Ward 2. (Household 38)

Name	Age	Color[a]	Free or captive	Birthplace	Marital status[b]	
Manuel da Cunha de Azeredo Coutinho Souza Chichorro	61	W	Free	Rio de Janeiro	M	Property owner, Commander, retired Judge of the High Court of Pernambuco; his plantation is for planting and produces coffee and foodstuffs, raises pigs and cattle, and yielded an income of 338000 reís; the ages of the slaves are what they said they were
[Slaves]						
Felicidade	41	M	Captive	Creole	M	
Rita	44	M	"	Creole	M	
Domingos	66	B	"	African	M	
Joana	39	B	"	African	M	
Benedito	20	B	"	Creole	S	
Isabel	15	B	"	Creole	S	
Benedito	18	B	"	Creole	S	
Isabel	12	B	"	Creole	S	
Luísa	11	B	"	Creole	S	
Antônio	50	B	"	African	S	
João	50	B	"	African	W	
Manuel	49	B	"	African	M	
Catarina	39	B	"	African	M	
Felícia	12	B	"	Creole	S	
Maria	11	B	"	Creole	S	
Inácia	2	B	"	Creole	S	
Sebastião	49	B	"	African	M	
Josefa	38	B	"	African	M	
Felisberto	15	B	"	Creole	S	
Manuel	12	B	"	Creole	S	
Helena	12	B	"	Creole	S	
Apolônia	8	B	"	Creole	S	
Matias	2	B	"	Creole	S	
João Benguella	40	B	"	African	M	
Rosa	38	B	"	African	M	
Felipe	10	B	"	Creole	S	
Elentéria	2	B	"	Creole	S	

(continued)

[List of the Inhabitants . . .] *(continued)*

Name	Age	Color[a]	Free or captive	Birthplace	Marital status[b]
Raimundo	30	B	Captive	African	S
José	36	B	"	African	M
Maria Rosa	38	B	"	African	M
Benedito	35	B	"	African	W
Maria	5	B	"	Creole	S
Tomé	2	B	"	Creole	S
Luís	25	B	"	African	S
Caetano	38	B	"	African	M
Ana	30	B	"	African	M
Feliciana	3	B	"	Creole	S
Agostinho	39	B	"	African	M
Florência	30	B	"	African	M
Lauriano	8	B	"	African	S
Caetano	6	B	"	Creole	S
José	5	B	"	Creole	S
Apolinário	4	B	"	Creole	S
Ricardo	2	B	"	Creole	S
Manuel	30	B	"	African	M
Joaquina	30	B	"	African	M
Domêncio	30	B	"	African	M
Benedita	16	B	"	Creole	M
Manuel Luís	30	B	"	African	S
[Daralo?]	35	B	"	African	S
Cipriana	35	B	"	African	S
João Congo	52	B	"	African	S
Jacinto	48	B	"	African	S

[a] Color: White (W); black (B); mulatto (M).
[b] Marital status: Married (M); single (S); widowed (W).

Source: 2° Distrito de Juiz de Paz da Vara de Santo Antonio de Paraibuna do Municipio da mesma, Quateirão N° 2, Arquivo do Estado de São Paulo, Seção de Manuscritos, Maços de População, Jacarhy, Santa Branca, Parahybuna, 1835, Maço 2, Caixa 86, Ordem 86, Fogo 38.

INÁCIA WILLS HER WAY

PATRIARCHY CONFIRMED

In 1857 an old woman made generous provisions for a family of slaves. This story tells of the inescapably human consequences that followed from her carefully worded instructions, and how her intentions collided with one man's sense of order.

The year before she died, Inácia Delfina Werneck, being eighty-six years old and "somewhat ill but getting about and in perfectly sound mind," prepared her last will and testament.[1] A will is first of all a legal document that disposes of and distributes property. For the historian who wants to recover the shape and sense of past lives, it is also a usefully complex cultural document revealing how people, who could not or did not otherwise write about their lives, chose to present themselves in relationship to their God, death, their families, and their goods. Nineteenth-century Brazilians were more often illiterate than literate, but even those with the skills to read and write did not frequently write, or at least not keep, bundles of personal letters or diaries, although of course some occasionally did both. The culture, not being literary, is better characterized as juridical. Brazilians authenticated myriad transactions – all contracts and transfers of property, including wills – through a notary, who in turn faithfully recorded them in large books

---

[1] Testamento, Ignacia Delfina Wernek, Paty do Alferes, 1857 (hereafter cited as Testamento, Ignacia Delfina Wernek, 1857), Centro de Documentação. Histórica, Universidade Severino Sombra, Vassouras, Rio de Janeiro (hereafter cited as CDH-USS), Caixa 241, fl. 1. Werneck is spelled variously with a "W," a "V," or earliest with a "B," and sometimes without a "c"; similarly, the modern spelling of Ignacia is Inácia, and for the masculine Ignacio it is Inácio; in this and other cases I use modern spelling, except when quoting or citing manuscript sources.

Figure 5. Vassouras in the late 1850s, center of the fabulous wealth generated by slaves and coffee. The church presides over the main square, and the elegant houses of important commercial families range along the far side. Barren hills are already visible behind the cluster of buildings. By 1872, the population for the entire county was estimated to be about 30,000, while the parish of Pati do Alferes counted about 14,000, of whom slightly more than half were slaves. (Victor Frond, "Vassouras," in *Brazil pittoresco* . . . (1861). Reproduced with the kind permission of the Instituto Histórico e Geográfico Brasileiro, Rio de Janeiro.)

Figure 6. The twin towers of the church in Vassouras's central square as they appear today. (Photograph by the author)

that by law were preserved for future consultation. Anyone with reputation, property, or personal well-being to protect – and that included just about everybody – might find reason to take matters to the courts. Luckily for historians their actions resulted in a repository of judicial sources rich in what they can help us to retrieve, or the subtle possibilities they can suggest, about the lives of persons who would otherwise be wholly lost to us.

My expectations for this will are not modest. In its pages, and in attendant documents, I want to discover not only what one woman from an illustrious planter family did with her life, but how she prepared to die. Her story is necessarily also the story of her extended family, the region this family so profoundly influenced, and the changes that came. It is about gender relations between this woman and the men who confined and protected her, especially her nephew, the baron, who played a key role in her later life; between a female mistress and a female slave and her children; and between a powerful man and far less powerful former slaves. Like other planter families around them, this family owned slaves with whom they lived in daily and intimate proximity and whose pervasive presence can be found on countless occasions and in countless exchanges. This story is centrally about the workings of slavery seen close up, in microcosm, and further dispels a view of slave owners as merely arbitrary and qualifies a view of slave women and men as merely victims. Yet I puzzle over the actions of both aunt and nephew and their differing relations with slaves and former slaves. The telling is unavoidably risky and imperfect because even dense sources often do not say what we most want to hear about what persons in the past thought and felt about what they did. And so I make the most of Dona Inácia's will and the way it unfolds to comment on two families, one slave, the other free, and their surprising and illuminating connections.

THE MAKING OF THE WILL

"I am the legitimate daughter of Sargeant Major Ignacio de Souza Wernek and Dona Francisca das Chagas, both deceased. I was born in and baptized at the Cathedral of Rio de Janeiro."

With this formulaic phrase, Dona Inácia established not only her prior right of inheritance, but also her lineage and social position.[2] Contemporaries would have recognized immediately the Werneck name, identifying Inácia as born to one of the great founding families of the

---

[2]   Testamento, Ignacia Delfina Wernek, 1857, fl. 1.

middle Paraíba River Valley, the region lying beyond the mountains northwest from Rio de Janeiro and destined to become in the nineteenth century the world's richest coffee-producing region. Their history illuminates the formation of a powerful planter elite.

Sometime in the early eighteenth century, Inácia's Portuguese grandfather, Manuel de Azevedo Mattos, emigrated from the Azores Islands to the mining fields of colonial Brazil, where he grew wealthy not as a miner but in the steadier, more predictable occupation of merchant. He traveled the ten or twelve days over the narrow, rough road that carried the precious gold from inland mines to the port and capital of the colony, Rio de Janeiro, to trade for the salt, iron implements, cloth, gunpowder, firearms and swords, olive oil, cheese, flour, glass, hats, and slaves needed in the mining towns. All but salt had to be imported from the other side of the Atlantic. In Rio de Janeiro he met and, in 1733, married Antônia da Ribeira, the daughter of another Portuguese immigrant who had earlier settled in Rio de Janeiro, and then, probably fleeing the French invasion of 1711, moved his family to the village of Iguaçu, a safe distance from the capital and a stopover for muleteers in the trading network that converged on the port. Although Manuel later took Antônia, together with her unmarried sister Angela, to live in the area of the general mines, or Minas Gerais as the region was called, he continued to do business in Rio de Janeiro.

Around midcentury as the gold wore out and men looked for other livelihoods, Manuel brought his family to the heavily forested and well-watered Paraíba River Valley he had so often crossed. There they settled on lands of a royal grant near the banks of the Sant'Ana River and produced, like other newcomers, sugar, corn, beans, pork, rum, and bananas for market in Rio de Janeiro. These years saw a resurgence in the growing and milling of cane, and sugar likely predominated among his crops. By 1765, when Antônia died, they owned fifty slaves on the fazenda Piedade, a second adjoining royal land grant, and additional lands at a place called Monsores. From the abundant supply of fine hardwood trees, Manuel built the first substantial house in 1771 (later called Sant'Ana), and in 1780 a second one more agreeably situated higher up on the opposite bank, where the occasionally rain-swollen river did not threaten, which became Piedade. He lived there with his grown children: Ana, who never married; Inácio and his family; and Manuel. At his death in 1788, the elder Manuel's vast lands were divided among the three children.[3]

---

[3]   On roads and trade, see André João Antonil, *Cultura e opulência do Brasil* (1711; rpt., São Paulo: Melhoramentos, 1976), pp. 186, 169–171; on the early Werneck

Figure 7. Entrance to the first house at the fazenda Piedade, built in the late eighteenth century by Werneck's great-grandfather, and which later became separated and known as Sant'Ana. (Photograph by the author)

Figure 8. The second and more luxurious house at the fazenda Piedade. Construction on the wings began during Werneck's father's time, continued during Werneck's residence, and was finished by his heirs after his death. The royal palms, originally imported from India, were probably planted after Werneck's tenure. (Photograph by the author)

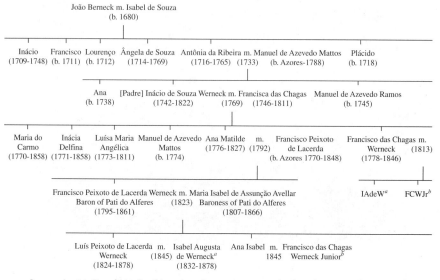

João Berneck m. Isabel de Souza
(b. 1680)

Inácio (1709-1748)   Francisco (b. 1711)   Lourenço (b. 1712)   Ângela de Souza (1714-1769)   Antônia da Ribeira m. Manuel de Azevedo Mattos (1716-1765) (1733) (b. Azores-1788)   Plácido (b. 1718)

Ana (b. 1738)   [Padre] Inácio de Souza Werneck m. Francisca das Chagas (1742-1822) (1769) (1746-1811)   Manuel de Azevedo Ramos (b. 1745)

Maria do Carmo (1770-1858)   Inácia Delfina (1771-1858)   Luísa Maria Angélica (1773-1811)   Manuel de Azevedo Mattos (b. 1774)   Ana Matilde (1776-1827) m. (1792) Francisco Peixoto de Lacerda (b. Azores 1770-1848)   Francisco das Chagas m. Werneck (1813) (1778-1846)

Francisco Peixoto de Lacerda Werneck m. Maria Isabel de Assunção Avellar
Baron of Pati do Alferes (1823) Baroness of Pati do Alferes
(1795-1861) (1807-1866)

IAdeW[a]   FCWJr[b]

Luís Peixoto de Lacerda m. Isabel Augusta Ana Isabel m. Francisco das Chagas
Werneck (1845) de Werneck[a] 1845 Werneck Junior[b]
(1824-1878) (1832-1878)

Sources: Anuário Genealógico Brasileiro 1 (1939): 141, 204, 322, and 4 (1941): 227–264; Francisco Klörs Werneck, História e genealogia fluminense (Rio de Janeiro: Edição do Autor, 1947), pp. 4–6, 16, 18; Belisário Vieira Ramos, Livro da família Werneck (Rio de Janerio: Cia. Carioca de Artes Gráficas, 1941); Eduardo Silva, Barões e escravidão: Três gerações de fazendeiros e a crise da estrutura escravista (Rio de Janeiro: Editora Nova Fronteira, 1984), pp. 47–50, 53–55, 60–61, 69–70.
[a] Isabel Augusta de Werneck, wife and also first cousin once removed to Luís Peixoto de Lacerda Werneck
[b] Francisco das Chagas Werneck Junior, uncle and husband to Ana Isabel de Lacerda Werneck
[c] José Inácio de Souza Werneck, uncle and husband to Carolina Isabel de Lacerda Werneck

With Inácio, whose Souza Werneck name came from his maternal grandparents, increase in both family and land continued. While in Rio de Janeiro to study for the priesthood at the São José seminary, in 1769 the young Inácio met and then married Francisca das Chagas, the daughter of his father's commission agent. Although they celebrated their wedding in Rio de Janeiro at the church of Our Lady of the Rosary

family, see Francisco Klörs Werneck, História e genealogia fluminense (Rio de Janeiro: Edição do Autor, 1947), based on extensive research in parish records, pp. 4–6, 18; Belisário Vieira Ramos, Livro da família Werneck (Rio de Janeiro: Cia. Carioca de Artes Gráficas, 1941); and Eduardo Silva, Barões e escravidão: Três gerações de fazendeiros e a crise da estrutura escravista (Rio de Janeiro: Nova Fronteira, 1984), pp. 47–50. The best account of the settling of the Paraíba Valley remains Stanley Stein, Vassouras: A Brazilian Coffee County, 1850–1900 (Cambridge: Harvard University Press, 1957), esp. pp. 3–13; for a history of fazenda Piedade, see Francisco de Paula e Azevedo Pondé, "A fazenda do barão de Pati do Alferes," Revista do Instituto Histórico e Geográfico Brasileiro 327 (April–June 1980): 84–90 (hereafter cited as RIHGB).

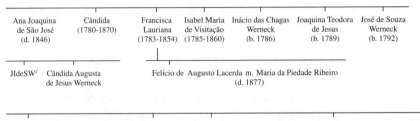

| Ana Joaquina de São José (d. 1846) | Cândida (1780-1870) | Francisca Lauriana (1783-1854) | Isabel Maria de Visitação (1785-1860) | Inácio das Chagas Werneck (b. 1786) | Joaquina Teodora de Jesus (b. 1789) | José de Souza Werneck (b. 1792) |

| JIdeSW^c | Cândida Augusta de Jesus Werneck | Felício de Augusto Lacerda m. Maria da Piedade Ribeiro (d. 1877) |

| Marina Isabel m. Francisco de Assis (1845) e Almeida | Manuel Peixoto (b. 1830) | Carolina Isabel m. (1845) | José Inácio de Souza Werneck^c (1825-1891) | Maria Isabel m. Dr. Joaquim Teixeira de Castro |

and Saint Benedict of Black Men, where the cathedral was temporarily housed, within a few years they, too, like his parents, left the city for the Paraíba Valley. Their first three children, including the second-born Inácia, were baptized at the same cathedral in Rio de Janeiro, while the other nine were christened in the country parish church at Pati do Alferes near Piedade.[4]

Inheriting Piedade and the surrounding lands of his father's royal grant made Inácio one of the region's great landowners when he was still in his prime, but did not satisfy his land hunger. By 1798 he had petitioned the Prince Regent through his Brazilian viceroy for another grant of "uncultivated public lands" in Pati do Alferes parish bordering his brother's grant and measuring half a league of frontage and half a league deep where they abutted the holdings of their neighbors. The ship

---

[4] F. K. Werneck, *História e genealogia*, p. 19; Pondé, "A fazenda," 84; Silva, *Barões e escravidão*, pp. 51–52. From 1737 until 1808 the cathedral and Rosário church were one and the same; only with the arrival of the Portuguese court in Brazil in 1808 was the cathedral transferred to the church of the Carmelites, where it remains today, explaining the seeming discrepancy between Werneck, who said Inácio and Francisca married in the cathedral, and Pondé, who said the Rosário church. See Noronha Santos, "Anotações a Introdução das 'Memórias,'" in Luiz Gonçalves dos Santos (Padre Perereca), *Memórias para servir à história do Reino do Brasil*, 2 vols. (1825; rpt., Belo Horizonte: Editora Itatiaia, 1981), vol. 2, pp. 99–100.

carrying the petition to Portugal was captured and lost at sea, delaying confirmation until 1804. By then Inácio had long possessed these lands according to informal squatter's rights, clearing and cultivating a part of them, an arrangement that benefited the crown in taxes, and that when made formal committed Inácio to certain terms. Any minerals found there belonged to the crown, as did the right to log specified hardwood trees wanted as masts for his majesty's ships, and the right to found a town. But land required other resources to make it productive. The viceroy supported the petition for land on grounds that Inácio already possessed the essential labor for successful cultivation: "a numerous family [and] slaves."[5] Like his father, Inácio took seriously the crown's injunction to build roads that made it easier to transport cane, and later coffee, to market, as well as to tax. In 1808 he wrote the viceroy that the Caminho Novo, or New Road, was open along the margins of the Paraíba River and across the mountain ridge, and indicated on an accompanying map where best to post a tax collector. He later participated in the mapping of Commerce Road, which further connected the highlands and his own fazenda with Rio de Janeiro when it opened sometime after 1813.[6]

As one of the big planters in the valley, Inácio also enjoyed the status of a militia officer. Having worked his way up through the ranks, in 1809 he was promoted to the highest post of sergeant major, effectively becoming the region's superior military officer. Since the 1790s, military service had carried as its principal duty a royal mandate to "civilize" local Coroado Indians along the northern Paraíba River, the strategy

[5]   Sesmaria, Captain Ignacio de Souza Werneck, 1802, Arquivo Nacional, Seção de Arquivos Particulares, Família Werneck, Cód. 128, vol. 70, fls. 40v–43v (hereafter cited as ANRJ-SAP, FW); in fact, Inácio received his first royal land grant at the age of sixteen in the Captaincy of Minas Gerais, which he left to attend seminary. See Ramos, Livro da família Werneck, p. 3.

[6]   Ignacio de Souza Werneck to Viceroy, Rio [Pirati], 9 March 1808, Biblioteca Nacional, Rio de Janeiro, Seção de Manuscritos (hereafter cited as BNRJ-SM), Cód. 7, 4, 6; ibid., Mappa do Certão do Rio Preto para baixo pertencente à Capital do Rio de Janeiro com os Seus Rios Principaes, e descrisão dos Caminhos de Paraiba abaixo notados com pingos, 1808 [copy, ms]; Pondé, "A fazenda," 91, 102, and maps, 150–151; Alexandre Joaquim de Siqueira, "Memória histórica do município de Vassouras, 1852," in Greenleigh H. Faria Braga, comp., Vassouras de ontem (Rio de Janeiro: Cia. Brasileira de Artes Gráficas, 1975), p. 109 (hereafter cited as Siqueira, "Memória histórica, 1852"). Roads did not always solve the problems of travel and could themselves be "oceans of mud," as described as late as the 1860s by Augusto Emílio Zaluar, Peregrinação pela província de São Paulo, 1860–1861 (Belo Horizonte: Itatiaia, 1975), p. 28.

being to contain them on lands conceded by the crown, although actual removal to that area required delicate and protracted negotiation. By 1816 Inácio could report with evident satisfaction that the Coroado no longer possessed the "ferocity" of those earlier "savages."[7]

To his military title Inácio was eccentric in adding another, that of priest. When Francisca died in 1811, after forty-two years of marriage and twelve living children, Inácio resumed a religious life, taking holy orders and saying his first mass in 1814 at Piedade's elegant small chapel before the painted-wood image of the Virgin of Piedade ordered from Europe years before by his father. As on many fazendas throughout the valley, the chapel at Piedade was not a separate building but contained within the Casa Grande. Gathering to celebrate the occasion, family would have filled the chapel and its two side alcoves, while neighbors occupied the marble-tiled entry that served both house and chapel, and slaves strained to hear from the portico. Padre Inácio was then seventy-one years old.

From this time on he shuttled between Pati do Alferes and Rio de Janeiro, preparing his will in the capital, but leaving appropriate funeral instructions for either place. By the time he did die in 1822, only two months before Dom Pedro I declared Brazil an independent empire, nine of his twelve children had married and one married daughter was already years dead. Just as property was once again divided among the heirs, including Inácia, of course, her generation would acquire new lands through marriage and purchase, repeating the cycle of expansion and contraction of family holdings.[8]

[7] Quoted in Joaquim Norberto de Souza Silva, "Memoria historica e documentada das aldêas de indios da Provincia do Rio de Janeiro," *RIHGB* 17 (1854), "Parte documentada," 498–499. On strategy into Indian areas in the Paraíba Valley, see "Memoria acerca dos meios facilitar e ampliar a civilização dos indigenas que habitam as margens do Rio Parahyba dos Sul . . . ," BNRJ-SM, Cód. 7, 4, 10, no. 2.

[8] Pondé, "A fazenda," 88–96, 108, and photographs, 109; Silva, *Barões e escravidão*, pp. 50–59; Inventário, Francisca das Chagas, Vassouras, 1812, CDH-USS, Caixa 74 (hereafter cited as Inventário, Francisca das Chagas, 1812); Testamento e Contas Testamentarias, Padre Ignacio de Souza Wernek, Vassouras, 1843, CDH-USS, Caixa 240 (hereafter cited as Testamento, Padre Ignacio de Souza Wernek, 1843); in this case the date of the document does not correspond with the date of the will itself, and probably indicates when all matters concerning the estate were finally closed. The fragmenting of land through partible inheritance was not unique to this region; on Bahia, see B. J. Barickman, *A Bahian Counterpoint: Sugar, Tobacco, Cassava, and Slavery in the Recôncavo, 1780–1860* (Stanford: Stanford University Press, 1998), pp. 105–108; Katia M. de Queirós Mattoso, *Bahia: A*

In the endless jockeying to enhance and extend property, power, and reputation, the Wernecks did well, forming alliances that ensured their prominence and establishing new family lines. Inácia's sister, Ana Matilde, followed family tradition by marrying a Portuguese immigrant, Francisco Peixoto de Lacerda, who, like Ana Matilde's grandfather, came to Brazil from the Azores as a boy.[9] That pattern of well-born local women taking immigrant men as husbands disappeared with her generation. With independence, Portuguese trading monopolies ended, the immigration of appropriate Portuguese men slowed, and well-off Brazilian women began to seek husbands among an increasing pool of suitable local men. Francisco had gone from Rio de Janeiro to the Paraíba Valley when he was fifteen, and received a royal land grant of his own from the Portuguese crown after he married. Ana Matilde and Francisco established what would become the illustrious Lacerda Werneck clan through their only child, a son and Inácia's nephew, Francisco Peixoto de Lacerda Werneck, who in turn married a daughter of the parish's other powerful and land-rich family, the Gomes Ribeiro de Avellars. The younger Francisco, who was to play an important part as executor of Dona Inácia's will, would one day be made a baron, while his wife, Maria Isabel, was the sister of three future barons and the niece of a viscount. The eldest son of their six children would marry, and father thirteen children. And so the clan branched out, establishing themselves on new holdings, extending the reach of their power, and making themselves prominent among the nation's coffee-producing elite.

Yet at the same time, as a counter to the fragmenting of property among numerous children and the diluting of family power, a strategy of near-relative marriages enabled a single extended family to reconsolidate its property. Cousins often married cousins, sometimes actually the child of a parent's sister or brother; sometimes "cousin" meant simply a relative. Occasionally, a widow married her dead husband's brother, or a widower his dead wife's sister, as when Inácia's brother married his brother's widow in 1815; sisters sometimes married men who were themselves brothers; even aunts married nephews and uncles their nieces. Three of Ana

cidade do Salvador e seu mercado no século XIX (São Paulo: Hucitec, 1978), pp. 40–44; Katia M. de Queirós Mattoso, *Bahia, século XIX: Uma província no império* (Rio de Janeiro: Nova Fronteira, 1992), pp. 462–463.

9   On the pattern of colonial-born women marrying Portuguese immigrant men in early São Paulo, see Alida Metcalf, *Family and Frontier in Colonial Brazil: Santana de Parnaíba, 1580–1822* (Berkeley: Univeristy of California Press, 1992), pp. 87–119.

Figure 9. The magnificent fazenda Pau Grande, built in the late eighteenth century by the baron of Capivary, was the birthplace of his niece, Maria Isabel de Assumpção Avellar, who became Werneck's wife and the baroness of Pati do Alferes. Pau Grande was first a major producer of sugarcane in the region and then of coffee. The living quarters are separated by a two-story chapel, with its pitched roof adorned by a cross. (Photograph by the author)

Matilde's grandchildren married her nieces or nephews. Inácia's sister Isabel Maria married the son of another sister's husband and his first wife. Such marriages clearly violated church rules and required dispensations, which might be earned by saying the rosary, making a confession, receiving holy communion or, most important, offering alms for pious works. The Lacerda Werneck family's full sponsorship for the construction of a new church in a remote part of the parish of Pati do Alferes surely credited them with innumerable dispensations.[10] No doubt they thought

---

[10] Carta de Sesmaria to Captain Ignacio de Souza Werneck, 20 March 1789 and 12 April 1799, Doc. 104 (1799), and Doc. 105, Confirmação de Sesmaria, 30 September 1805, ANRJ-SAP, FW, Cód. 112, Vol. 1 (PY 104.2 and PY 105.1). In piecing together the genealogy of this complex family, I have relied on *Anuário Genealógico Brazileiro* 1 (1939): 141, 204, 322, and 4 (1941): 227–264. Werneck, *História e genealogia*, pp. 16, 29–40, 63–64; Pondé, "A fazenda," 102–103. On sponsorship of church building, see Francisco Peixoto de Lacerda Werneck (baron of Pati do Alferes) to Vicente Houet de Bacellar Pinto Guedes, Monte Alegre, 21 April 1854, ANRJ-SAP, FW, Cód. 112, Vol. 3, Copiador, fls. 177–178 (PY 691.162–162A); and his letters to [?], Monte Alegre, 22 July

their strategies reasonable and even necessary, not because there were too few potential marriage partners, even eligible ones, but because any marriage outside the family unavoidably meant the dispersal of property and influence through partible inheritance.

"I am a parishioner . . . of Our Lady of the Conception of Paty do Alferes in whose cemetery I shall be entombed . . ."

Beyond the Wernecks' concern with real estate during their lifetimes, at death their funerals became symbolic and tangible displays of class. Men scripted slightly grander funerals recalling their more public roles, while women arranged their burials and fulfilled their benevolent duties in domestic or personal terms. Inácia's father directed that his body should be "shrouded in the habit of my patron saint, St. Peter" and buried in church lands at Our Lady of the Conception in the village near his fazendas. If he died in Rio de Janeiro, however, his remains were to be buried at the monastery of the Third Order of Mount Carmel, where he was a brother. The parish register, however, described him as "solemnly entombed" inside Pati do Alferes church and near the altar, an honor reserved for a select few. Inácia's brother-in-law was content to leave the shrouding, commending, and burying of his body to the discretion of his executor, but was precise as to an appropriate show of his benevolence. Alms were to be distributed to 200 of the poor, each receiving a note of 1,000 réis, worth about 52 cents, paid on the day

1852, ANRJ-SAP, FW, Cód. 112, Vol. 3, Copiador, fl. 7 (PY 691.8); to Luiz Antonio Barbosa, Monte Alegre, 20 November 1853, ANRJ-SAP, FW, Cód. 112, Vol. 3, Copiador, fls. 122–124 (PY 691.116–116B); to Bernardo Ribeiro de Carvalho, Monte Alegre, 2 February 1854, ANRJ-SAP, FW, Cód. 112, Vol. 3, Copiador, fl. 144 (PY 691.135); to Baron of Rio Bonito, Monte Alegre, 21 May 1854, ANRJ-SAP, FW, Cód. 112, Vol. 3, Copiador, fls. 189–191 (PY 691.171–171B); to Ignacio Dias Paes Leme, Monte Alegre, 8 June 1854, ANRJ-SAP, FW, Cód. 112, Vol. 3, Copiador, fls. 200–201 (PY 691.180–180A); to Baron of Palmeiras, Monte Alegre, 21 June 1854, ANRJ-SAP, FW, Cód. 112, Vol. 3, Copiador, fls. 209–210 (PY 691.186–186A); to Ignacio Dias Paes Leme, Monte Alegre, [June 1854?], ANRJ-SAP, FW, Cód. 112, Vol. 3, Copiador, fls. 202–203; and to Luiz [Werneck's son], Monte Alegre, 6 October 1856, ANRJ-SAP, FW, Cód. 112, Vol. 3, Copiador, fl. 374 (PY 691. 329); Manoel do Monte Rodrigues d'Araujo, *Elementos de direito ecclesiastico em relação á disciplina geral da igreja e com applicação aos usos da igreja do Brasil*, 3 vols. (Rio de Janeiro: Livraria de Antonio Gonçalves Guimarães, 1857–1859), vol. 3, p. 202. In subsequent notes, as well as frequently in the text, I refer to Francisco Peixoto de Lacerda Werneck (baron of Pati do Alferes) as Werneck.

Figure 10. Dona Inácia's church, Nossa Senhora da Conceição in Pati do Alferes, where she was a member of the lay sodality. (Photograph by the author)

of his death and burial. Such sums of money encouraged the poor to swell the procession of mourners who accompanied the deceased to his grave, offering prayers for his soul. Evidently, local people knew who qualified as "poor" without the will having to specify, whereas the priest announced, and a newspaper notice repeated, that all the godchildren who were to receive legacies must present baptism certificates. Inácia's sister Francisca was tighter with her purse strings than her brother-in-law, but equally generous in those she nominated to receive alms and equally careful to demonstrate her ability to act charitably. Coins were to be distributed to "all the poor who gather on the day my body is buried." Unlike the others, Inácia said she wanted a simple burial, without either pomp or alms.[11]

[11] Testamento, Padre Ignacio de Souza Werneck, 1843, fl. 1; "Publica forma do testamento de Francisco Peixoto de Lacerda," ANRJ-SAP, FW, Caixa 379, Doc. 176, fl. 1v (PY 005/91 176.1) (hereafter cited as Publica Forma do Testamento, Francisco Peixoto de Lacerda, 1848); the original will is Testamento, Francisco Peixoto de Lacerda, Vassouras, 1848, CDH-USS, Caixa 241, fls. 24, 63 (hereafter cited as Testamento, Francisco Peixoto de Lacerda, 1848); Testamento, Francisca Lauriana das Chagas, Vassouras, 1849, CDH-USS, Caixa 241, fls. 1–2 (hereafter cited as Testamento, Francisca Lauriana das Chagas, 1849); Werneck, *História e genealogia*, p. 21; Testamento, Ignacia Delfina Wernek, 1857, fl. 1v.

Just as important as funerals were the masses. Inácia, like the others, requested masses to be said for her soul and the souls of her parents and relatives. Her brother-in-law added masses for his recently deceased wife, as well as his brothers and sisters. Here the women presented themselves as the more generous. Francisca ordered masses for "all persons with whom I had relations of friendship," and both sisters asked that masses be said for the souls in purgatory. They endowed not single masses, but *capellas de missas*, each capella counting fifty masses. A difficulty arose because these deceased (not untypically) asked that the many masses for their souls be said "with the body present" – that is, as soon after death as possible and during the first seven days, when the body was considered still present and ending with the seventh-day mass at the completion of the soul's migration from the body. In tropical Brazil, where burial must occur within twenty-four hours after death, the body is present only symbolically. Even so, masses accumulated, and no single priest could comply in the few days allowed. So many were the masses Inácia's father endowed that the priests took four years to say them all, as their signed receipts meticulously verified.[12]

Christian burial in this style did not come cheap. For Inácia's five capellas, or 250 masses, her estate would pay the parish church a standard altar fee – as "established by custom" – of one mil-réis for each low mass prayed, without singing or candles. Local churches received a substantial 50 mil-réis for praying a high mass, wax for candles being extra. Internment itself cost another 10 mil-réis, and for the burial of each free person the church expected to receive a pound of wax and 750 réis, presumably a tip for the grave digger and other lay assistants. Burial expenses and masses for Dona Inácia came to nearly 600 mil-réis, or more than the cost of hiring a prime male slave for three years.[13] As everyone could see, only those who were affluent in life could afford to be buried so well.

[12] Testamento, Padre Ignacio de Souza Werneck, 1843, fls. 1, 9–12; Publica Forma do Testamento, Francisco Peixoto de Lacerda, 1848, fl. 1v; Testamento, Francisca Lauriana das Chagas, 1849, fls. 1–1v; Testamento, Ignacia Delfina Wernek, 1857, fl. 1v; on masses for the dead in midcentury Bahia, see João José Reis, A morte é uma festa: Ritos fúnebres e revolta popular no Brasil do século XIX (São Paulo: Companhia das Letras, 1991), pp. 203–227.

[13] Siqueira, "Memória histórica, 1852," p. 92; Inventário, Ignacia Delfina Wernek, Vassouras, 1858, CDH-USS, Caixa 106, fls. 22, 48 (hereafter cited as Inventário, Ignacia Delfina Wernek, 1858). I base the cost of hiring a male slave on rates recorded by Werneck; see Inventário, Ignacia Delfina Wernek, 1858, fl. 130.

"...on this Fazenda de Sant'Anna, Parish of Paty do Alferes and [in] houses belonging to the Illustrious Baron of Paty do Alferes..."

As only the second daughter and with all her family's material resources and social standing to dower her, Inácia might have expected to take a husband; instead, she was one of three sisters in her generation who never married, while the other five sisters and all the brothers did. Inácia was the eldest of the spinsters, already nine years old when Cândida was born and twelve the year of Francisca Lauriana's birth. None of the sisters sought the cloistered life of the convent, but instead chose actively secular lives. It hardly seems likely that spinsterhood was encouraged as a strategy to limit the number of heirs when clearly the family saw benefit in extending themselves. Nor is there any reason to think these three daughters did not marry for lack of a dowry.[14] Perhaps acceptable husbands could not be found, or these daughters agreed to supervise their father's household, or perhaps they simply preferred to remain unmarried. In the end, each sister retains a measure of privacy, her reasons for not marrying going unrecorded in any of the sources available to historians.

Being without a husband did not leave Inácia poor. Following Portuguese law, adopted by an independent Brazil after 1822, Inácia and her siblings inherited in equal shares from their parents' jointly owned property. Although the law provided that children inherited from each parent based on an inventory and division of the entire estate, families frequently agreed to postpone the actual distribution until both parents had died in order to avoid fragmenting family property any sooner than necessary. Somewhat unusually, then, the Werneck heirs inherited from their mother at her death, perhaps because the probate judge sought to protect the interests of a minor son and grandchildren, or because an impatient adult heir requested his or her share. For this family the decision made sense. All but one of the children had reached their majority; and their father, preferring to devote his attention to priestly business, may have found it convenient to shift the responsibility for administering his fazendas to his children. An inventory of the estate in 1812,

---

[14] Writing about colonial Bahia, Susan Soeiro suggests that sugar-planting families placed their daughters in convents rather than have them marry below their station because they could not supply dowries adequate to attract socially appropriate husbands. See "The Social and Economic Role of the Convent: Women and Nuns in Colonial Bahia, 1677–1800," *Hispanic American Historical Review* (hereafter cited as *HAHR*) 54, no. 4 (May 1974), esp. pp. 218–219, 223.

a year after their mother's death, listed: twenty-two slaves; extensive land holdings, including one section bought at auction and another from the royal grant "confirmed by his Royal Highness" in 1804; outbuildings, including a water-driven sugarcane mill; a press used in preparing manioc flour; stables; and cattle, loaves of sugar, clothes, and some gold and silver items.[15] Notably, coffee fields did not yet figure among the family's assets and the slaves were relatively few. As her share Inácia received a parcel of land and some cash. With the transfer of this property having taken some eight years, three years later their father died, and each received an equal share of the remainder, roughly doubling the value of their maternal inheritance. This time Inácia took her portion entirely in cash. As an extra protecting gesture toward each of his unmarried daughters, Inácio left a bequest in cash from the third of the remaining estate over which he exercised the right to distribute as he chose. Perhaps he thought of these bequests as compensation for any income earned from the dowries his other daughters had earlier received – Ana Matilde had taken into her marriage a slave, china, and gold. The dowries themselves would have been counted as part of each daughter's share of their parents' estate.[16]

With Inácio's death, and the property divided into twelve equal parts, Piedade was broken up. The more gracious house and some land went to Ana Matilde and her husband, Francisco, while the youngest son, José, received land and the original, smaller house, which he quickly sold to Francisco's nephew, a member of the Lacerda Brum family. This now separate fazenda became known as Sant'Ana. At a time when land was thought to be most profitably worked in great tracts, the sensible strategy for family members was to sell their several, smaller portions to one sibling, sometimes on credit or at most retaining informal usufruct rights, and thereby insuring family, if not personal, control over the

[15] Werneck, História e genealogia, pp. 21–22; Inventário, Francisca das Chagas, Vassouras, 1812, fls. 4–9v, 14, 18–18v; Candido Mendes de Almeida, comp. and ed., Codigo Philippino; ou, Ordenações e leis do reino de Portugal, recopiladas por mandado d'el-rey D. Philippe I. 14 ed. segundo a primeira de 1603 e a nona de Coimbra de 1824. Addicionada com diversas notas . . . (Rio de Janeiro: Typ. do Instituto Philomathico, 1870), Liv. 4, Tit. 96, esp. paras. 7 and 8 (hereafter cited as Codigo Philippino, 1870).

[16] Testamento, Padre Ignacio de Souza Wernek, 1843. Unless a prenuptial contract stated otherwise, the law assumed a couple's property to be owned communally, half belonging to each spouse; two-thirds of each half went to the heirs, while each spouse exercised testamentary freedom over one-third of his or her half, or one-sixth of the total. See Codigo Philippino, 1870, Liv. 4, Tit. 46, 82, and 97.

original holding. By just such an arrangement of buying back land from the other heirs, Ana Matilde and Francisco reconstituted the major part of the fazenda Piedade.[17]

Inácia's place in the family provided her not only with continued residence in family houses but also male protectors and the security of an income. An artificial world? Not according to the standards of her class and the times. Having always lived in her parents' household, Inácia was already forty years old when her mother died in 1811, and fifty-one at her father's death eleven years later. In his will written in Rio de Janeiro in 1820, her priest-father referred to his three unmarried daughters "who find themselves still in my company," a description more of their reliance on his household than his physical presence.[18]

For Inácia, her brother-in-law came to replace her father as the central male figure in her life. Inácia, who remained at Piedade; her sister Francisca, whose residence is more difficult to trace; and their brother-in-law Francisco, by then a widower, formed a strong working relationship. Francisco demonstrated his regard for them in his will written shortly before his death. Acknowledging that they lived on his lands, some part of which each had inherited and then sold to him, but where they continued to own buildings, slaves, and productive coffee bushes, he explained that he acted as their agent: "I always invested their moneys, lending them out in my name." In addition to a generous legacy for each, he paid them verbal tribute. His instructions to his son and executor, their nephew the younger Francisco, affirmed his unqualified trust: If they presented any claim to his estate, they should be paid without hesitation, "seeing that I know them incapable of asking for anything not owed them."[19]

The arrangement continued for more than twenty years, until 1848, when Francisco died. Inácia was seventy-seven that year. Piedade then passed to Francisco's only son and Inácia's nephew, Francisco Peixoto de Lacerda Werneck, who restored the property to its original size by buying

---

[17] The buyer of Sant'Ana was Francisco Peixoto de Lacerda Brum, a name confusingly similar to his uncle's, Francisco Peixoto de Lacerda, and to his cousin's, Francisco Peixoto de Lacerda Werneck, yet the difference in their final names crucially identifies them with distinct families. Pondé, "A fazenda," 93, 102–103 n. 37. For a detailed description of Piedade and its assorted outbuildings, see Inventário, Anna Mathildes Wernek, Vassouras, 1827, CDH-USS, Caixa 320, fls. 1v–5 (hereafter cited as Inventário, Anna Mathildes Wernek, 1827).

[18] Testamento, Padre Ignacio de Souza Wernek, 1843, fl. 6v.

[19] Publica Forma do Testamento, Francisco Peixoto de Lacerda, 1848, fls. 2v–3.

Figure 11. The original entrance, once gated, at the fazenda Monte Alegre, where Werneck lived from at least 1853 and where he died in 1861. The brick paving is recent. (Photograph by the author)

Sant'Ana back from his cousin Lacerda Brum. Married with children of his own, and soon to be named the baron of Pati do Alferes by an appreciative emperor, the wealth and power of the Lacerda Wernecks reached its apogee during this Werneck's administration. Inácia now relied on her nephew's business acumen and family loyalty. She had every reason to trust him, having known him since he was born and being present at Piedade while he was a boy growing up. Although by 1853, when Werneck had left Piedade to live a considerable distance away at his recently acquired and more luxurious fazenda Monte Alegre, Inácia stayed on at the dilapidated Sant'Ana house with its sparse, well-worn, and familiar furniture where she would make her will and die.[20]

[20] Ibid., fls. 1, 4v; Pondé, "A fazenda," 93, 100 n. 35, 102–103 and 103 n. 37;
      Inventário, Francisco Peixoto de Lacerda Werneck (baron of Paty do Alferes),

Figure 12. The main house at Monte Alegre, facing a garden and steps that lead down to a lower level and the road that winds from entrance gate to house. Glass-paned windows and doors were notable architectural features of the great houses of the Paraíba Valley, a sign of the region's wealth. (Photograph by the author)

Despite a difficult journey between the two places, Werneck played a pivotal role in the last years of Inácia's life and then as executor of her will.

" . . . I only dictating it, and not knowing how to read or write I ask Luiz Henriques to sign [for me]."

This woman who had lived eighty-six years, owned slaves, produced coffee, realized an income from its sale, and whose family built one of the empire's great coffee fortunes was illiterate. Not knowing how to read or write, Inácia spoke her last wishes to the notary summoned to Sant'Ana, who wrote them out for her, filling five and a half sheets of paper. He then read her words aloud to her and, Inácia having found her will "in every way according to what she had dictated," the notary declared it "firm and valid" and certified it to be enforceable by the Justices of His Imperial Majesty. Before the four witnesses, someone

Vassouras, 1862, CDH-USS, Caixa 115 (hereafter cited as Inventário, Francisco Peixoto de Lacerda Werneck, 1862), fls. 41v, 42, 212v.

named Luís Henriques, who was perhaps the notary's assistant, signed on her behalf.

Inácia's illiteracy was peculiar not only to her times but to her gender. As a daughter, Inácia was never schooled, although Piedade boasted a library whose listed contents covered several pages in the estate inventory. An education for her would have required a resident tutor at Piedade, and while her brother would later educate his nephews by bringing a tutor to his fazenda, there is no mention of hiring a teacher for the girls. Not even Rio de Janeiro, much less Pati do Alferes or any of the surrounding villages, provided a school for girls when Inácia was growing up in the 1770s and 1780s. The men in this planter family not only were better educated than Inácia but relied on regular and detailed written communication with their agents in Rio de Janeiro to market their coffee; they authored books on the economic and political issues of their day and read newspapers to keep abreast of world events, especially those affecting the international coffee trade. A single brief scene dramatizes the gender differences in literacy that further cut across the condition of slave and free: The son of Inácia's slave woman copied and signed in a clear and graceful hand a legal document for his mother, while Inácia, like her slave woman, could not form the letters of her own name.[21] Gender more than race, legal condition, or class determined a person's chances to learn to read and write.

In the course of her lifetime, Inácia saw all that begin to change and the opportunities for girls widen. By the time she died, in the town of Vassouras where the region's public life concentrated, two public school teachers, a man and a woman, offered primary school instruction to both boys and girls, while a private school for girls taught French, piano, and singing as well as reading and writing. By then even in Inácia's smaller home parish of Pati do Alferes, families could hire the services of a private teacher for their daughters. The boys were still favored, however, with more specialized teachers and subjects: calligraphy, geography, drawing,

---

[21] Testamento, Ignacia Delfina Wernek, 1857, fls. 3v–4v; the document copied and signed by the slave woman's son is in Inventário, Ignacia Delfina Wernek, 1858, fl. 137; Inventário, Francisca das Chagas, 1812, fls. 14–17v; Ramos, *Livro da família Werneck*, p. 10; Silva, *Barões e escravidão*, pp. 134, 168, and for a bibliography of the Werneckys' writings, see pp. 259–261. The practice continues; while doing research at the notary office in Vassouras in the 1980s, I observed the notary, seated on a bench next to his client, quietly read a document while she listened intently, ear down, her face turned from the paper.

Latin, French, English, philosophy, rhetoric, and music, but not yet mathematics or history.[22]

By the next generation, prominent women more often held their own among the men of their class by making their ideas known in writing. The baroness, wife of Inácia's nephew, after her husband died and she assumed management of the Werneck fazendas, wrote an articulate and stinging sixty-page account of local agricultural practices, calling her fellow planters to account for their rapacious depletion of the soil and the ruin they had brought to the valley.[23]

Another woman's literacy stands in even greater contrast to Inácia's illiterate and thoroughly provincial life. More than a generation younger than the baroness and nearly four generations younger than Inácia, Eufrásia Teixeira Leite was born in 1850, eight years before Inácia died. She lived audaciously by the standards of her day. The daughter of the Vassouras money-lending family with whom the Wernecks did business, Eufrásia inherited a fortune as a young woman, left Brazil in 1874 to live independently in Paris, and acting on her own through astute investments in European stock markets became even richer. Through frequent letters and telegrams written over a span of twelve years, she conducted a remarkable transatlantic love affair with Joaquim Nabuco, descendant of a northeastern sugar-planting family, son of a renowned statesman, and the man who would lead the campaign to abolish slavery in Brazil, a campaign he fought with words in speeches, tracts, newspaper editorials, letters, and a book, *Abolitionism*, published in 1883. Eufrásia and Joaquim first met in Bordeaux, traveled in Italy together, then met most often in Paris, and in Brazil on only one occasion in December 1885, when she returned briefly and they stayed together at the fashionable English-owned Whyte Hotel in the lush, rain-forested hills outside Rio de Janeiro. Despite their love, she repeatedly refused to marry him, explaining in letters that she could not be happy in Brazil, the place where

---

[22] *Almanak administrativo, mercantil e industrial da corte e provincia do Rio de Janeiro* (Rio de Janeiro: Laemmert, 1856), pp. 115, 119 (hereafter cited as *Almanak Laemmert*).

[23] Maria Isabel de Assumpção Avellar (baroness of Paty do Alferes), "Relatorio do Estado da Nossa Caza desde 6 de Dezembro de 1861 até 6 de Dezembro 1862" (hereafter cited as Avellar, "Relatorio do Estado da Nossa Caza, 1862"), at one time said to be in Inventário, Francisco Peixoto de Lacerda Werneck, Vassouras, 1862, quoted in Stein, *Vassouras*, pp. 46, 50, 51. The report is now lost and cannot be consulted or cited directly, although the Inventário seems to be a complete unit bound with the original thread.

his ambitions were firmly rooted, nor could she surrender her independ-ence to attach herself to his life. In April 1886 Nabuco wrote his only surviving letter to her, resigning himself again to friendship and asking her to return the "chaotic mass" of letters he had written, promising to do the same if she wished. A year later, in May 1887, she wrote him from Paris for what would be the last time, although in the meanwhile she had offered to finance his efforts to regain the seat in parliament he so passionately wanted, something she did, she said, because she luckily had money and preferred not to invest it with strangers, and something he adamantly refused to accept – all through letters. Having never married, Eufrásia returned permanently to Brazil in 1926, then seventy-six years old. She outraged her relatives by ignoring them in her will and instead devoted her entire estate to charity, directing the major portion to the founding and maintenance of two schools, one for educating poor girls "without regard to color or social class," the other for poor boys. Eufrásia's financial dealings and her literary love affair are impossible to imagine in Dona Inácia's spoken, face-to-face world of eighty years earlier.[24]

"I was always single and never had any children..."

When Inácia declared she had never had a husband, she echoed words her younger sister Francisca Lauriana used in her will nearly a decade earlier: "I have always lived as a single woman...." But from there on the similarity in words and experience falls away. Francisca continued, "and in this state I had a son...." An unmarried woman, member of a widely influential and respected family, a woman who followed Catholic practices, formally recognized her natural son and instituted him as her legitimate and only heir.[25] By our imagined notions of early nineteenth-century sensibilities it seems a startling revelation.

[24] Eufrásia Teixeira Leite to Joaquim Nabuco, [Rio de Janeiro], 8 December 1885; Paris, 22 January 1886; Paris, 4 July 1876; Paris, 16 April 1887; Paris, 11 May 1887, all transcribed in Ernesto José Coelho Rodrigues Catharino, *Eufrásia Teixeira Leite: Fragmentos de uma existência, 1850–1930* (Rio de Janeiro: Edição do Autor, 1992), pp. 110, 113–114, 106, 118–119, 120; Joaquim Nabuco to Eufrásia Teixeira Leite, Rio de Janeiro, 18 April 1886, in Joaquim Nabuco, *Cartas a amigos*, ed. Carolina Nabuco (São Paulo: Instituto Progresso Editorial, 1949), pp. 147–148; Testamento, Eufrásia Teixeira Leite, Rio de Janeiro, 1930, tran-scribed in Catharino, *Eufrásia Teixeira Leite*, p. 158. For an account of their relationship, see Monika Kittiya Lee, "The Ungrateful Art of Correspondence: A Love Affair," Honors thesis, University of Texas at Austin, 1995.

[25] Testamento, Ignacia Delfina Wernek, 1857, fl. 1; Testamento, Francisca Lauriana das Chagas, 1849, fl. 1.

In fact it was neither a revelation nor startling. Nothing in the wording of Francisca's will suggests that she had ever attempted to deny her maternity, something that would be difficult at best given the steady comings and goings of fazenda life; the casual talk among domestic slaves, at least one or two of whom probably assisted at the birth; and the closely commented-on nature of local social life. Rather than make a dramatic acknowledgment explaining a heretofore denied son, Francisca was merely setting the legal record straight: Her son should be treated as such within the law as he was outside it, inheriting her property as any legitimate child would. Through her will she made Felício's rights incontestable.

Although admittedly the sources offer only an outsider's view, and despite whatever tongue wagging Francisca's pregnancy may have provoked at first, no lasting stigma appears to have attached to her as a single woman with a child. Rather than bringing shame to her numerous and powerful family, who might have repudiated her, the family's name and power continued to shield her. Family treated her much as they did her two unmarried sisters. Her brother-in-law, Francisco Peixoto de Lacerda, held her in high regard, managing her business interests just as he did Inácia's. Francisca and Inácia shared parts of their lives, probably living under the same roof at Sant'Ana, or at least near enough to each other that Francisca knew her sister's favored domestic slave well enough to make her more than a token bequest in her own will, taking further care to specify that in the event of the slave woman's death, the legacy should pass to her children. For her part, Inácia became godmother to one of Felício's daughters, baptized "Ignacia" in her honor.[26] These bequests suggest a domestic familiarity between the sisters, a comfortable life together either in the same house or with frequent and casual exchanges between their two households.

Even more tellingly, Francisca's son became not only a successful planter but a prominent public figure in Vassouras County. By the time Francisca made her will in 1849 as an older woman of sixty-six years, Felício was a planter in his own right and, with a growing reputation, participated actively in civic affairs. Beginning that year he served until 1852 as a member of the exclusive Municipal Council, the governing body for the county, prominent as the only member of this family to do so during the two central decades of his career. Within his family's

---

[26] Publica Forma do Testamento, Francisco Peixoto de Lacerda, 1848, fls. 2v–3; Testamento, Francisca Lauriana das Chagas, 1849, fls. 2–2v; Testamento, Ignacia Delfina Werneck, 1857, fl. 2v.

home parish of Pati do Alferes, he went on to be deputy police commissioner from 1857 to 1861, a post appointed by the central government, unpaid and typically reserved for the affluent – someone with a following of his own – a post that combined extensive police and judicial powers. He sat on the electoral board that screened potential voters, determining who could vote in elections; he had the odious job of recruiting men to the army, but with it came the power to exempt others and gain their loyalty; to these powers were added those of arresting suspected criminals, gathering evidence and preparing their cases for submission to a judge, and, for some lesser charges, actually deciding the case. All his duties came under the general rubric of keeping order. Subsequently, Felício was several times a justice of the peace, by then still a prestigious, locally elected position, although its earlier powers had been largely transferred to police commissioners and their deputies. The men chosen to vote in the second tier of elections – known as electors – were few, only twelve in Pati do Alferes during this period, and Francisca's son was one. For at least nine years, during the 1860s and into the '70s, he administered the Sodality of Our Lady of the Conception in Pati do Alferes (of which his aunt Inácia had been a lifetime member), an honorary position that reflected his good reputation. His services, together with his prominence as a landowner, earned him the emperor's accolade first as a cavalier in the Order of Our Lord Jesus Christ, then as a commander in the Imperial Order of the Rose.[27] If he shone less brightly than the Gomes Ribeiro de Avellar brothers, who together with the Wernecks dominated the parish, and less than his older cousin, who became a baron and whose wealth far outweighed that of his neighbors, among others of his generation Felício clearly did better than most.

In public life. At home, his marriage to Maria da Piedade Ribeiro produced, besides eight living children, ill-feeling and mistrust. Strangely, he made his will in 1855, when still a youngish man at the height of his career and when most men in like circumstances did not plan for dying. And even more strangely, he named as executors not only his wife, but

---

[27] *Almanak Laemmert*, "Municipio de Vassouras," 1849–1852, 1856–1868, 1871; Lei 261, 3 December 1841, Brazil, Laws, statutes, etc., *Coleção das Leis do Brasil* (hereafter cited as *Leis do Brasil*); Richard Graham, *Patronage and Politics in Nineteenth-Century Brazil* (Stanford: Stanford University Press, 1990), pp. 53, 59–60, 89, 93; Thomas Flory, *Judge and Jury in Imperial Brazil, 1808–1871: Social Control and Political Stability in the New State* (Austin: University of Texas Press, 1981), pp. 171–179.

also his "compadre" Lacerda Brum and one other man, specifying that together the three were to administer his property, and that his wife was not to dispose of any property without the others' approval. He further denied her exclusive authority over their children by also granting that to the three executors jointly. And, he continued, if "my wife [re]marries, my two executors will be called to oversee my children and my property." This he did, he said, not because he knew of any inability on her part, but because he "fear[ed] the stepfather of my children will not treat them with the same friendship and affection as my two executors." Did he have in mind a particular husband/stepfather? Did he know of an affair between his wife and another man? Or was there merely an animosity between them that bred suspicion? And whereas many husbands left the free third of their property to the surviving spouse, Felício left his to Lacerda Brum and his sister, Gertrudes Mariana, with whom he had a rural partnership in the neighboring province of Espírito Santo, where together they owned land and slaves. Twenty-two years later, when Felício died and was buried in Espírito Santo, his widow simply ignored the dispositions of his will for six years until finally called to an accounting by a judge.[28]

Just as his mother and his aunt Inácia had benefited from having a male family patron, success in Felício's own enterprises and good family connections put him in a position to offer patronage to other women in the family. In 1869, his cousin's daughter, Ana Isabel de Lacerda Werneck, was widowed with four young children; both her parents were dead (the baron and baroness of Pati do Alferes); and her estate was mired in debt. She accepted Felício's offer of help. Through Felício, who enlisted the influence and resources of the most prominent member of the Teixeira Leite banking family, she was able to arrange her business affairs, and in a short time her former wealth was restored. When an old illness returned and she found herself bedridden, Felício took over the supervision of her household and fazenda. And he came with "all speed" from the adjoining province and his own fazenda when she made her final testamentary declarations in the hours before she died,[29] another occasion of familial male patronage toward a vulnerable woman.

[28] Testamento, Felicio Augusto de Lacerda, Vassouras, 1878, CDH-USS, Caixa 507, fls. 1–2, 2–6v, 16, 17–18, 20v, 21, 24 (hereafter cited as Testamento, Felicio Augusto de Lacerda, 1878). The will is dated 1855, while the registered date is 1878, the year following his death, and includes documents dated 1883.

[29] Testamento, Anna Izabel de Lacerda Werneck, Vassouras, 1869, CDH-USS, Caixa 242, fls. 2–2v.

Although no disapproval impeded his career, Felício is nevertheless absent from family genealogies published in the 1940s (usually by family descendants), and Francisca is noted as being "without succession," an epitaph that denies her the role of mother, which deeply distinguished her from her two also unmarried sisters. Is this omission of a natural child from the published record, strange given the relative frequency of natural children among planter families, a gesture of moral condemnation, a show of family shame? For one family genealogist the omission was not merely an oversight. He felt compelled to explain: Commander Felício Augusto de Lacerda never took the Werneck family name, "and so we consider him as a family foreign to ours."[30]

For us the question persists: Who was the father? Francisca did not reveal the father's name in her will, and whether she had a legal reason to do so remains unclear. In nineteenth-century Brazilian law two categories distinguished between those we refer to simply as illegitimate children: natural and spurious. Natural children were those born of parents who were free to marry – were without ecclesiastical impediment – but for some reason of their own choosing did not. Once formally recognized, these children could inherit from either or both parents and inherit equally with any legitimate children either parent might have had in either a prior marriage that had ended in widowhood or in a subsequent one. Spurious children were those born of adulterous, incestuous, or sacrilegious relationships, and they were treated very differently in law. These parents were prevented by canon law from marrying each other, and their children, thought to have been born in sin, were barred from ever inheriting. An 1847 law, in effect at the time Francisca prepared her will, repeated explicitly that only natural children could inherit, and that among commoners testamentary recognition sufficed to qualify them. The implication is that Francisca would have had to identify the father in order to demonstrate that their relationship was not condemned, something she did not do. If, however, Francisca's son could inherit unilineally from her without regard to the father, as historian Linda Lewin has argued was increasingly the case by the 1820s, then Francisca had no necessity to reveal his identity.[31] Because the law

---

[30] *Anuário Genealógico Brasileiro* 4 (1942): 255; Ramos, *Livro da família Werneck*, p. 8.

[31] Decreto 463, 2 September 1847, *Leis do Brasil*; and reprinted in *Codigo Philippino*, 1870, Liv. 4, "Additamentos," together with interpretive notes by contemporary jurists, pp. 1141–1144, and the original law regarding commoners Liv. 4, Tit. 92. Linda Lewin discusses a third category, the child of an unknown father,

and actual legal practice may have been at odds, it is impossible to draw any confident inference about whether the father was single or already married.

Francisca's son, Felício Augusto de Lacerda, was not named for her family of Wernecks, the Souza Wernecks, or the Chagases, but for a Lacerda. In Francisca's generation the most visible Lacerda was her brother-in-law, Francisco Peixoto de Lacerda, married to her sister, Ana Matilde. Was he the father of Francisca's son? His own marriage to Ana Matilde was not overly fertile. At a time when couples often had their first child in the first year of marriage, their child was born after three long years. This child was Francisco Peixoto de Lacerda Werneck, an older cousin to Felício, and the nephew who figures prominently in Inácia's story. There were no more children after him.[32] Could they conceive no other children, or would further pregnancies have endangered her health, even her life? Ana Matilde died in 1827, at the age of fifty-one, after thirty-five years of marriage. Either then as a widower or earlier had Francisco formed a relationship with his unmarried sister-in-law? She was forty-four when her sister died, not too old to marry, but old to bear a healthy first child. But the church prohibited marriage to a deceased wife's sister (or to a deceased husband's brother), or at least attempted to. Such marriages occurred, and had occurred among this generation of Wernecks. Francisco was legally free at any time to acknowledge a second son, although a child born before 1827 would have been born to an adulterous father and could never inherit. But if born to a widower father after 1827 and recognized by him as his natural son, he would divide his father's estate equally with the first son.[33] Was this something

---

who, therefore, cannot be identified with certainty as either spurious or natural. See "Natural and Spurious Children in Brazilian Inheritance Law from Colony to Empire: A Methodological Essay," *The Americas* 48, no. 3 (January 1992), esp. p. 378.

[32] Publica Forma do Testamento, Francisco Peixoto de Lacerda, 1848, fls. 1, 5; *Anuário Genealógico Brasileiro* 4 (1942): 252.

[33] Inventário, Anna Mathildes Wernek, Vassouras, 1827; Werneck, *História e genealogia*, p. 21; Sebastião Monteiro da Vide, *Constituições primeiras do Arcebispado da Bahia. Feitas e ordenadas pelo... 5° Arcebispo do dito Arcebispado e do Conselho de Sua Magestade: Propostas e aceitas em o synodo diocesano que o dito Senhor celebrou em 12 de junho do anno de 1707. Impressas em Lisboa no anno de 1719 e em Coimbra em 1720...* (São Paulo: Typ. "2 de Dezembro," 1853), Liv. 1, Tit. 67, no. 11 (hereafter cited as *Constituições primeiras, 1856*); the authority of the *Constituições primeiras* and of Canon Law was extended to independent Brazil by Decreto e Resolução, 3 November 1827, and recommended by Aviso, 25 June

Francisco chose to avoid out of prior agreement with Ana Matilde or loyalty to their son? Or perhaps it was Francisca who chose not to marry for her own reasons. Unlikely, but not impossible. Yet it remains mere speculation, for not a scrap of actual evidence in the existing record supports it. Not unusually, Felício's date of birth is not mentioned either by his mother in her will or in his own will. And if Felício knew who his father was, he did not identify him in the sources I could consult.

The first Francisco, brother-in-law to Francisca and Inácia, an immigrant from Portugal without antecedent family in Brazil, must have had a brother or sister with children, because he had a niece and two nephews who also bore the Lacerda name and with whom he was especially close. In his will he remembered them with affection and substantial legacies in land, slaves, and cash for their constant kindness and support, even crediting his niece with having increased the fortunes of his household through her alert administration. If Francisco had a brother, was he the father of Francisca's son? Or had a Lacerda, perhaps Francisco, merely offered the family name, giving the boy the additional social acceptance and identity that a male kinsman could bestow, while simultaneously dismissing or disguising the real father's identity? Felício owed Francisco a large sum of money, suggesting they were on intimate terms, which Francisco contrived to forgive by leaving him a nearly equivalent amount in cash. More telling of his trust and respect, he named Felício as alternate executor after his son and before his favorite nephew, Lacerda Brum.[34]

This small group of Lacerdas stuck together. The death of their brother-in-law in 1848, and the property transfers that followed, provoked both Francisca and Inácia to newly affirm their family allegiances. Inácia remained with the Wernecks, continuing at Sant'Ana, where she had lived, probably with Francisca, since as early as 1827; their nephew, the younger Francisco, now the owner of Sant'Ana, replaced his father as manager of her financial dealings. Francisca chose differently. She moved away from her Werneck branch of the family and more firmly into the orbit of the Lacerdas, her sister's in-laws – an unusual choice

1828, quoted in M. J. de Campos Porto, *Repertorio de legislação ecclesiastica desde 1500 até 1874* (Rio de Janeiro: Garnier, 1875), p. 191; Lewin, "Natural and Spurious Children," 373–374; *Codigo Philippino*, 1870, Liv. 4, Tit. 92 and 93, and "Additamentos," pp. 1141–1141; *Anuário Genealógico Brasileiro* 4 (1942): 262.

34 Publica Forma do Testamento, Francisco Peixoto de Lacerda, 1848, fls. 1v–2v; Testamento, Francisco Peixoto de Lacerda, 1848, fls. 23–23v.

among clannish people who counted blood kin above all others. By the time Francisca put her affairs in order a year later, she was already living apart from Inácia at the fazenda São José, which belonged to Lacerda Brum, the same relation who had owned Sant'Ana for more than twenty years before selling it back to Werneck in 1848.[35] With his uncle's death, Lacerda Brum became Francisca's protector, despite being related only through marriage. Had he taken over until a young Felício could assume responsibility for his mother's affairs? The Lacerda connection evidently proved supportive. By the time Francisca died in 1854, Felício had achieved a well-respected place in county life, something he could not have done without family backing. We know of his later business association with Lacerda Brum and his sister, and the enduring affections that linked them.[36]

CHOOSING HEIRS

"I leave to my nephew..."

Her parents long dead, the unmarried and childless Inácia nonetheless appears in her will encircled by assorted family. At first it is a perplexing, seemingly disconnected grouping: Why these relations? By the time Inácia made her will, many of her siblings, her closest kin, had died, including three sisters and two brothers. Information for another three is incomplete, although they, too, were aging and possibly also dead. At least three sisters, including her only older sister, Maria do Carmo, were still alive. Inácia made a gift – her gold necklace – to only one, her younger sister Isabel, who was then seventy-two years old, suggesting that she occupied a special place in Inácia's affections.

Instead, Inácia went to the next generation of her nieces and nephews, and even to their children, whom we would call great-nieces and -nephews. Perhaps these were her favorites, the ones she knew best being also their baptismal godmother, for the full list of nieces and nephews is many times longer. In naming them she carefully singled out at least one child belonging to each brother or sister (except Cândida, who had no

---

35 Testamento, Padre Ignacio de Souza Werneck, 1843, fl. 18. This Lacerda Brum was Francisco Peixoto de Lacerda Brum, nephew to Inácia and Francisca's brother-in-law and cousin to Francisco Peixoto de Lacerda Werneck. Testamento, Francisca Lauriana das Chagas, 1849, fl. 2v; Pondé, "A fazenda," 102–103.

36 Testamento, Felicio Augusto de Lacerda, 1878 [1855], fls. 1v.

children), thereby honoring her own generation as nearly as she could. Inácia nominated a succession of three nephews to act as her executor, the second being called only if the first could not serve, and the third only if neither of the first two could serve. She remembered each of the other nephews and nieces with token bequests, small amounts of money or pieces of simple jewelry. The most substantial sums went to a nephew, son of Maria do Carmo, who was also her godson and a fellow godparent with her to another child; to his wife (who was also his first cousin and Inácia's niece); and to their daughter, another of Inácia's goddaughters. Inácia saved her gold bracelets for another niece and goddaughter who was also married to her first cousin, that is, to another of Inácia's nephews.

A venerable aunt and godmother, Inácia kept a formal place in this densely interrelated family, although how often she saw any of them can only be guessed, scattered as they all were on distant fazendas and difficult to visit because of persistently bad roads. At the end of her life Inácia was one of the last in her generation. Maria do Carmo died two months after Inácia, and Inácia seemed to have little contact with Cândida, who lived until 1870, leaving Inácia with the possible company of only one sister who could remember their days growing up at Piedade, although they would remember them differently, Inácia being fourteen years older.[37]

"I institute as my heirs in equal parts ... Bernardina and all her children ..."

Yet for all that Inácia spoke of family in her will, she lavished most attention on her slaves. When she declared that she had no children and her parents were deceased, it was to establish that having no "forced" heirs – that is, no ascendant or descendant kin prescribed by law to receive her property – she was free to nominate anybody she pleased as her heirs.

Inácia chose her favorite slaves: Bernardina Maria de Jesus and Bernardina's five children, José, João, Rosa, Maria, and Manuel. Although Bernardina's age is never given, she was getting on in years. By 1857 she was not only a mother, but a grandmother of three, one of whom was herself already married, putting Bernardina in line for

---

[37] Testamento, Ignacia Delfina Wernek, 1857, fls. 1, 2–2v; *Anuário Genealógico Brasileiro* 4 (1942): 227, 245, 261–262.

BERNARDINA MARIA DE JESUS FAMILY TREE

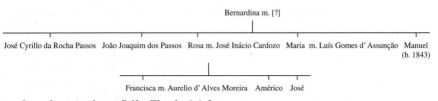

Source: Inventário, Ignacia Delfina Wernek, 1858, fls.2–3, 10.

great-grandmotherhood. At the time of the will Bernardina headed this durable family alone, although in the past there had been a partner-father; whether they married in church or lived together by their private agreement was not said, nor whether he was a freeman or a slave. While Bernardina's two daughters were identified by their role as wives – Rosa, wife of José Inácio Cardozo, and Maria, wife of Luís Gomes d'Assunção – the sons, including the first and last born of the five children, all bore the same last name of Passos, suggesting Passos was father to all five and present at least intermittently in Bernardina's life over at least ten years.[38]

The family's status as slaves was, in fact, ambiguous; like many others, they occupied an uncertain position somewhere between enslaved and freed. After 1871 and passage of the Rio Branco Law, or the law of the Free Womb, as it was popularly called, conditional freedom could be imposed for seven years at most. In Inácia and Bernardina's time, however, customary practices, stitched into a network of unequally reciprocated obligations, regulated the granting of freedom. Sometime in the past Dona Inácia had given Bernardina her letter of manumission, making her a freed woman, but freed conditionally with the obligation that she must continue to serve Inácia for as long as she lived, far longer than seven years, as it turned out. Her freedom incomplete, Bernardina in effect remained a slave until her owner's death, but at the same time, as a provisionally freed woman, she could count on a contract of sorts with some force. By custom Inácia could not sell her slave without also passing on to the new owner the commitment to free her, nor should a promise of freedom be withdrawn once given, a protection against free

---

[38] Testamento, Ignacia Delfina Wernek, 1857, fls. 2, 2v, 3; Inventário, Ignacia Delfina Wernek, 1858, fl. 10. José was at least ten years older than the youngest son, Manuel.

persons becoming enslaved as much as the honoring of a pledge made to a slave. With her freedom acknowledged at Inácia's death, Bernardina was transformed into a fully freed woman.[39]

Any children born to a slave mother were born slaves regardless of the father's status. As if to cancel this stubborn truth, Inácia explained that she had had each of Bernardina's children baptized as if born free, adding "they have ever since been reputed as free."[40] Because she did not provide them with freedom papers, her declarations, although not unique, carried uncertain legal weight, and demonstrated the fine confidence by which Inácia put her private authority as slaveowner above the law that sought to maintain strict distinctions between free persons and slaves. Inácia assumed her instructions to the parish priest once recorded were binding, but just in case of error or doubt she arranged for each of the children to receive a letter of manumission after her death, something the law did recognize. Paradoxically, Inácia continued to think of them as her slaves until her dying day.[41]

How unusual was Inácia in freeing slaves? In this moral economy of favors exchanged between persons tightly bound in often markedly

[39] Lei 2040, 28 September 1871, *Leis do Brasil*, especially Art. IV; a translation of the 1871 Rio Branco Law appears in Robert Conrad, *The Destruction of Brazilian Slavery, 1850–1888* (Berkeley: University of California Press, 1972), Appendix II, pp. 305–309; arguing from Roman law as the basis for Portuguese, and then Brazilian law, the nineteenth-century jurist Agostinho Marques Perdigão Malheiro examined the ambiguities of conditional freedom as understood before 1871 in *A escravidão no Brasil: Ensaio histórico-jurídico-social*, 3 parts in 1 vol. (Rio de Janeiro: Typ. Nacional, 1866–67), Part 1, Par. 112–113, pp. 144–145, and Par. 125, pp. 160–172; Testamento, Ignacia Delfina Wernek, 1857, fls. 2–2v, 3. A. J. R. Russell-Wood notes that in colonial Brazil, a slave's conditional freedom might be withdrawn for ingratitude. See *The Black Man in Slavery and Freedom in Colonial Brazil* (London: Macmillan Press and St. Antony's College, Oxford, 1982), p. 40. It appears that in practice masters rarely revoked manumission; in a survey of secondary sources, Matt D. Childs found only twenty-one cases of revoked freedom out of 4,971 cases of manumission counted before 1871. See "'A Peculiar Sight, and Very Fit for a Photograph': Master-Slave Rituals of Power at a Gold Mine in Nineteenth-Century Brazil," *History Workshop Journal* 53 (Spring 2002), forthcoming.

[40] Testamento, Ignacia Delfina Wernek, 1857, fl. 2.

[41] For an excellent discussion of the legal, practical, and emotional tangles of conditional freedom, the status of children born to conditionally freed mothers, and the continued dependence of conditionally and even fully freed slaves in Rio de Janeiro in the decades following these stories, see Sidney Chalhoub, *Visões da liberdade: Uma história das últimas décadas da escravidão na corte* (São Paulo: Companhia das Letras, 1990), pp. 102–143.

unequal relationships, it was not uncommon for Brazilian slaveowners to free a favored slave at death or at the celebration of a birthday or wedding as remuneration for "the good services she rendered me," as Inácia put it. A doctor and his wife went beyond this familiarly repeated sentiment, granting freedom to their African woman, Clementina, for "the care and patience she took with [our] son . . . during the long and dangerous illness he suffered in his infancy." At the "presumed age of forty-nine," Clementina probably had few good years left to "enjoy" her new freedom.[42] In 1838 another Vassouras planter and his wife freed the five slaves born and raised in their household, gave them land and to one some cash, and in exchange required that they arrange, and submit receipts for, four masses to be said annually. He also ordered five masses for the souls of his slaves. Earlier another planter freed his house slave, dowered her daughter, and provided an even more sizable amount to educate her two sons.[43]

Among Inácia's family, those with children preserved their property. Her father, Padre Werneck, desiring, as he said, to "leave my house in good order to the benefit of my family," freed no slaves, nor did Francisca, who reserved all her real property of land and slaves for her son. Inácia's brother-in-law, despite owning more slaves in more affluent times but having a son who would inherit, was scarcely more generous in freeing only two slaves outright, including the light-skinned Manuel Antônio, although he conceded that six others who had only partially paid for their freedom should nevertheless receive their letters of manumission. The slave woman Sebastiana, who had fully purchased her freedom and that of her children, their letters of manumission already registered in the notary office, received an extra legacy for continuing to serve him even after she became free. Cândida, unmarried like Inácia and without heirs to take her slaves, freed five slaves either outright or conditionally, and gave each of her other slaves over ten years old a small sum of cash.[44]

[42] Testamento, Ignacia Delfina Wernek, 1857, fls. 1v–2; Carta de liberdade, Francisco de Paula Barboza Leite Brandão, Rio de Janeiro, 31 December 1875, ANRJ-Seção do Poder Judiciário, Cartório do Segundo Ofício (hereafter cited as SPJ), Livro de Escrituras, 114, fl. 62v.

[43] Testamento, Francisco Antonio Xavier, Vassouras, 1843, CDH-USS, Caixa 242, fls. 1v–2; Testamento, Domingos Justino Pereira da Fonseca, Vassouras, 1800, CDH-USS, Caixa 242, fl. 1v.

[44] Testamento, Padre Ignacio de Souza Werneck, 1843, fl. 5; Publica Forma do Testamento, Francisco Peixoto de Lacerda, 1848, fls. 2v, 3; Inventário, Candida Maria Werneck, Vassouras, 1870, CDH-USS, Caixa 327, fls. 7v, 8–8v.

Rather than receiving their freedom, slaves sometimes appeared in wills, and then at funerals, as the collectively deferential recipients of a deceased owner's charity and to pray for her or his soul. Francisca left 4,000 réis to each of her female slaves, without saying anywhere in her will how many slaves she owned, male or female, referring to them only as a "portion" of slaves who were well known to her executor, as was the rest of her property: slave women brought to mourn their mistress publicly and visibly.[45] But Inácia provided no rewarding alms for public mourners. And if she risked going to her grave with few witnesses to pray for her soul, it was because their anonymous, collective, and symbolic presence held no interest for her. Her consuming preoccupation was with the named and known slaves whose immediate lives she wanted to influence.

Dona Inácia's testamentary provisions for this slave family were eccentric and extravagant not because freedom, money, or even land were altogether unusual bequests to privileged slaves, but for the elaborate manner of the giving and the equally elaborate instructions for their administration. She favored the daughters, confirming her earlier gift of money to Bernardina's daughter Maria to a buy a slave for her own having, a woman called Inés, and her gift of the slave Helene to Rosa, Bernardina's other daughter. She perhaps worried that Rosa's and Maria's ownership of slaves might be challenged and wanted to set the record straight. It was not unheard of in nineteenth-century Brazil for former slaves to own other slaves, although typically they were able to buy them only after years of work and saving, and often only after other family members were safely freed. (And in this case the freedom of Maria and Rosa was itself questionable, although not in Inácia's mind.) In 1856 an African freedwoman, Albina Barbosa, with a daughter to think about, left her only goods, a slave, to her, but calculated that money earned from the slave woman's labor would one day pay her own (Albina's) funeral expenses. The black Maxima Maria Joaquina da Conceição (a surname frequently chosen by freed women) could afford to be more open-handed. Once a slave herself and now the widow of a former slave, she had raised three slaves in her household: One she freed before her marriage, the other two were to be freed at her death. But slaves as endowments to former slaves, as Inácia arranged, departed notably from standard slaveowner conduct, and was possible because Inácia had no required family heirs to whom she owed a legal accounting.[46]

---

[45] Testamento, Francisca Lauriana das Chagas, 1849, fls. 1v–2.

[46] Testamento, Albina Barbosa, Salvador, Bahia, 1856, Arquivo Publico do Estado da Bahia, Seção Judiciária, 07/3001/20 (hereafter cited as APEB-SJ); Testamento,

And Inácia went further. If slaves were sometimes freed conditionally, Inácia arranged for the rarity of conditional and temporary ownership. She assigned two of her slaves, Antônio Congo (an African who took, or was issued, the name of his birthplace as his surname) and Teresa, to serve Bernardina for two years, after which time they, too, were to become free. Bernardina's ownership was further restricted: by the terms of the will she could not sell or transfer them, and at the end of the period, just as Inácia had scripted it, Antônio and Teresa declared in notarized documents that they had been released and received their freedom, while Bernardina said they had never been out of her possession – that is, she had not profited by hiring them out for cash wages.[47] Inácia intended to keep tight rein on her slaves in their freedom, and even after her death.

But there was still more. Just as her father, brother-in-law, and then nephew one by one had acted as the protecting male in her life, Inácia now chose to play the characteristically male role of household head, stewarding the interests of her slave heirs. After expenses and legacies were paid by the estate, Bernardina and her children were to inherit the remainder of Inácia's goods – namely, eight slaves (discounting Antônio and Teresa), and an outstanding loan owed to Inácia by a neighboring planter. Her will is centrally concerned with the administration of this remainder, matters on which Inácia surely received legal advice, probably from her niece's husband and second-named executor, the Vassouras attorney Francisco de Assis e Almeida.

Bernardina and the four older children, having reached their majority, were to inherit immediately, while Manuel, being fifteen years old and still a minor when Inácia died, was to remain under the care of a guardian until his twenty-fifth birthday. (Women were considered adults at the younger age of twenty-one.) Inácia instructed her executor, her

Maxima Maria Joaquina da Conceição, Salvador, Bahia, 1837, APEB-SJ, Livro do Registro de Testamentos, 25, Capital, 15/8/1837–9/8/1838, fls. 30v–33. Cases in which an unmarried or widowed man endowed a former slave woman, his companion and sexual partner, with slaves and even land comprise a category of their own; see, e.g., Testamento, Joaquim Ribeiro de Avellar (baron of Capivary), Vassouras, 1863, CDH-USS, Caixa 242, who first bequeathed to his ex-slave companion seventeen slaves for her use, and then revised the number to eight, presumably on the objections of his natural son and only heir (fls. 3v–4, 6v, 7v), and Codicilio, Joaquim Ribeiro de Avellar, Vassouras, 1863 [enclosed in the will], fls. 1–2. (This man was the uncle of Werneck's wife.)

47 Testamento, Ignacia Delfina Wernek, 1857, fl. 2; Inventário, Ignacia Delfina Wernek, 1858, fls. 134, 137.

nephew the baron, to act also as guardian, with the obligation to care for any minors, namely, Manuel. The guardian was to assume a parent's traditional obligations toward a child (and also a slaveowner's ideal obligations toward a slave): care for his physical well-being (understood to include shelter, food, clothing, and medicine, as it also would for a slave), training in the trade or skill at which he was most apt, and punishment when he deserved it. The guardian was to administer Manuel's property "in the best way he knows," applying the income to his maintenance and training. What was left over, if anything, should be added to the principal or be used to purchase real property.[48] Inácia gave the guardian wide but customary powers, trusting unreservedly in his judgment. These uncompensated duties would take time and imposed responsibility and worry.

Why such detailed instructions? Did Inácia think Bernardina incompetent to look after her own son? Was she undermining a mother's authority in preference for a male guardian? Or if a male guardian was necessary, why not appoint the oldest son, José? In fact, Inácia's instructions were consistent with standard practice in cases in which a father died, minor children inherited property, and their property was held in trust. Although authority routinely passed to the widowed mother, she, too, was seen as vulnerable, and the probate court, or Court of Orphans, as it was called, often appointed a guardian to watch over the children's physical well-being and administer their property. In the reverse situation, when a wife and mother died, the father remained in authority, of course, and no guardian was appointed unless the father was suspected of malfeasance.[49] And being illiterate herself, Inácia might have been especially mindful of Bernardina's illiteracy and vulnerability in a culture that wrapped even the simplest transactions in pages of written language and official stamps. José, although literate, scarcely compared to the baron in his power to be an influential guardian. Inácia had acted toward her heirs according to the understandings of the domestic and legal culture of her day. Nothing in the provisions was exceptional, only their application by a prominent white woman to a family of former slaves.

---

48 Inventário, Ignacia Delfina Wernek, 1858, fl. 10; Testamento, Ignacia Delfina Wernek, 1857, fls. 3–3v; *Codigo Philippino, 1870*, Liv. 4, Tit. 99; *Almanak Laemmert*, 1856, p. 121.

49 Testamento, Ignacia Delfina Wernek, 1857, fl. 3; *Codigo Philippino, 1870*, Liv. 1, Tit. 88, para. 3, 6; Liv. 4, Tit. 95, nn. 2, 5.

"...the goods that I now possess are the slaves..."

Dona Inácia fixed a hierarchy among her slaves by granting some their freedom and withholding freedom from others. It was surely not by chance that she freed only the Brazilian-born, while leaving the Africans, nearly all men, enslaved.[50] The seven who remained slaves were Caetano, Luís, Antônio Monjollo (who, like Antônio Congo, was identified by an African place name), José, Pedro, Simão, and Joana, the only woman not freed. All were Africans, but from diverse parts of the continent without a common African language or culture. How did these "goods" understand their fates? Had they known they would not be freed, or had they, too, waited anxiously until the reading of the will only to feel the dull, tight ache of disappointment? Was their chance gone, or did they nourish a hope that if there was freedom for the others theirs might yet come? Years ago had they competed with Bernardina, Teresa, Antônio Congo, and Maria Rosa to be among the favored and lost? Had Inácia's ranking of her slaves always been apparent? Apparently, such distinctions could drive a wedge between slaves, revealing fragile loyalties and ambivalence. In currying favor with an owner, one slave in 1866 hesitated to surrender friendship with a fellow slave, knowing as he surely did that his chances for full freedom were not great and ties with the slave quarters would continue to matter.[51] With Inácia's death her slaves faced what all slaves deeply dreaded: sale to a new and unfamiliar owner.

[50] Testamento, Ignacia Delfina Wernek, 1857, fls. 1v–2; Inventário, Ignacia Delfina Wernek, 1858, fl. 47. Across time and place Brazilian slaveowners disproportionately granted freedom to their female slaves, and tended to favor creole or Brazilian-born slaves over Africans. See Stuart B. Schwartz, "The Manumission of Slaves in Colonial Brazil: Bahia, 1684–1745," *HAHR* 54, no. 4 (November 1974): 612; Mary C. Karasch, *Slave Life in Rio de Janeiro, 1808–1850* (Princeton: Princeton University Press, 1987), pp. 345–352; Mieko Nishida, "Manumission and Ethnicity in Urban Slavery: Salvador, Brazil, 1808–1888," *HAHR* 73, no. 3 (August 1993): 374–376.

[51] Testamento, Ignacia Delfina Wernek, 1857, fl. 1v; Inventário, Ignacia Delfina Wernek, 1858, fls. 47, 104; on the question of divisiveness among slaves, especially ethnic differences, see Manolo Florentino and José Roberto Góes, *A paz das senzalas: Famílias escravas e tráfico, Rio de Janeiro, c. 1790–c. 1850* (Rio de Janeiro: Civilização Brasileira, 1997); on competition between slaves, see Robert W. Slenes, "Senhores e subalternos no oeste paulista," in *História da vida privada no Brasil*, ed. Fernando A. Novais, vol. 2: *Império: A corte e a modernidade nacional*, ed. Luiz Felipe de Alencastro (São Paulo: Companhia das Letras, 1997), pp. 278–280.

Inácia also made distinctions among the privileged. Whereas Bernardina had been conditionally freed earlier and now was named Inácia's heir, another slave woman, Maria Rosa (unrelated to Bernardina), was to be freed only at Inácia's death. She would have known, as all slaves knew, that such promises were not always kept. Freedom was something anxiously awaited; it would come with a death at some uncertain time, and then only if others knew and honored the promise.[52] Antônio Congo and Teresa were not freed outright even then, but were assigned to a woman once a slave herself to work as slaves for two more years before being freed. Did they resent the delay, the transfer to a woman whom they had known for years as a fellow slave, now suddenly elevated to a position of temporary ownership, but with neither the full rights of ownership nor the resources to benefit them as a proper mistress might? They, too, had to wait and trust that Dona Inácia's wishes would be carried out, in the meanwhile serving Bernardina. It made sense from Inácia's point of view to provide her favorite Bernardina with a slave couple who could help her establish what would now be her own, independent household: haul water, chop wood, cut and sew clothes, plant, hoe, weed, harvest, hull beans, boil sugar, cook, wash, clean – the work was endless and Bernardina was not young. Her children had families and work of their own, except Manuel, who at fifteen was strong and could help out. Nothing in the sources, however, can tell us what Antônio Congo and Teresa thought of the arrangement: apprehension, resentment, relief, or just something to be gotten through?

Why this exceptional treatment toward Bernardina, her children, and, by extension, her grandchildren? Such treatment was certainly possible within the ambiguous and often idiosyncratic social relations that formed between Brazilian owners and their slaves. Inácia supplied no straightforward answer. She offered no fond, explaining words as sometimes appeared in wills. It is nonetheless tempting to see these slaves as surrogate family to an aging spinster, more daily present for Inácia than her many nieces, nephews, and other godchildren, the counterpart to Francisca's son and granddaughters. Some thought them so. The baron was to say later that his aunt Inácia had loved Rosa and Maria "as if they

---

[52] An example of freedom promised and then withheld was the subject of a suit in which the court awarded the slave woman her freedom. See Juizo de Direito da 1ª Vara Civel, defendant, Serafina (preta), Rio de Janeiro, 1882, ANRJ-SPJ, Maço 555, N. 3498.

were her daughters." As a house servant, Bernardina certainly lived in daily and proximate contact with Inácia, raising her children in Inácia's household, Inácia arranging their baptisms, getting the daughters safely married, and starting them off with a slave each as a kind of dowry. José, Bernardina's oldest child and at least twenty-five years old by the time Inácia died, had been her overseer for three years, a position of responsibility that put him in charge of the field slaves and meant regular discussions about planting and harvesting not only with Inácia, but also with her nephew or his administrator. It was agreed Inácia would pay José for the work, although when she died she was in arrears to him for the entire time. Judging by a document included among the probate records that José evidently copied and signed, he was educated beyond mere literacy, also something Inácia would have arranged. He was a young man with some authority in Inácia's life, albeit the son of a slave. With Francisca at the Lacerda Brum fazenda by 1849, and Werneck's move to Monte Alegre after his father's death in 1848 and not later than 1852, for the last years of her life Inácia was alone at Sant'Ana with her slaves for company and ever greater reason to draw closer to them.[53]

It is tempting to think of Bernardina's children as transformed into Inácia's children. But it is also misleading. Despite the affection, regard, and dependence that bound them, an impassable line irrevocably separated them. Differences in race, legal condition, and status were powerful barriers; the social distance that separated owner and slave was not so easily or thoroughly collapsed. Each side knew where she or he stood. And the will acknowledged their differences. Inácia's godchildren needed no such special provisions; they were among the most privileged children in all of Brazil, whose parents' position and wealth offered advantages beyond any Inácia could add to, except, of course, by her reputation and illustrious name, which she had already given by acting as their godmother. Bernardina's children, although privileged among slaves, nevertheless remained poor and black, the visible marks of a slave heritage. Yet Bernardina, her children, and grandchildren constituted Inácia's immediate social world, and Inácia occupied a central place in their daily lives. There was the possibility for authentic emotional confusion on both sides.

[53] Testamento, Francisca Lauriana das Chagas, 1849, fl. 2v; Pondé, "A fazenda," 100; Inventário, Ignacia Delfina Wernek, 1858, fls. 92v, 137; Testamento, Ignacia Delfina Wernek, 1857, fls. 2–3.

The making of a will was a public act with its own audience. Numerous people contributed to its production, both on and off the fazenda and from as far away as the county seat of Vassouras, where Inácia's second-named executor practiced law and the life-tenured notary recorded legal business for the county's three parishes. A frail Inácia did not travel the dusty, rutted road into Vassouras for the signing, but, rather, a notary, his assistant, and four male witnesses were summoned the long distance to Sant'Ana. Their coming would have been an occasion of some preparation. Was Bernardina called on to provide an elaborate midday meal of the kind that Brazilians of Inácia's class expected? Or perhaps only a lighter afternoon tea? Inácia was in the habit of stocking her larder with delicacies fit for visitors. She could offer them port wine and cheese, a bowl of figs, or at least coffee. These men would certainly take some refreshment. Well before they assembled, there would likely have been consultations within the family about who should be asked to serve as executor, details about the provisions, and long reflection by Inácia about who should receive what.[54] As the principal object of the will, was Bernardina consulted, informed, or perhaps indifferently allowed to overhear snatches of conversations that vitally concerned her? Had word spread generally among Inácia's slaves, reporting, speculating on who would be freed, who not? Inácia was old, her death not far off, making it a time of mounting uncertainty and tension for her slaves. No one would have misunderstood Inácia's intent to direct lives as she dictated her will or its importance for them and her. Were the men who witnessed her peculiar generosity surprised, even dismayed? It was not their place to say.

THE WILL REVEALED

A will is not only a statement of last wishes, but also a set of instructions that must be carried out in circumstances that do not always match those imagined by the testator, or which change in the course of probate. So it was with Inácia's will.

"I appoint as my executor ... baron Paty do Alferes. ..."

Nothing in the initial days after Inácia's death on 31 January 1858 suggested anything out of the ordinary. The priest, Father Manuel Felizardo

---

[54] *Almanak Laemmert*, 1857, pp. 175–176; Testamento, Ignacia Delfina Wernek, 1857, fls. 3v–4v; Inventário, Ignacia Delfina Wernek, 1858, fl. 28.

Nogueira, someone long known to the family and a landowner himself with property bordering on Werneck lands, opened the will on the day of death to carry out the deceased's funeral dispositions. Eleven days later the municipal judge turned the will over to the notary to be registered and copied into the public record. In early February, Francisco Peixoto de Lacerda Werneck, "the Most Excellent baron of Pati do Alferes," having been informed of his duties as executor, accepted. But being an important and busy man with weighty responsibilities to attend and living far from the town of Vassouras where the will would be processed, the baron assigned power of attorney to Inácia's alternate executor and nephew, Francisco de Assis e Almeida, to file the necessary pieces of paper with the court. By the middle of March, Almeida had in his turn appointed a replacement.[55] Inácia was dead and buried, the first masses said, her soul commended to God. Earthly matters were now in the hands of her nephew Werneck, who, although he had efficiently distanced himself from the inconvenient legwork, actively decided key events that followed.

Probate moved slowly. Even the provisions Werneck treated as straightforward and readily complied with took time to be carried out. In December 1858, Bernardina's son, José Cyrillo da Rocha Passos, came forward, asking to be paid the three years of wages owed him as overseer. Werneck immediately acknowledged his claim as correct and authorized payment. The debt remained unsettled for another three and a half years, however, and in the meanwhile an impatient and shrewd José sold the debt to a third party, a friend of the Werneck family who later collected from the estate. Werneck issued Maria Rosa her promised letter of manumission: "I give full liberty and complete exemption from captivity to the slave Maria Roza, and as a freed woman from today and forever she enjoys all the rights, freedoms, privileges, and prerogatives belonging to the free state." Then he finished in words that departed from the formula: "and without obstacle she may dispose of herself as she sees fit," as though she were still property, even to herself. It was November 1858, nearly a year after Inácia's death, before Maria Rosa received these precious (and wordy) lines confirming liberty. Not knowing certainly when liberty would come must have made those last months of waiting seem a very long time. Werneck acted more quickly to name a guardian for Bernardina's minor son, Manuel,

55 Testamento, Ignacia Delfina Wernek, 1857, fls. 4v, 5–5v; Inventário, Ignacia Delfina Wernek, 1858, fls. 7v–9, 10.

thereby divesting himself of a responsibility that Inácia had particularly requested of him.[56]

But if Werneck hoped to remain apart from the heirs, his hope was lost. He soon found himself in the middle of a dispute brought by Bernardina's two sons over the two slave women Dona Inácia had given their sisters some time before she died. Through their lawyer the sons argued that the two slaves should be counted as part of the estate to be shared equally among all heirs, not as gifts given separately to their sisters. It was customary in probate proceedings for any gifts, including loans and dowries, made to the heirs (typically, a couple's children) to be returned to the estate for the final calculations of its total worth and deducted from the recipient's final share of the estate, thereby insuring that one heir was not favored over others.[57] Werneck, acknowledging he could not offer a legal opinion, nonetheless favored the sisters, knowing, he said, that his aunt had in mind to give the slaves as gifts to these young women raised in her house, whom she loved. The sons' lawyer turned this argument around: Precisely because Inácia loved them all, she intended them to inherit the entire estate in perfect equality. The sisters' lawyer countered that, although being an "ignorant country woman," Inácia's will left no doubt about her intentions. He scoffed at the suggestion that affection for two "slaves of the house" could become "poetically metamorphosed into maternal love." Treasury officials, who wanted to assess an estate tax on the two slaves, as well as the judge, agreed with the brothers: The two slaves should be counted as part of the estate.[58] Werneck had spoken on behalf of the sisters against a locally influential lawyer, his son-in-law's colleague, and lost, only a momentary defeat when seen against his enormous prestige, but still a defeat. If Inácia's wishes were frustrated in this matter, two heirs, not Werneck, were to blame.

On other matters, too, Werneck showed himself to be an exemplary executor. In the routine settling of an estate, amounts owed to the estate were collected and counted as part of the assets. Accordingly, Werneck

---

[56] Inventário, Ignacia Delfina Wernek, 1858, fls. 40, 126, 158, 70, 13.

[57] Ibid., fl. 84. In Portuguese, the term for this process is *colação*. See *Codigo Philippino, 1870*, Liv. 4, Tit. 9. Apparently no one brought up the question of whether Maria and Rosa were legally freed and could receive gifts of property.

[58] No value was ever assigned to the slaves, however. Inventário, Ignacia Delfina Wernek, 1858, fls. 92v, 102–102v, 119–120v, 117, 121.

immediately agreed to pay the estate for forty-seven bags of coffee weigh-
ing about 7,500 pounds and worth 419,000 réis, or about $218, which
belonged to the estate, having been harvested and sold before Inácia's
death. No doubt he had handled the transaction, keeping her money
on account against current or future bills. As guarantor for the sizable
loan still owed to his aunt by Manuel Francisco de Azevedo (probably
a relative of the family), who had evidently defaulted, Werneck repaid
the estate.[59] On the other side of the ledger, bills allowed to accumu-
late during Inácia's lifetime were submitted to her estate for payment.
From Monte Alegre, where he was Werneck's resident fazenda doctor
and the husband of one of Werneck's daughters (Inácia's great niece),
Dr. Joaquim Teixeira de Castro sent a sizable bill for 835,000 réis, or
about $434, covering the eight years since 1849, when he had doctored
Dona Inácia and her slaves on an annual retainer, which, he said, was
"very accommodating and cheap" in view of the distance he traveled
to her house. In this economy in which cash was chronically in short
supply and transactions regularly conducted on credit and trust, Inácia's
doctor had no reason to bill her annually. He knew he would be paid
eventually. Inácia also owed merchants for goods purchased during the
last year she lived: fifty-eight lengths of cotton cloth, two fatted hogs,
a large horse, nearly 250 pounds of white sugar, and a long list of other
foodstuffs. There were cash amounts advanced to Inácia by Werneck,
and a fee for revising her will.[60] Acting either privately as manager of
Inácia's finances while she lived or as executor, Werneck paid some of
these amounts, just as he paid the funeral costs, masses, legacies, and the
estate tax that followed her death. He submitted them all as expenses
to his aunt's estate; he expected to be reimbursed and the others to be
paid.[61]

---

[59]   For currency conversions into U.S. dollars at the time, see Julian Smith Duncan,
Public and Private Operation of Railways in Brazil (New York: Columbia University
Press, 1932), p. 183; an *arroba* weighed approximately 32 pounds, and there
were five arrobas of coffee to a bag. See Stein, *Vassouras*, p. 293, and Joseph
E. Sweigart, *Coffee Factorage and the Emergence of a Brazilian Capital Market,
1850–1888* (New York: Garland Publishing, 1987), pp. 15–16, 52 n. 2, and
pp. 302–304; Inventário, Ignacia Delfina Wernek, 1858, fls. 89, 21.

[60]   Inventário, Ignacia Delfina Wernek, 1858, fls. 21, 22, 35, 36, 47–48. I can add
nothing about the original will because, of course, having been replaced, it was
never recorded; we will never know what changes Inácia made.

[61]   Ibid., fls. 22, 47–48.

"Of the remainder of my goods after the dispositions and legacies are complied with . . ."

Up to this point probate proceeded routinely. Oddly, however, the inventory documents do not include a customary final tally sheet showing the estate's assets, expenses, and the balance. Nonetheless, it is possible to reconstruct an approximate balance from amounts entered at several places in the inventory. It confirms what those involved already recognized. By March 1860, when all accounts were in, a troubling deficit became clear: The estate could not pay all that was owed. There was no "remainder" for Bernardina and her children, and, still worse, the heirs were liable for the estate's outstanding debts.[62] Inácia's will was revealed as not only naive, but damaging.

It is worth pausing here to consider how Inácia's plans had gone so wrong. Being unable to read, write, or count, and relying all her life on others to manage her money, Inácia was out of touch with her own wealth and greatly overestimated what she had to give away. Had she kept her own accounts she would have seen that only by selling the slaves could she pay her debts. But it was the legal peculiarities of Inácia's will that made this miscalculation carry such disappointing consequences for her heirs. Inheritance law was particularly intended to protect family property, so that if there were living children, they were assured of receiving (in equal shares) two-thirds of their parents' jointly owned property after all funeral expenses, masses, and other bills were paid. Only the remaining one-third, or *terça*, as it was called, of the total conjugal estate (one-sixth from each spouse) could be assigned to anyone, whether the surviving spouse, the children, or, as was often the case, distributed as cash legacies to others, both kin and nonkin.

Debts posed a further problem. At the time of Inácia's death, Brazilian law made the heirs of an estate equally and personally liable for any debts the estate owed. In the usual proceedings, the debts were paid and the remaining one-third went to the legatees and the required two-thirds to the heirs. If, however, debts exceeded the assets, the heirs were liable for the shortfall. An heir who anticipated a deficit in the estate could refuse to inherit, but not all heirs knew in advance the balance of an estate, or how to protect themselves.[63]

---

[62] Ibid., fls. 47–48.

[63] The law simply assumed the principle of liability and stated only its variations and qualifications. See, e.g., *Codigo Philippino*, 1870, Liv. 2, Tit. 52, para. 5; Liv. 4, Tit. 51, para. 3, and Tit. 83, para. 4; on refusing to accept inheritance, see,

Inácia's will departed in two important ways from the model. First, because there were no forced heirs, there was no legal requirement to divide the estate, reserving the specified two-thirds portion of the property for them and leaving one-third to be distributed at the discretion of the testator. Not only could Inácia nominate her heirs, she had complete discretion to distribute freely all her property as she wished. Second, mistakenly assuming that her estate was ample, Inácia made numerous small bequests to family and godchildren that added up to a considerable sum with instructions that her legatees were to be paid first, a decision that ended up favoring her blood kin at the expense of her appointed heirs.[64] The problem was that when all the estate's assets had been spent, expenses still remained to be paid. The amount they owed – more than one *conto*, or about $522 – was an impossible burden. Without meaning to, Inácia had left an irritating mess for her executor and only spoiled hopes and debt for her heirs. There is no evidence that Bernardina knew or was informed that she and her children could refuse their inheritance as a way to avoid liability for the debts.

Werneck said plainly that there was nothing to be done but to sell the remaining assets – that is, put the slaves up for auction.[65] He could have covered the estate's debts himself, of course, just as he had probably paid

e.g., Livro 3, Título 18, Paragraph 9. For an example in which the heir owed the creditors more than the value of the property, see Inventário, Luisa Maria da Conceição, Salvador, Bahia, 1816, APEB-SJ, 04/1725/2195/12, fls. 41v, 43v, 44, 45v. Muriel Nazzari, "Transition toward Slavery: Changing Practices Regarding Indians in Seventeenth-Century São Paulo," *The Americas* 49, no. 2 (October 1991): 132, 142, 145, 148, argues that in settling an estate after the deaths of the spouses, over time the courts increasingly favored creditors rather than debtors who, in the case of bankrupt estates, were the heirs. Some who did know to refuse were the daughter and granddaughter heirs of Alexandre Gomes de Brito in 1826, while the wife and children of Domingos Henrique Azevedo desisted from their inheritance in favor of the creditors and in their own interest. See Inventário, Alexandre Gomes de Brito, 1826, Salvador, Bahia, APEB-SJ, 08/3470/01, fls. 5, 12, and Inventário, Domingos Henrique Azevedo, 1866, APEB-SJ, 07/2973/05, fl. 5. Portuguese and Brazilian law were not alone in holding the heirs liable for the debts of the deceased. Writing about a seventeenth-century Dutch notary, Donna Merwick notes that on inheriting his father's estate, he took "steps to relieve himself of all liability for his father's debts," and could even produce a witness to certify that he had received no part of the estate. See *Death of a Notary: Conquest and Change in Colonial New York* (Ithaca: Cornell University Press, 1999), p. 81.

[64] Testamento, Ignacia Delfina Wernek, 1857, fl. 3.

[65] Inventário, Ignacia Delfina Wernek, 1858, fl. 47.

Table 3. *Reconstructed Balance Sheet: Estate of Inácia Delfina Werneck, 1861*

	1st appraisal[b]	Sale price[c]	2nd appraisal[d]	Sale price[e]	Subtotals	Totals
I. Estate assets (in réis[a])						
A) Seven slaves						
Pedro Nação	1,800,000	1,801,000				
Antonio Nação	1,500,000	1,501,000				
Luiz Nação	1,450,000		300,000	321,000		
Simão Nação	1,200,000		800,000	480,000		
Caetano Cabinda	1,000,000		400,000	200,000		
José Monjollo	1,600,000		600,000	600,000		
Joanna Mozambique	1,200,000		600,000	600,000		
Subtotals		3,302,000		2,201,000	5,503,000	
B) Sale of coffee[f]					419,000	
C) Loan owed to Inácia[g]					645,000	
D) Rental for slaves[h]					449,380	
					7,016,380	7,016,380
II. Estate expenditures (in réis)		Amount				
A) Doctor's bill[i]		835,000			835,000	
B) Overseer's salary[j]		705,000			705,000	
C) Amounts paid by Werneck[k]						
Inácia's expenses		441,360				
Merchant		109,000				
Funeral		278,257				
Masses		116,000				
Legacy[l]		300,000				
Subtotal		1,244,617			1,244,617	

D) Amounts still owed by Werneck[m]

Estate tax	80,000
Merchants	1,681,300
Masses	191,800
Legacies	923,000
Unexplained Legacies[n]	2,360,647
Subtotal	5,236,747

III. *Final balance* (in réis)

$$
\begin{array}{r}
5,236,747 \\
8,021,364 \quad -8,021,364 \\
\hline
-1,004,984
\end{array}
$$

[a] At the 1861 conversion rate of 1,000 réis = 52 cents (U.S.), the deficit was $522.59. See "Appendix: Statistical Tables," in Julian Smith Duncan, *Public and Private Operation of the Railways in Brazil* (New York: Columbia University Press, 1932), p. 183.

[b] Inventário, Ignacia Delfina Wernek, 1858, fl. 73.

[c] Ibid., fl. 77.

[d] Ibid., fl. 104.

[e] Ibid., fls. 111–111v

[f] Ibid., fl. 89.

[g] Ibid., fls. 21, 89.

[h] Ibid., fl. 130.

[i] Ibid., fls. 35, 47, 130v–131.

[j] Ibid., fls. 40, 126, 158.

[k] Ibid., fls. 48, 22.

[l] The sum of 300,000 réis plus the legacy above of 923,000 réis (1,223,000 réis) nearly equal the total legacies specified in the will of 1,250,000 réis.

[m] Ibid., fls. 47, 48, 130v.

[n] Ibid., fls. 47, 130v; Werneck never explained this amount; it is much too large, however, to plausibly refer to the total legacies to the unspecified number of poor godchildren mentioned in Inácia's will.

bills from time to time for Inácia when she was alive and coffee sales were down. Such a solution would have allowed Bernardina and her children to keep the slaves, as Inácia had intended and assumed they would. But the outstanding sum was large, Inácia was no longer alive, and Werneck's loyalty to his aunt did not extend so far. Why should it? Standard legal procedure in any probate required that all expenses attributable to an estate be met before the remaining property passed to the heirs.

Probate proceedings having dragged on for more than two years, events for Bernardina and her children, for the slaves, and for Werneck finally came to a head during the year between March 1860 and April 1861.

Werneck arranged the auction. Income from the sale of the slaves would go for "payment of legacies and debts," as Werneck said it, the heirs being understood as debtors and their inherited property to be converted into payment of debt.[66] For the two years since Dona Inácia died, all seven slaves had been in Bernardina's possession on lands where previously they had worked for Inácia with Bernardina's son, José Cyrillo, as their overseer. By 1869 a law prohibited selling slaves "under the gavel," but in 1860 the local probate judge approved Werneck's request for a public sale. When in mid-March the auction was held, it drew no bids. In a hastily called second auction a few days later, a notice was posted and for nine days the slaves appeared in front of the judge's house in Vassouras, the notary being on hand to verify any sales. The same Dr. Castro from Werneck's fazenda offered a token amount more than the appraised price for Pedro and Antônio, although the price he finally paid was discounted by the amount Inácia owed him for medical services. He was reimbursed from the proceeds of the sale of the two slaves.[67] Nonetheless, with only two low bids and five slaves still unsold, the second auction was also seen as a failure.

A disgruntled Werneck wasted no time. Before the end of March, acting through the judge, he ordered the heirs to reimburse him for expenditures he had made on behalf of the estate; if not, he would call for a third auction. For Bernardina and her children it was an impossible choice: Either assume the estate's debts or surrender the slaves. Although

---

[66] Ibid., fl. 77.

[67] Decreto 1695, 15 September 1869, in *Codigo Philippino, 1870*, Liv. 4, Appendice, pp. 1395–1396; Inventário, Ignacia Delfina Wernek, 1858, fls. 40, 71v, 73, 75–77, 130–131v.

Werneck's request was consistent with the law as it applied both to families and even to business partnerships, in the situation in which the heirs were a family of newly freed slaves without resources, it seems either a futile course or one intentionally punitive. But these people were his aunt's former slaves, not his; he had no special bonds with them. His duty was to carry out his aunt's will, a duty that became increasingly difficult and time consuming. As Werneck surely must have guessed would happen, Bernardina and her children sent neither money nor an explanation, and did not appear.[68]

As a way out of the impasse, but one that also removed the slaves from Bernardina's use, Werneck decided to hire the slaves himself. With no reply to his demand for reimbursement, on 1 April 1860 four of the unsold slaves were quickly transferred to his authority at Monte Alegre. Werneck later supplied a detailed accounting of the days each slave worked or was laid off by sickness, the daily rate at which each worked, and the total he owed the estate for their year's labor. Caetano worked a full schedule of 288 days at 500 réis, or about 26 cents per day, while José Monjollo, his hip joints damaged, was unable to work for 20 days and Simão, sick with yaws, missed 55 days. Luís, whom Werneck described as "very old," worked only 184 days at the lesser rate of 320 réis, or 16 cents per day. Werneck further noted that the black woman Joana had stayed with Bernardina while nursing her child.[69] The slaves repaid Werneck with their labor, a portion of what the estate owed him. Income that would normally have gone to the heirs, as the owners of the slaves, was instead used by Inácia's estate to cover part of the deficit.

In December 1860, when the heirs had still not appeared, and perhaps wishing to be rid of the burdensome slaves, yet insistent on recovering his costs, Werneck called for a third auction. This one, staged a few months later, in March 1861, at the doors of the Municipal Council chambers on Vassouras's main square, finally produced results, the value of the slaves having been reappraised "more reasonably and in accord with the times and [their] condition," as Werneck instructed. There were buyers even for the old and infirm, useful for menial tasks when bought cheaply enough.[70]

[68] Inventário, Ignacia Delfina Wernek, 1858, fl. 83; *Codigo Commercial do Imperio do Brazil*, annotated by Salustiano Orlando de Araujo Costa, 4th ed. (Rio de Janeiro: Laemmert, 1886), Parte 1, Tit. 15, Cap. 3, Secs. 6 and 7.

[69] Inventário, Ignacia Delfina Wernek, 1858, fl. 130.

[70] Ibid., fls. 77, 95, 104, 111–111v.

The slaves – including a nursing mother, an old man, and another with a serious skin disease – had been shunted from Inácia to Bernardina, then to Werneck, and now sold to new owners; distressing uncertainty had led to further uncertainty. It was not at all as Inácia had planned, although Bernardina might have sold the slaves herself, preferring whatever cash she could get to their sickly, unreliable labor and the cost of feeding them. What reason would she have had to observe ideal slaveowner behavior to care for aging or sick slaves, and what means? Such slaves would have been an ambivalent gift at best and, as it turned out, no gift at all.

Looking back, the failed second auction in March 1860 marked a radical turn in Werneck's conduct toward the heirs. Up to this point, as executor he had kept strictly within the law. Then, with only two slaves sold for disappointingly low prices, he not only toughened his stand by calling on the court to enforce the heirs' liability for the estate's remaining debts, but he also stepped outside his role as executor. Within days of this auction, the court summoned Bernardina and her four adult children to verify their signatures on a rental contract they had earlier signed with Werneck. When eight months later, in December 1860, they had not paid the agreed-on amount, Werneck initiated a civil suit against them. The suit represents a set of events that ran parallel to the probate proceedings, legally unrelated, but apparently related in Werneck's thinking as a second debt owed him by the heirs; five copies of the contract, one for each heir, together with a notarized transcription of the suit were included in the probate record.[71]

The matter of the contract had been brewing since May 1858 when, a few months after Inácia's death, Werneck leased them land at Sant'Ana, the same lands Inácia had inherited from her parents, sold to her brother-in-law, and had long benefited from, an arrangement Werneck accepted and administered along with Inácia's other business affairs after his father died. Although Werneck used the term "usufruct" to describe his aunt's claim to certain fields, Inácia made no reference at all to land in her will, and the legality of the arrangement remains ambiguous. More likely, she simply had an informal working agreement first with her brother-in-law and then her nephew. But because in either case the agreement would have lapsed with her death, there was no reason to mention it in her will. It was Werneck who extended to Bernardina and her children the favor of access to land, fields for both coffee and food crops, and the use

---

[71] Ibid., fls. 83, 140–150v, 151v–152.

of two houses.[72] Just as Inácia had enjoyed the profits from the coffee produced on those lands, so would her heirs (in equal parts).

But with a crucial difference: They were to pay rent, 100,000 réis each, for a total of 500,000 réis, or about $260, annually, due in installments every six months. Werneck further bound them to each other and to the contract by stipulating that if any of the five renters wanted out of the agreement, he or she must sublet his or her part to one of the other four, who was then obligated for an additional 100,000 réis. If any one renter defaulted, all five were subject to eviction. The contract was drawn up and read to them, they agreed, and all five signed, or had someone sign for them. Two and a half years later, in December 1860, they were in arrears for the staggering amount of about $890, including principal, interest at 1 percent per month, court costs, and stamp duty. Without a response from either Bernardina or the children, in March 1861 the remaining five slaves were sold at auction, and in April the court handed down a judgment in the civil case against Bernardina and her children. Still, they paid nothing, and nowhere in the documents does any of them explain, defend, object, or attempt to negotiate. How well had they even understood the paper they signed? A month later the court again ordered them to comply and gave them ten days. Again, nothing. In June 1861, a court official went out from town to the fazenda Sant'Ana, easily a day's round-trip on horseback, to notify the family they had twenty-four hours to pay up.[73]

The outcome remains uncertain. The implication of the ultimatum was clearly eviction, although Werneck himself had not carried through by the time he died a few months later in November 1861, and neither did his heirs. The second executor, seeking to settle Dona Inácia's estate in 1864, noted that the amount Werneck owed for hiring the slaves had not yet been paid to the estate. On the other hand, several amounts were still outstanding to Werneck (now his estate), notably, rent on the "land and its improvements," which, according to the executor, Bernardina and her family continued to "enjoy after [Werneck's] death." A year later, in November 1865, they were summoned to appear before the judge to reply to the executor's accounting. The record of Inácia's

[72] Inventário, Ignacia Delfina Wernek, 1858, fls. 140–150v.

[73] The principal amount owed was 1,250,000 réis, and interest and costs came to another 461,252 réis, for a total of 1,711,252 réis, which at an exchange rate of 52 U.S. cents per mil-réis was the equivalent in 1860 and 1862 of $890. See Duncan, *Public and Private Operation of the Railways in Brazil*, p. 183; Inventário, Ignacia Delfina Wernek, 1858, fls. 140–142v, 143, 150v, 151, 152v, 153v, 154v.

estate ends there, with money still outstanding. A year later, however, when Werneck's widow also died and the inventory of the couple's joint property was revised for final settlement, among the "small irregularities" that remained was the matter of accounts owed by Dona Inácia's estate to Werneck's. As late as 1866, Bernardina was still on the land, and Werneck's heirs still bothered about payment.[74]

And being still on the land meant that Bernardina's family could farm, growing food crops to feed themselves and even some coffee from aging coffee bushes, which they might have sold. They had no slaves for the work, of course, but they were themselves a competent if small labor force: the four young men, two sons and two sons-in-law, together with the two daughters. They could get by.

With the deaths of Werneck and his widow, the fazenda Piedade, including Sant'Ana and Bernardina's fields, went to their oldest son Luís, who, having taken up a diplomatic post in Switzerland, sold it to his sister and brother-in-law, the same Dr. Castro from Werneck's fazenda who also had prescribed for Inácia's slaves.[75] So, although Bernardina and her five children stayed on, they were handed from one landlord to another, anxiously dependent on yet another man's uncertain favor while their case dragged on. Dona Inácia's effort to see them securely established on the place where they had always lived remained in doubt, and instead they lived with the nagging possibility of eviction. Things were at a stalemate.

THE CONTRACT

There is more to say, however, about Werneck and his puzzling decision to lease land at Sant'Ana to Bernardina and her children. Because in all aspects the contract he signed with them was oddly out of keeping with land and labor practices at the time, it calls attention to the man and his actions.

It was not unheard-of for owners, through their wills, to free their slaves and simultaneously grant them land, sometimes in generous amounts, sometimes nothing more than a narrow strip of poor land

---

[74] Inventário, Ignacia Delfina Wernek, 1858, fls. 160–160v, 163; Inventário, Francisco Peixoto de Lacerda Werneck, 1862, fls. 273, 288–288v (because the inventory was not completed before his widow died, it continues beyond her death in 1866, although the document bears the earlier date of 1862).

[75] Pondé, "A fazenda," 105, 123; Silva, *Barões e escravidão*, p. 90.

within a larger holding that was kept for family heirs. And of course it was slaveowners without heirs – unmarried or widowed men or women or priests without necessary heirs – who were more likely to make such provisions. The practice seems to have been more frequent in the last decades before the abolition of slavery in 1888, although Maria Helena Machado finds examples in eastern São Paulo province as early as the 1840s and 1850s. The current community of Cafundó in western São Paulo began as a donation of land to freed slaves sometime in the last years of slavery. The donation was not an outright gift from the owner, however, but came with strings attached. These former slaves were to use the land for their benefit and pass it on to their descendants, but they could not sell it. In piecing together the remarkable story of this small community, authors Robert Slenes, Carlos Vogt, and Peter Fry are careful to set it in the context of other donations of land to other freed slaves, typically in groups, in the same county, where they discover a recognizable pattern not only in the last years before abolition, 1876 to 1887, but also earlier in the 1840s. And like Cafundó, these donations frequently were encumbered with restrictions, and the parcels of land modest. Nor was the practice confined to southern coffee areas. In 1860 in Bahia, João Simões Coimbra, long separated from his wife and childless, gave his slaves freedom, money, and the use of a plot of land.[76] But of course it was not a solution Inácia could offer on any scale, not owning land in her own name.

The more usual arrangement for accommodating freed slaves willing to stay on a fazenda (or those with no other place to go or those from somebody else's plantation) was to settle them as *agregados*, dependents who continued to work according to the abilities of their age, health, sex, and skill, typically at subsistence farming on a plot of ground within the larger plantation. Writing in 1855, Werneck's own son Luís caught the condescension of the practice: "The slave himself, scarcely freed, abandons the great fazenda and goes to practice small-scale farming on

---

[76] Maria Helena Machado, *O plano e o pânico: Os movimentos sociais na década da abolição* (Rio de Janeiro: Editora Universidade Federal do Rio de Janeiro; São Paulo: Editora Universidade de São Paulo, 1994), pp. 29–30, 40–41, 44; Robert W. Slenes, Carlos Vogt, and Peter Fry, "Histórias do Cafundó," in Carlos Vogt and Peter Fry with the collaboration of Robert W. Slenes, *Cafundó: A África no Brasil – Linguagem e sociedade* (Campinas: Editora da Universidade de Campinas; São Paulo: Companhia das Letras, 1996), pp. 37–102; Inventário e testamento, João Simões Coimbra, Salvador, Bahia, 1860, APEB-SJ, 03/1242/1711/07, fls. 30–31v.

a few feet of land charitably bestowed in a spirit of beneficence by the great landowner."[77] In exchange for favors from their powerful patron, one of which could be avoiding recruitment into the army or securing justice in some dispute, they also owed services, usually labor for a special project organized by the landlord, such as building a chapel or a road. For freed men who could vote, an essential part of the bargain involved marking a ballot for the patron's candidate at election time. Even if dependents also received wages, as happened only occasionally, they often continued informally to owe services, and their dependence was not much diminished. They formed part of the extended residential household, ranking below family members and above those still slaves with whom they were sometimes confused, depending on color and rank. In this way a former slave became a client, trading work, services, and deference for favors. A common phrase made the unequal relationship explicit: He lives "at the favor" of his patron. It applied just as well to women.[78]

In the aftermath of the abolition of slavery in 1888, planters in Werneck's district, desperate to salvage and harvest their crops, found themselves admittedly dependent on any laborers they could persuade to work, and anxious to strike a bargain. Only then did they consider formally renting land to newly freed slaves. But while rental agreements were discussed as something to be experimented with, not yet something tested by wide experience, they settled on a third course that avoided

---

[77] Luiz Peixoto de Lacerda Werneck, *Idéias sobre a colonisação, precedidas de uma succinta exposição dos princípios geraes que regem a população* (Rio de Janeiro: Laemmert, 1855), pp. 61–62, quoted in Machado, *O plano e o pânico*, p. 51.

[78] For an early discussion of the *agregado*, see Eni de Mesquita, "O papel do agregado na região de Itú – 1780–1830," *Coleção Museu Paulista* 6 (1977): 13–121; on the central role of male agregados as voters in local elections, see Graham, *Patronage and Politics*, esp. pp. 20–21, 105–106, 137, 177, 193; Hebe Maria Mattos de Castro, *Das cores do silêncio: Os significados da liberdade no sudeste escravista, Brasil século XIX* (Rio de Janeiro: Arquivo Nacional, 1995), p. 89. Maria Sylvia de Carvalho Franco was the first to examine the dependence of free men. See *Homens livres na ordem escravocrata* (São Paulo: Ática, 1976), pp. 91–106, esp. p. 95. On the "ethic of favor," see Emília Viotti da Costa, "Brazil: The Age of Reform, 1870–1889," in *The Cambridge History of Latin America*, vol. 5: C. *1870 to 1930*, ed. Leslie Bethell (Cambridge: Cambridge University Press, 1986), pp. 746–747; and *The Brazilian Empire: Myths and Histories* (Chicago: University of Chicago Press, 1985), esp. pp. xxi, 61, 76–77. On agregados confused with slaves, see Silvia Hunold Lara, *Campos da violência: Escravos e senhores na Capitania do Rio de Janeiro, 1750–1808* (Rio de Janeiro: Paz e Terra, 1988), p. 180.

using agregados. Sharecropping won out as the predominant solution for Paraíba Valley planters who, having just lost the right to own their labor force, refrained from surrendering control over their land.[79]

A written agreement of the kind Werneck had drawn up with Bernardina and her children was exceedingly rare in 1858. Writing about a county south and east over the escarpment from Vassouras in lower-lying lands, Brazilian historian Hebe Maria Mattos de Castro traced land use practices from 1850 into the 1890s using notarial and judicial sources. Finding only three written rental agreements (meaning notarized ones) before 1860, she concludes they were completely atypical for the region. And these lands were further unusual in being sizable, well-established holdings that rented for large sums; the construction of any new buildings or the planting of new crops was prohibited; and these lands were rented in special and temporary circumstances to benefit minor heirs pending the settlement of an estate. Not until the 1870s were seven contracts recorded by the local notary for small, uncultivated blocks of land of the kind a poor man or woman, perhaps a former slave, might farm.[80]

Unwritten agreements are especially hard to recover, of course, but landowners preferred them. If less reliable because more easily broken, informal, spoken agreements had the compelling advantage of allowing planters the final say on how their land was used. The vocabulary for these renters changed. They were not called agregados, but *moradores*, tenants or settlers, or *arrendatários*, renters – that is, "free people in the lower ranks of life," with the important difference that they paid some small rent. Their rent bought them little security, however. Landlords who wanted their lands back did not hesitate to evict tenants even before the agreed-upon terms were up, once the land became productive. At best, a renter with verbal authorization to make improvements on a plot could hope to be indemnified for the rough house or shed he might have built. The French cotton merchant L. F. Tollenare, who visited the northeastern sugar region around Recife early in the nineteenth century, reported that even the sugar farmers who owned slaves but farmed land belonging to big mill owners, white men for the most part and not poor blacks or freed slaves, made a point of saying that without written

[79] Stein, *Vassouras*, pp. 266, 273, refers to a discussion in 1888 about the possibility of renting land, but offers no evidence that any such agreements followed.

[80] Hebe Maria Mattos de Castro, *Ao sul da história: Lavradores pobres na crise do trabalho escravo* (São Paulo: Brasiliense, 1987), pp. 136–137.

contracts they invested in slaves and cattle, which they could take with them, and chose to live in "miserable cabins" rather than see their efforts lost in constructing more comfortable housing.[81]

In this sense Werneck's desire to sign a contract not only was unusual but can be construed as offering Bernardina's family secure access to land without fear of their being arbitrarily expelled. On the other hand, the contract was silent about whether they would be reimbursed for any improvements they made on the land and mentioned only that they were to build fences and, by implication, do so at their own expense. It was unclear whether they were to be reimbursed for any new coffee bushes they planted, or whether they could count on seeds or seedlings from the baron's other holdings to start food crops. Furthermore, the contract became a trap if the rent was too high for the tenant to meet, as happened with Bernardina and her children.[82]

Rents in goods or cash were a complex business, varying from place to place and over time. Tenants customarily paid an agreed amount of what they produced, either a marketable export crop such as coffee or sugar or a locally consumed staple such as corn; in the early part of the century perhaps one-tenth of the crop or in the 1870s an annual rent in cash. Earlier in the century a minimal cash rent in the sugar zone around Recife might increase if a man had a laborer to help him cultivate more land than he could farm alone. The lower the rent, the greater the likelihood the tenant also owed services, making a man answerable to a landlord's arbitrary demands. According to historian B. J. Barickman, nineteenth-century tenant farmers in the coastal sugar-, tobacco-, and manioc-growing hinterland of Salvador in southern Bahia, although they frequently were made to pay in kind, chose cash when they could

---

[81] Henry Koster, *Travels in Brazil in the Years from 1809 to 1815* (Philadelphia: M. Carey and Son, 1817), 2: 135–136; Castro, *Ao sul da história*, p. 137; L[ouis] F[rançois] de Tollenare, *Notas dominicais tomadas durante uma viagem em Portugal e no Brasil em 1816, 1817, e 1818* (Salvador: Progresso, 1956), pp. 93, 95.

[82] Tollenare, *Notas dominicais*, pp. 95–96. On the importance of reliable access to land, see Castro, *Das cores do silêncio*, pp. 89–90. In discussing land and labor practices in the Paraíba Valley in the latter years of the nineteenth century, Nancy Priscilla Smith Naro stresses the importance to renters of whether they could claim a right to the improvements they made, including both buildings and crops. See "Customary Rightholders and Legal Claimants to Land in Rio de Janeiro, Brazil, 1870–1890," *The Americas* 48, no. 4 (April 1992): esp. pp. 487, 504, 510.

in order to free themselves to grow whatever crops they thought most profitable.[83]

Having contracted to receive payments in cash from his renters, how should we evaluate the amount Werneck charged? In Rio de Janeiro province as well as in Bahia, ground rents generally were modest. In a coastal area of what would later be included in the province of Rio, poor farmers paid rents for sugarcane land that ranged from 320 réis to 1,000 réis, while others squatted and paid no rent. In 1854, a man and his wife rented by verbal agreement approximately six acres with 150 old coffee bushes, together with another similar plot with a thatched-roof house and kitchen, all for 25,000 réis annually. In Bahia rents typically amounted to no more than the equivalent of the standard yearly ration of manioc flour for one person – that is, tenant farmers had to produce and sell only slightly more manioc, for example, than they needed to feed themselves and their slaves. We do not know how much land certain tenants rented, but in 1854 one farmer got a small farm for 16,000 réis per year, and the highest annual rent for a farm in Bahia was 80,000 réis, while the lowest was a mere 3,000 réis.[84] In Bahia at about the same time as the Werneck lease, the prosperous owner of several small farms and a substantial number of slaves freed some and gave to them not only money but usufruct of one of the best-producing farms. He charged no rent.[85] In contrast to any of these examples, the 500,000 réis Bernardina and her four adult children agreed to pay yearly for their few unmeasured fields is striking.[86] Werneck's rent was extravagant.

Why offer them land at all? Was he honoring an understanding he had with his aunt to keep them at Sant'Ana, a reward-for-services from a decent mistress, arranged by a respectful nephew on her behalf? But then why make their staying so difficult? Did he want them gone? Or

---

[83] Tollenare, *Notas dominicais*, p. 95; Castro, *Ao sul da história*, p. 137; Koster, *Travels in Brazil*, vol. 2, p. 136; B. J. Barickman, *A Bahian Counterpoint*, pp. 123–124.

[84] Sheila de Castro Faria, *A colônia em movimento: Fortuna e família no cotidiano colonial* (Rio de Janeiro: Nova Fronteira, 1998), pp. 115, 119–120. The measure of land was a *quartel*, the equivalent of an *alqueire paulista*, or 5.97 square acres. Castro, *Ao sul da história*, p. 140; Barickman, *Bahian Counterpoint*, p. 124.

[85] Inventário e Testamento, João Simões Coimbra, Salvador, Bahia, 1860, APEB-SJ, 03/1242/1711/07, fls. 31–32; and [his second] Inventário, João Simões Coimbra, Salvador, Bahia, 1870, APEB-SJ, 03/1052/1521/02, fl. 65v.

[86] Inventário, Ignacia Delfina Wernek, 1858, fl. 142.

perhaps wishing to be rid of a patron's obligations, did he try to transform traditional ties into a formal contract between independent parties, land leased for cash, a contract that put the responsibility on them and dispensed with the necessity of further favors from him?

If so, the terms were contradictorily personal and paternalistic. He leased to them not only Inácia's coffee fields, from which they could produce a marketable cash crop, but additional land suitable for food crops to provide their own subsistence. He included two houses for them to live in – not to sublet to other tenants was the implied proviso. The first house belonged with the coffee fields; he instructed that the second was for Bernardina and one of her children or a son-in-law and his family. If the offer was generous, it was also undisguisedly condescending: They must keep the house clean (as if they would not) and reserve space to store coffee, something he would not provide and they might not think of without prompting; the stipulation to fence in their food crops was unusual in a region where lands were rarely surveyed and boundaries were deliberately vague (there was no mention of cattle to be kept out); and, finally, when clearing to plant food crops, they were instructed not to burn beyond their particular fields.[87] Werneck evidently worried that they would be careless and a nuisance to his neighbors; he clearly was speaking to subordinates.

Out of the first puzzle, a second one forms. Having leased the land, why then sue Bernardina and her children for the unpaid rent after only two and a half years? In this face-to-face society in which borrowing and lending were common and banks scarcely existed in the late 1850s, credit was often personal and carried for years, as with the doctor's bill or the overseer's salary. One female tenant in Bahia owed her landlord twenty-seven years' back rent for her farm.[88] A lawsuit against Bernardina so soon was extreme, not at all the usual way of doing things.

Had Werneck provided land so that the inherited slaves could be used productively, with the lease a lesson in the commerce in which this family of former slaves now participated? The alternative was to hire the slaves out as day laborers in town, but keeping track of them might prove messy and involve him. Better perhaps to keep both heirs and their slaves on his property and under his watch. Or had he foreseen that the estate would finish in the red and insisted on the lease as a way for Bernardina and her children to work off whatever debt they inherited? Possibly, yet if the slaves had sold at the originally

[87] Ibid., fl. 142v.   [88] Barickman, *A Bahian Counterpoint*, p. 124.

appraised values, the estate's costs could readily have been met. The lease was signed in 1858, two years before the estate's deficit was declared, although Werneck handled his aunt's finances and surely could have anticipated the problem. With the slaves still not satisfactorily sold in the second auction in March 1860, had he become fed up and decided to recover his expenditures by collecting on the rent? Perhaps, but even by my conservative estimate, his final loss from administering the estate was small compared with the amounts he daily transacted through his Rio de Janeiro commission agent during the period the suit was pending: the equivalent of approximately $157 against an astonishing $47,000 on one day, or the more regularly mentioned amounts of $1,200, $2,600, or $3,941 on other days.[89] Was it worth suing for?

And was there any point? Surely, Werneck did not think the family could produce enough to pay him, or that once behind in payments they could catch up. Having sold coffee for his aunt, Werneck knew how much these fields returned. The last sale he reported to the estate not only fell well short of paying Inácia's final bills but fell short of the annual rent he now asked from Bernardina and her children. How could he expect Bernardina to pay him? Even more telling, in 1858, about the time of Inácia's death, Werneck wrote his Rio de Janeiro agent that the fazenda Sant'Ana was "very old and sterile" and "left completely destroyed" by his father, who had "taken his fortune from its soil." A month later, he again described the fazenda as in its final decline, and said the coffee bushes "yield dry and poorly formed fruit" from "barren soil [terras frias]." Although the 140 slaves at Sant'Ana, 90 of them field slaves, produced between $6,000 and $7,000 income from coffee, Werneck reckoned that half as many slaves on his other fazendas produced four times as much.[90] Bernardina and her children would have to scratch their living and the rent money from worn-out fields.

[89] Werneck to João Baptista Leite e Cia., Monte Alegre, 16 February 1861, ANRJ-SAP, FW, Cód. 113, Vol. 3, Copiador, 2° maço, fl. 245 (PY 692.227); 28 March 1861, ANRJ-SAP, FW, Cód. 113, Vol. 3, Copiador, 2° maço, fl. 256 (PY 692.238); 22 April 1861, AN-SAP, FW, Cód. 113, Vol. 3, Copiador, 2° maço, fl. 263 (PY 692.245).

[90] Werneck to Bernardo Ribeiro Carvalho, Monte Alegre, 16 January 1858, ANRJ-SAP, FW, Cód. 112, Vol. 3, Copiador, fls. 465–466 (PY 691.410–410A); 20 February 1858, ANRJ-SAP, FW, Cód. 112, Vol. 3, Copiador, and fls. 471–473 (PY 691.415–415B).

WERNECK'S SENSE OF ORDER

How then are we to understand Werneck in his puzzling dealings with Bernardina and her family? He was not a careless man who acted arbitrarily. And he certainly cannot be reduced to the one-dimensional image of an ugly, brutal master who beat work from his slaves until they broke, then freed them to be rid of them. His instructions to his son Luís on establishing and running a fazenda, written in 1847 and published a year later, reveal a thoughtful and articulate man, informed in conserving the resources of the land and forests, astute in the business of growing coffee, and rational in the care of his slaves.[91] It is worth pausing to consider his treatment of his slaves more generally, his views on the correct running of society, and the crises he faced in the 1850s, exactly when Inácia died and he came to deal directly with her dependents. In these contexts the man becomes more visible.

He knew his slaves to be human beings and recognized his dependence on them. He recommended that slave quarters be built with verandas, so that a black might visit a fellow slave without getting his feet wet in the rain and risk catching cold; he recommended medicines and a diet that by contemporary standards was more adequate than some and consisted of three meals a day rather than two – his criticism of other planters was scarcely disguised. Punishment should be timely and fitting to the fault, and nursing women should have a year off from field work. Acknowledging such practices as both humane and in the planter's interests, he cautioned Luís that "extreme oppression dries up their hearts."[92]

In the routine running of fazenda life, he took serious account of his slaves' needs. In the fall of 1854, Werneck worried that he could wait no longer for the 600 blankets ordered from Portugal. "The cold

---

[91] Francisco Peixoto de Lacerda Vernek, *Memoria sobre a fundação de huma fazenda na provincia do Rio de Janeiro, sua administração e épocas em que se devem fazer as plantações, suas colheitas, etc., etc.* (Rio de Janeiro: Laemmert, 1847).

[92] Vernek, *Memoria*, pp. 9, 17–18. When Luís and his wife (who was also his first cousin once removed), Isabel Augusta de Werneck, inherited a fazenda from her father (his great-uncle, Werneck's uncle and Inácia's brother), they returned from Europe, where Luís had done brilliantly studying law. The fazenda was Monte Alegre, the same fazenda Luís later sold to his father sometime between 1848 and 1852, so that he might return to Europe, and where Werneck lived until his death. On Isabel Augusta's family's vast property, see Inventário, Francisco das Chagas Werneck, Vassouras, 1846, CDH-USS, Caixa 87; on Luís's life, see Silva, *Barões e escravidão*, pp. 85–90; Pondé, "A fazenda," p. 123.

has hit," he wrote his agent in Rio de Janeiro, "and the slaves are need-
ing them."[93] Werneck was among plantation owners in both sugar and
coffee zones who advocated setting aside land for slaves to plant in
coffee, corn, beans, bananas, potatoes, yams, manioc, or sugar. The produce could supplement their rations, but Werneck generally assumed a
slave would sell his harvest in order to "buy his tobacco, special food, or
fine clothing for his wife . . . and children." He strictly insisted, however,
that slaves should sell only to their masters, who in turn should pay a
fair price. "This is to avoid their hanging around and being corrupted
at the store," which often doubled as a drinking place. In December
1853, when slaves at Piedade sold him their coffee worth about $217,
Werneck wrote his agent to send the money "in the smallest change
possible," to be divided into the necessary amounts among many slave
growers.[94]

Consideration for his slaves meant that collectively they had some
voice and could present him with a dilemma. In 1858, Werneck keenly
wanted to transfer the slaves from Sant'Ana's exhausted fields (where
Bernardina and her children remained) to his newly purchased and fertile, but distant, fazenda Conceição. He knew the move would be difficult
for them, and he hesitated. Writing his agent, he explained: To "separate
them from each other and divide them among other fazendas when they
are accustomed to living as a family, aside from being impolitic, would
displease them." It was like breaking up a "tribe," he said. Nonetheless, when Werneck's property was inventoried in 1862, a year after his
death, all slaves were gone from Sant'Ana.[95] Evidently, regard for their
preferences had been set aside, perhaps by Werneck himself, anxious
to increase production at his other fazendas, or at his death, when the
Baroness took over as executrix. But we know Werneck had not treated
the decision casually.

93 Werneck to Bernardo Ribeiro de Carvalho, Monte Alegre, 27 March 1854,
    ANRJ-SAP, FW, Cód. 112, Vol. 3, Copiador, fl. 162 (PY 691.151).
94 Verneck, *Memoria*, pp. 16–17; Werneck to Amigo e Sr. [Bernardo Ribeiro de
    Carvalho], Monte Alegre, 9 December 1853, ANRJ-SAP, FW, Cód. 112, Vol. 3,
    Copiador, fl. 130 (PY 691.121–121A). B. J. Barickman provides a useful discus-
    sion of the prevalence and use of slave garden plots in "'A Bit of Land, which
    They Call Roça': Slave Provision Grounds in the Bahian Recôncovo, 1780–
    1860," *HAHR* 74, no. 4 (November 1994): 649–687.
95 Werneck to Bernardo Ribeiro de Carvalho, Monte Alegre, 16 January 1858,
    ANRJ-SAP, FW, Cód. 112, Vol. 3, Copiador, fls. 465–466 (PY 691.415–415B);
    Inventário, Francisco Peixoto de Lacerda Werneck, 1862, fl. 212.

Figure 13. The chapel at Monte Alegre, as it is today restored. It was here that Werneck arranged for a priest to say mass on Sundays for his slaves. A further way, he made clear, of disciplining them. (Photograph by the author)

At the same time, however, he was candid in his manipulation of his slaves. "This small property right," as Werneck referred to slave garden plots, encouraged them to "acquire a certain love for their country" and, more concretely, a connection to the place and its master. He said he had "a very good result," especially with slaves unskilled at picking coffee, in paying them for whatever they harvested above a quota set deliberately low. The trick was that the slaves easily exceeded the goal, payment stopped, and the higher amount (40 percent more than the original quota) "was then established as the general rule."[96] Hearing mass, learning Christian doctrine, and confessing once a year, he said,

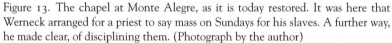

[96] Verneck, *Memoria*, pp. 20–21.

were a "brake" on slaves' bad habits. In 1857, he asked permission from the Bishop in Rio de Janeiro for a priest to say mass and preach to the slaves every Sunday at the chapel of his fazenda Monte Alegre, just as a priest had lived and said mass at Piedade for some twenty-six years during his father's time. A confessor "who knows his part" could urge slaves to adopt good morality and good manners, and instill "blind obedience to their masters and those who govern them."[97]

On the other hand, Werneck met open insurrection of any slaves with swift and violent repression. In November 1838, when more than 80 or 100 slaves fled (officials soon talked of more than 200), the majority of them reportedly armed, and principally from one fazenda (although a scattering of slaves from other fazendas gave alarming proof of communication across fazenda boundaries), Werneck, as commander of the regional National Guard, hurriedly mustered four divisions with 150 troops and civilians, some mounted, most on foot. Two long and tiring days' pursuit, sustained by the men's "extraordinary will for combat," ended in bloody confrontation. Although two soldiers were killed and another two wounded, the runaways took the worst of it: twenty-two dead or captured, and of the prisoners, seven or eight gravely wounded. One woman, an "esteemed" slave of the fazenda from which the majority of the runaways had come, refused to turn herself over, shouting that she would die, yes, but return, no. Werneck did not say if they shot her. The bags and crates of food, clothing, tools, arms, even gunpowder – all "stolen," probably gathered over some time – together with the skilled carpenters, blacksmiths, stone masons, and sugar masters who participated, including a number of women, convinced Werneck and other authorities that the slaves had intended to set themselves up as an insurgent settlement – an intolerable threat to white order. Werneck either burned or carried away their supplies. By month's end, a local official hastened to assure the provincial president that nearly all the fugitives had been captured, there was nothing to fear from the remaining few, and public order was generally restored.[98]

---

[97] Ibid., p. 16; Werneck to Bernardo Ribeiro de Carvalho, Monte Alegre, 21 June 1857, ANRJ-SAP, FW, Cód. 112, Vol. 3, Copiador, fls. 433–435 (PY 691–381–381A); Testamento, Francisco Peixoto de Lacerda, 1848, fl. 103.

[98] Francisco Peixoto de Lacerda Werneck (Colonel in Charge) to President of the Province, Command Headquarters, Valença Legion, 13 November 1838; President of the Province to Minister of Justice, Rio de Janeiro, 20 November 1838; President of the Province to Justice of the Peace [Parish of Pati do Alferes], Rio de Janeiro, 20 November 1838; President of the Province to Minister of

Also by month's end, Werneck publicly blamed the slaves' owner, Manuel Francisco Xavier, for provoking their flight. In a letter to the president of the province, written a brief three days after the insurrection, Werneck denounced his fellow planter for the disorder that reigned on his fazenda with his knowledge and tolerance. He cited a litany of events that had occurred within the previous few months: a slave shot dead by another slave and buried secretly at Xavier's order; slaves who arranged to buy gunpowder with their own money in a nearby town; white men wounded and overseers mortally beaten – crimes, Werneck said, that this planter sought to hide, and were known only by his dependents and slaves who spoke about them "tight-lipped" and "with the greatest secrecy." In the space of four years, so many similar events had occurred at this fazenda as to make the other planters of the parish fearful that insubordination could have "deadly consequences." He went on to alert the provincial president that Xavier owned more than 500 slaves, and that within the radius of a league four other fazendas each operated with more than 300 slaves, besides all those with lesser numbers of slaves. Werneck worried that the "contagion could spread to other fazendas," inciting a general uprising in the region.[99] One planter's delinquent conduct put them all at risk.

While Werneck put his condemnation in writing, no doubt others shared his views, and no doubt they talked among themselves. Werneck's accusation was sobering, if not also shocking: A planter's inability or re-fusal to govern his own slaves was the cause of their insurrection. If slave disobedience warranted swift retaliatory violence, a planter's en-dangering actions warranted serious rebuke and justified one planter's intrusion into the affairs of another. The exercise of slave-owning power was not a private, within-the-fazenda matter, but public, and a slave-owner should be held publicly accountable. Werneck had challenged a prominent planter whose wealth and prestige, far from exempting him,

Justice, Rio de Janeiro, 5 December 1838; County Judge to President of the Province, Vassouras, 13 November 1838; all in ANRJ-Seção do Poder Execu-tivo (hereafter cited as SPE), IJ1–860; see also José Antônio Soares de Souza, "O efêmero quilombo do Pati do Alferes em 1838," *RIHGB* 295 (April–June 1972): 33–69; for interpretation from the insurrectionists' point of view, see Flávio dos Santos Gomes, *Histórias de quilombolas: Mocambos e comunidades de senzalas no Rio de Janeiro, século XIX* (Rio de Janeiro: Arquivo Nacional, 1995), pp. 179–321.

[99] Francisco Peixoto de Lacerda Vernek (Colonel in Charge) to President of the Province, Command Headquarters, Valença Legion, 8 November 1838, quoted in Souza, "O efêmero quilombo," pp. 43–44.

increased the requirement for exemplary conduct. In his view, to retain their legitimacy, slaveowners had to demonstrate the justness of their authority.[100]

Werneck was not a man of the Enlightenment, and he had scant patience for the liberalism that stirred impassioned political debate and action in his own region and in the upper levels of imperial government. He believed in and valued an Old Order where everybody, not only slaves, knew their place. And knowing society to be carefully and hierarchically ranked, he insisted on the proper expression and observance of a person's position. Werneck's son, writing in 1855, took the view that people were distinguishable "according to the order, scale, or category into which [they are] placed in society."[101] In this society people did not meet as equals, but always as superior or inferior to someone else. The patronage of those with more authority, wealth, or connections should be sought. Werneck readily admitted his strategy in encouraging his younger son, Manuel, to cultivate a friendship with the son of one of "our best men of state" who later would be able to help him in his own career, but only if Manuel was a good example to his friend: studious, prudent, and well behaved. Everything he did would lose merit, however, if he allowed his friend to catch on to his motives.[102] So, if he

[100] As it turned out, Werneck's explanation largely agreed with the one offered by Manoel Congo, the slave accused of leading the uprising, at his trial: They fled out of fear of the violence that went unchecked on Xavier's fazenda. See Homicídio, Manoel Congo, Juiz de Paz, Freguezia de N.S. da Conceição do Pati do Alferes, 1838, CDH-USS, Caixa 464, fls. 18v–19. For a transcription of the trial, see *Insurreição negra e justiça, Paty do Alferes, 1838*, transcribed by João Luiz Pinaud, Carlos Otavio de Andrade, Salete Neme, Maria Cândida Gomes de Souza, and Jeannette Garcia (Rio de Janeiro: Ed. Expressão e Cultura – Exped Ltda. e Ordem dos Advogados do Brasil, 1987). Portraits of Captain-Major Manuel Francisco Xavier and his wife can be seen in the parish church in Pati do Alferes, to which they generously contributed. See Aurélio Stulzer, *Notas para a história da vila de Pati do Alferes* (Rio de Janeiro: Lito-Tipo Guanabara, 1944), pp. 7–8, 15. This is likely the same Francisco Xavier reprimanded by royal officals in 1799 for the poor treatment of a slave who fled in self-defense, whom they returned and who in the future should be treated, they said, "with humanity and leniency." See Lara, *Campos da violência*, p. 297. On planter culture and the presumption that a planter's power did not normally extend beyond his own fazenda, see ibid., p. 175.

[101] Luiz Peixoto de Lacerda Werneck, *Idéias sobre colonização, precedidas de uma sucinta exposição dos princípios que regem a população* (Rio de Janeiro: Laemmert, 1855), p. 28.

[102] Werneck to Manoel, Monte Alegre, 31 March 1854, ANRJ-SAP, FW, Cód. 112, Vol. 3, Copiador, fls. 165–166 (PY 691.154–154A).

considered himself worthy of deference from some, he reciprocated by offering it to those who deserved it from him, all the while candidly acknowledging the nature of the exchange.

When others failed to know their place, Werneck quickly voiced his displeasure at their offense. He grew irate when he thought his assistance to a friend's orphaned son, for whose schooling he paid, was abused. He was willing to pay for everyday clothes, but not to send him to a fine tailor. It was not only the money he objected to, but the fact that the boy's expenses were "not in harmony with his position." "I will not have him there like a *lord*, incurring expenses his circumstances do not warrant," he snapped. He wanted a stop put to the boy's pretentiousness.[103] Two years later he refused to endorse a promissory note for a young man who had shown the disrespect of sending a messenger to ask for Werneck's signature rather than coming personally. Werneck returned the note unsigned, saying that "such behavior irritated me." "This fellow has become intolerable." Although the man "is obligated to me in many ways," Werneck remarked, "he pretends to be equal to persons long established here and who are of another social position." The man paid for his impertinence: Werneck announced he would "cut all relations with him."[104] He had even less patience with a certain Antônio José Vianna, who was writing letters to the black woman Eugênia, who had been sent from Rio de Janeiro to Monte Alegre's infirmary to recover from an illness and to give birth. Werneck wanted the "scoundrel" "horsewhipped" not only for the intimacy the letters expressed – he blamed Eugênia's poor health on the "excesses she would have done for him" – but because they were sent behind Werneck's back through his administrator.[105] He reserved his good opinion for those who did not presume too much.

A slave's insubordination drew more than irritation or threats. Werneck sent his slave Sebastiano to the House of Correction in Rio de Janeiro to be severely whipped and afterward put to hard labor for an indeterminate time. For sixteen years Werneck had known him as

[103] Werneck to João Baptista Leite e Cia., Monte Alegre, 15 March 1859, ANRJ-SAP, FW, Cód. 112, Vol. 3, Copiador, 2° maço, fl. 87 (PY 692.74); Werneck to João Baptista Leite e Cia., Conceição, 12 September 1859, ANRJ-SAP, FW, Cód. 112, Vol. 3, Copiador, 2° maço, fl. 98 (PY 692.85).

[104] Werneck to João Baptista Leite e Cia., Monte Alegre, 2 April 1861, ANRJ-SAP, FW, Cód. 113, Vol. 3, Copiador, 2° maço, fl. 257 (PY 692.239).

[105] Werneck to João Baptista Leite e Cia., Monte Alegre, 7 April 1861, ANRJ-SAP, FW, Cód. 113, Vol. 3, Copiador, 2° maço, fl. 258 (PY 692.240).

a "good slave," a master stone mason who had never set foot off the fazenda, until recently when he became a liar and a drunk to the point of becoming insolent. Werneck thought the man might do him some harm, and judged it was time to "take him down a peg or two." "About a month ago," Werneck wrote his agent, "I laid open his back." It is a startling moment that reveals a twisted intimacy of violent physical contact between master and slave. Not an overseer, not someone paid to do the job out of the owner's sight and hearing, but Werneck himself had brought the whip down across Sebastiano's back and torn open the flesh. "He only became worse." Werneck had lost control over his slave, and both men knew it. "The only thing to do is to kill him, and this I will not do," wrote Werneck. He arranged to sell him instead to some remote corner of the province.[106]

Werneck's own career duplicated the rankings of the hierarchy he defended. Born to the privileges of property, as a young man nineteen years old in 1814 with no land of his own, but already cultivating an enormous section half a league square, Werneck petitioned the Portuguese crown for a royal grant. He had slaves "to cultivate the lands" and would "set up a fine establishment and increase the Royal Tithes...."[107] In his lifetime he multiplied his grandfather's twenty-two slaves, and his father's two fazendas with "plenty of slaves." By the time he died he owned vast property: seven fazendas, covering approximately 44 square miles, and more than 600 slaves, having owned nearly another 1,000 over the years who had since died, fled, or been sold.[108]

With property came the further privileges of power and reputation. Werneck enjoyed an officer's status first in the local militia, then in

[106] Werneck to Bernardo Ribeiro de Carvalho, Monte Alegre, 31 March 1856, ANRJ-SAP, FW, Cód. 112, Vol. 3, Copiador, fl. 352 (PY 691.310); Werneck to Bernardo Ribeiro de Carvalho, Monte Alegre, 5 April 1856, AN-SAP, FW, Cód. 112, Vol. 3, Copiador, fl. 353 (PY 691.311).

[107] Sesmaria, Valença, Francisco Peixoto de Lacerda Werneck, ANRJ-SPE, Sesmarias, Caixa 156, Doc. 31, fl. 1.

[108] Inventário, Francisca das Chagas, 1812, fl. 6v; Publica Forma do Testamento, Francisco Peixoto de Lacerda, 1848, fls. 3–3v; Werneck to Bernardo Ribeiro de Carvalho, Monte Alegre, 16 August 1858, ANRJ-SAP, FW, Cód. 112, Vol. 3, Copiador, 2° maço, fls. 32–33 (PY 692.29–29A); Inventário, Francisco Peixoto de Lacerda Werneck, 1862, fls. 199–234, 65v–69; Avellar, "Relatorio do Estado da Nossa Caza, 1862," quoted in Stein, *Vassouras*, p. 46 and n. 41. By my calculation, using Stein's figures to convert leagues to kilometers, the total plantation area was 108.9 square kilometers, not 81 square kilometers, as he has it; to arrive at square miles, I multiplied square kilometers by 0.4.

the newly organized National Guard, and by 1839 as commandant of regional forces. At the time of the Liberal Revolt of 1842, he successfully led some 300 troops, armed and outfitted at his private expense, against Liberals at the provincial border, a fight on behalf of the central authority of the monarchy and for "good order," as he later put it. An appreciative emperor repaid his loyalty with honorary titles that further enhanced his reputation: Knighthood in the Imperial House, Commander in the Order of the Rose in 1842 for his services in restoring "public order," Cavalier in the Order of Christ, and, in 1852, he became the second Baron of Pati do Alferes.[109] In 1859, a year after Inácia died, Werneck nervously welcomed a "gracious and agreeable" Emperor on his first visit to Pati do Alferes, afterward pressing his agent and kinsman in the capital: "I ask you to tell me with the frankness of a friend what you have heard . . . regarding the reception of the Monarch at my house."[110] A chapel, together with a cemetery and vicarage, built with Werneck's money and vision to serve local parishioners, dedicated to God and named for the Emperor's daughter Isabel, neatly entwined the double hierarchies of church and state in one grand gesture.[111] Werneck knew what "good order" meant.

Yet he also knew by the mid-1850s that there were widening cracks in the world he believed in, defended, and relied on. By the time Inácia died in 1858 and Werneck became landlord as well as executor to her heirs, plantation life in the valley was changing.

Coffee was in decline. By 1856, the crisis was undeniable. A majority of trees throughout the middle Paraíba Valley had been planted more than twenty-five years earlier; they were old and bore little fruit. Aging,

[109] Silva, *Barões e escravidão*, pp. 70–71; Pondé, "A fazenda," 100–101; Greenleigh H. Faria Braga, *De Vassouras: História, fatos, e gente* (Rio de Janeiro: Ultra-Set, 1978), p. 26.

[110] Werneck to Commander Domingos José Leite, Monte Alegre, 10 February 1859, ANRJ-SAP, FW, Cód. 112, Vol. 3, Copiador, 2° maço, fl. 81 (PY 692.68); Werneck to Bernardo Ribeiro de Carvalho, Monte Alegre, 18 February 1859, ANRJ-SAP, FW, Cód. 112, Vol. 3, Copiador, 2° maço, fl. 83 (PY 692.70).

[111] For an account of the building of the chapel, its partial collapse, the escalating expense, and the celebration of its blessing, see Werneck to Luiz Antonio Barbosa, Monte Alegre, 20 November 1853, ANRJ-SAP, FW, Cód. 112, Vol. 3, Copiador, fls. 122–124 (PY 691.116–116B); Werneck to Baron of Rio Bonito, Monte Alegre, 21 May 1854, ANRJ-SAP, FW, Cód. 112, Vol. 3, Copiador, fls. 189–191 (PY 691.171–171B); Werneck to Ignacio Dias Paes Leme, Monte Alegre, 8 June 1854, ANRJ-SAP, FW, Cód. 112, Vol. 3, Copiador, fls. 200–201 (PY 691.180–180A); and Silva, *Barões e escravidão*, p. 84.

poorly nourished trees were especially vulnerable to insect blights and ever-present ants. An 1859 photograph of the denuded hills, backdrop to Vassouras's handsome buildings, reveals what was becoming generally visible throughout the region. The soil was wearing out; coffee bushes were producing fewer full, red berries. New plantings in virgin soil were necessary. The effects of erosion were similarly apparent on the abandoned hillside fields behind the fazenda that bordered on Werneck property.[112] At Werneck's fazenda Manga Larga, 400,000 of the 479,000 bushes were described in 1862 as old and pruned back, while 120,000 of the 160,000 bushes at Piedade were also old. Harvests on Werneck's fazendas that once yielded 50,000 to 60,000 *arrobas* of coffee fell to 16,000 or 18,000. And in the especially bad year of 1858, only two of his fazendas produced any coffee at all. In the 1860s Werneck's widow sharply denounced what she and others called *rotina*, the repeated practices of clearing new fields by felling and burning virgin forests, careless planting that accelerated erosion, and yearly harvests with nothing to replenish the soil. She noted tersely that in all their vast holdings they did not possess even "200 square *braças* of virgin forest of first quality."[113]

Even where forested land still existed, the heavy work of preparing and planting new fields in virgin soil required strong, younger slaves to replace the slaves who, like the bushes they tended, had grown old and weak. The chronic complaint of too few slaves at high prices took on

---

[112] Victor Frond, "Vassouras" and "Interior da fazenda do Governo, oficinas e senzalas," both about 1859. The original photographs, like all those Frond took in Brazil in the late 1850s and 1860s, are believed lost; what remain are the lithographs made from them for *Brazil pittoresco: Album de vistas, panoramas, paisagens, monumentos, costumes, etc., com os retratos de Sua Magestade Imperador Don [sic] Pedro II et [sic] da Familia Imperial, photographiados por Victor Frond, lithographiados pelos primeiros artistas de Paris . . . e acompanhados de tres volumes . . . sobre a historia, as instituições, as cidades, as fazendas, a cultura, a colonização, etc., do Brazil, por Charles Ribeyrolles* (Paris: Lemercier, 1861), plates 14 and 24. For background on Frond and his authorship of this photographic project, see Gilberto Ferrez and Weston J. Naef, *Pioneer Photographers of Brazil, 1840–1920* (New York: Center for Inter-American Relations, 1976), p. 85; for a schematic map of the early land grants surrounding Piedade, see Pondé, "A fazenda," 94.

[113] Avellar, "Relatório do Estado da Nossa Caza, 1862," quoted in Stein, *Vassouras*, pp. 46, 50–51; 200 square braças equaled approximately 47 acres. Condemnation of exploitative land and labor practices is at the center of Stein's study of the Paraíba Valley coffee economy. See *Vassouras*, esp. pp. 45–54, 214–225; and on aging coffee trees, see p. 221. Silva, *Barões e escravidão*, pp. 172, 174; Pondé, "A fazenda," pp. 127–130.

new significance after 1850, when the traffic from Africa was effectively halted. Prices for prime slaves bought through the internal Brazilian trade almost doubled in the two years between 1852 and 1854. But Vassouras planters were not troubled by prices alone. They perceived danger from the slaves they imported from the north – planters said those slaves "always enjoyed an unfortunate fame" as instigators of insurrections, small-scale but insurrections nonetheless. Neither costs nor fear deterred them, however, from bringing into the province an estimated yearly average of 5,500 slaves during the 1850s.[114] Planting went on apace.

As a solution to both their fears and the labor shortage, in 1854 a group of prominent Vassouras planters proposed replacing dwindling numbers of slaves with free workers, but not just any free workers. They particularly had in mind white, European immigrants, whose discipline and enterprise they surely exaggerated, and whose mere presence they believed would diffuse the danger posed by restless slaves. By 1858 a draft contract was drawn up setting out terms and responsibilities for both planter and laborer. The laborer, for example, should not be asked to work side by side with slaves nor for more than ten hours per day.[115] Werneck scoffed at such schemes, as he had since 1847, seeing clearly the dilemma planters faced: Why would an immigrant settler submit himself to a planter's authority and the necessary discipline of a plantation when he might be offered land to work for himself elsewhere in this land-rich country or a higher salary outside agriculture? Werneck granted, however, that the Portuguese he had hired as skilled workers, administrators, and overseers served him better than Brazilians.[116]

As coffee yields in the valley dropped, planters responded by planting coffee on every available acre of ground. Consequently, they grew fewer

[114] Sebastião Ferreira Soares, *Notas estatísticas sobre a produção agrícola e carestia dos gêneros alimentícios no Império do Brasil* (1860; rpt., Rio de Janeiro: IPEA/INPES, 1977), pp. 135–136; *Instrucções para a Commissão Permanente nomeada pelos fazendeiros do municipio de Vassouras* (Rio de Janeiro: Typ. Episcopal de Guimarães e Cia., 1854), p. 65.

[115] *Instrucções para a Commissão Permanente*, pp. 65–68; Baron of Muritiba to Francisco Peixoto de Lacerda Werneck (baron of Paty do Alferes), Rio de Janeiro, 12 October 1858, ANRJ-SAP, FW, Cód. 112, Vol. 4 (PY 246.1); Werneck to Baron of Muritiba, Paty do Alferes, 25 November 1858, ANRJ-SAP, FW, Cód. 112, Vol. 3, Copiador, 2° maço, fls. 60–61 (PY 692.53–53A).

[116] Verneck, *Memoria*, p. 16; Werneck to Baron of Muritiba, Paty do Alferes, 25 November 1858, ANRJ-SAP, FW, Cód. 112, Vol. 3, Copiador, 2° maço, fls. 60–61 (PY 692.53–53A).

food crops. Their folly soon became apparent. Werneck had long advocated self-sufficiency: an orchard, "vegetables in variety for your table," sugar, and tea; along the roads within a fazenda, plant oranges, bananas among the groves, yams below, and cotton for spinning and weaving the rough cloth for slaves' clothes and even cloth for household use. In this way, he continued, a planter "need only purchase wine and salt, or some delicacy with which to welcome guests; the rest he has plentifully at home." He warned: "Every planter should plant enough food to meet his needs, so that he need not purchase to eat, even with insufficient harvests."[117]

Planters desperate to increase their revenues nevertheless preferred coffee to corn. By the early 1850s, a serious decline in the supply of locally grown food crops was causing planters to buy staples, especially corn, at high prices from farther away. Fazenda life depended on corn. The mules that transported coffee and all other goods from and to the fazenda were fed corn, as were cattle, horses, and fowl; domestic animals in turn provided the meat, poultry, and eggs that fed the human population. Slaves especially relied on cornmeal as the staple of their daily diet. Paradoxically, importing more food from Rio de Janeiro required more pack animals, which in turn required more corn. An extraordinary coffee harvest, such as the one in 1854, only accelerated the shift away from planting corn, beans (the other staple), and rice. Werneck's oldest son, Luís, himself a planter during these years, commented on the crisis in an article first published in Rio de Janeiro's leading newspaper, the *Jornal do Comércio*, in the fall of 1854. He described the "unprecedented" price of corn and chided planters for thinking only about export crops and their own "fabulous fortunes." To buy victuals for a coffee fazenda was equivalent, he wrote, to inviting "the horrible presence of hunger"; he thought that when forced to pay good money for provisions, planters scrimped, and slaves ate poorly. Good times for avaricious planters meant bad times for their hungry slaves.[118]

Werneck nonetheless blamed bad weather and ruined crops when he, too, was forced to buy food for his slaves. In 1853 he ordered twelve sacks of beans from his Rio agent, saying, "[I]t is the first time I buy such a commodity." A month later he ordered another ten sacks. "Even the elements revolt against us," he wrote. And because of persistent rain,

---

[117] Verneck, *Memoria*, pp. 10–11.
[118] Luiz Peixoto de Lacerda Werneck, "Breves considerações sobre a posição atual da lavoura de café," *Almanak Laemmert*, Rio de Janeiro, 1855, Supplemento, pp. 96–100.

beans rotted in the fields, coffee berries fell to the ground, and "the devil takes everything." Two years later he bought corn, which "fortunately was needed only at Sant'Anna and Piedade," where Inácia and her slaves were. A poor harvest again in 1857 and drought in 1859 meant more purchases. In 1859, as he waited for his aunt's former slaves to make good on the rent, he spent the equivalent of nearly $1,500 on corn and a similar amount on other staples, a small fortune by most men's standards. Writing to his agent in February 1861, he complained that provisions had not yet arrived; he said he was having to borrow food in order to eat. Later in the same month he ordered thirty sacks of black beans, "without bugs and quickly." When the invoice arrived, he replied that "it is the first time in my life that I have bought [beans]."[119] It was not, of course, and the defeat sounds in his words.

Then he ignored his own sound advice, and joined the rush to plant coffee and still more coffee. He felt the paradox of his decisions: Assigning more men and mules to search locally for foodstuffs and transport them back to his fazendas meant fewer mules for carrying coffee to market. He complained that the twenty-five new mules he bought in 1856 ate up in corn the profits they carted on their backs. In May 1861, a month after the court decided in his favor against Bernardina, he apologized to his agent for sending such a small quantity of coffee, but his mules (he owned 105 of them) were occupied carrying corn and beans.[120]

Despite the bleakness, there were small and large pleasures. Amidst shortages, delays in shipments, and soaring food prices, Werneck relished

[119] Werneck to Amigo e Sr. [Friend and Senhor], Monte Alegre, 16 January, 20 February, 20 and 23 May 1853, ANRJ-SAP, FW, Cód. 112, Vol. 3, Copiador, fls. 55, 65, 73, 75 (PY 691.52, 691.61, 691.68, 691.70); Werneck to Ilmo. Amigo e Sr. [Illustrious Friend and Senhor], Monte Alegre, 7 December 1855, ANRJ-SAP, FW, Cód. 112, Vol. 3, Copiador, fl. 309 (PY 691.275); Werneck to Bernardo Ribeiro de Carvalho, Monte Alegre, 28 March 1857, ANRJ-SAP, FW, Cód. 112, Vol. 3, Copiador, fls. 407–408 (PY 691.360–360A); Werneck to João Baptista Leite e Cia., Monte Alegre, 1 December 1859, ANRJ-SAP, FW, Cód. 112, Vol. 3, Copiador, 2° maço, fls. 125–126 (PY 692.110–110A); Werneck to João Baptista Leite e Cia., Monte Alegre, 2 October 1860, ANRJ-SAP, FW, Cód. 112, Vol. 3, Copiador, 2° maço, fl. 210 (PY 692.192); Werneck to João Baptista Leite e Cia., Monte Alegre, 16 and 26 February, 13 March 1861, ANRJ-SAP, FW, Cód. 112, Vol. 3, Copiador, 2° maço, fls. 245, 249, and 251 (PY 692.227, PY 692.231, PY 692.233).

[120] Werneck to Bernardo Ribeiro de Carvalho, Monte Alegre, 16 December 1856, ANRJ-SAP, FW, Cód. 112, Vol. 3, Copiador, fl. 382 (PY 691); Werneck to João Baptista Leite e Cia., Monte Alegre, 20 May 1861, ANRJ-SAP, FW, Cód. 112, Vol. 3, Copiador, 2° maço, fl. 269 (PY 692.251).

a gift of "excellent salted fish" sent him from the capital by an associate. In January 1858, the month of Inácia's death, with coffee yields collapsing, he found time and money to purchase a sugar plantation at the foothills of the mountains, justifying it to his commission agent as a sound investment despite its distance from the rest of his holdings. With good lands, watered plains, and virgin forests, good for corn, manioc, and "extraordinary cane" – everything he saw depleted on his other fazendas – he thought he could not have gotten it more cheaply. The "magnificent" water-driven mill and, especially, the solid grace of the old stone dam pleased him deeply.[121]

In the few years before and after Inácia's death, accumulating debts weighed heavily on Werneck. To pay for essential food he borrowed from his commission agent against future – and declining – coffee sales. More often the income did little more than reimburse his agent. In 1859, a generally bad situation grew worse. Werneck's long-time commission agent, Bernardo Ribeiro de Carvalho, closed his business and returned to Portugal, leaving Werneck to find an agent who would assume his debt, which by then had risen to 24 contos, or more than $12,000. Werneck had paid no interest to Carvalho, a kinsman through his wife's family. To the new agent, who would also serve as his private banker, however, he was to pay 9 percent a year compounded monthly, so that his debt of more than 32 contos in 1860 ballooned to 38 contos by the end of the year. Worried about bad harvests and mounting debt, he resolved to sell the house and coach he maintained in Rio de Janeiro, an admission that he could no longer keep up appearances, or perhaps that it no longer mattered. Anyway, by then he probably traveled to the capital only occasionally, if at all.[122]

In his last years, adding to other worries, Werneck was a sick man. Among the instructions he sent his commission agent in April 1861, he asked him to send a pair of elastic stockings, which he much needed,

[121] Werneck to João Baptista Leite e Cia., Monte Alegre, 13 March 1861, ANRJ-SAP, FW, Cód. 113, Vol. 3, Copiador, 2° maço, fl. 251 (PY 692.233); Werneck to Bernardo Ribeiro de Carvalho, Monte Alegre, 16 January 1858, ANRJ-SAP, FW, Cód. 112, Vol. 3, Copiador, fls. 465–466 (PY 691.410–410A).

[122] Werneck to João Baptista Leite e Cia., Monte Alegre, 7 February 1859, ANRJ-SAP, FW, Cód. 112, Vol. 3, Copiador, 2° maço, fls. 78–79 (PY 692.66–66A); Werneck to Bernardo Ribeiro de Carvalho, 27 January 1857, ANRJ-SAP, FW, Cód. 112, Vol. 3, Copiador, fl. 394 (PY 691.348); Werneck to João Baptista Leite e Cia., Monte Alegre, 16 February 1860, ANRJ-SAP, FW, Cód. 112, Vol. 3, Copiador, 2° maço, fl. 147 (PY 692.130); Silva, Barões e escravidão, p. 173.

he said, because of the swelling in his legs. A symptom perhaps of a poorly functioning heart? A later photograph shows him looking tired and slightly slumped, his clothes loose-fitting as though he had lost weight.[123] In letters he sounds tired, no longer a vigorous man able to face the challenges of his time. In July 1861, a month after a court official rode out to Sant'Ana to deliver an ultimatum to Bernardina and her children regarding their overdue rent, he despondently wrote his agent: "Money is worth nothing; everything is spent on labor. If the curse on coffee continues, it will mean bankruptcy." Having already suffered a series of lesser strokes, he died the following November from a cerebral hemorrhage.[124]

Despite his apprehensions, he did not end a ruined man, although the postmortem inventory of his property shows that debts to many creditors including his agents, totaling nearly $294,000, consumed two-thirds of the estate he owned jointly with his wife. Rather than burden their children and grandchildren with debt and to prevent the forced sale of land or slaves, Werneck's widow worked at gradually paying creditors up until her own death in 1866. She went so far as to sell her jewelry, all but one set of buttons "with two diamonds." Gone were the days when the soft rustle of his mother's imported French silk skirts trailed through the rooms at Piedade; and the large gilt-framed mirror in Monte Alegre's dining room now hangs serenely empty of all it once reflected.[125]

Did Inácia's death, coming as it had during leaner times, mean bad luck for Bernardina and her family? Did Werneck tighten the credit for his debtors, just as his new agents had done to him? Earlier, would a healthier, less troubled man have handled matters differently? Possibly. Yet Werneck's double-edged generosity always showed a firm, practical side. He appears a stern man, a disciplined man, a man who never doubted his authority or the rightness of his views. Certainly, he brooked no presumption from those who should know their place. Yet this time

[123] Werneck to João Baptista Leite e Cia., Monte Alegre, 22 April 1861, ANRJ-SAP, FW, Cód. 113, Vol. 3, Copiador, 2° maço, fl. 263 (PY 692.245); the photograph, taken about 1855, is reproduced in Graham, *Patronage and Politics*, p. 15.

[124] Werneck to João Baptista Leite e Cia., Monte Alegre, 5 July 1861, ANRJ-SAP, FW, Cód. 112, Vol. 3, Copiador, 2° maço, fl. 279 (PY 692.261); Pondé, "A fazenda," 120–121, 122.

[125] Inventário, Francisco Peixoto de Lacerda Werneck, 1862, fols. 273–273v, 276–277, 286–286v. A listing of her clothes filled four pages; see Inventário, Anna Matildes Wernek, 1827, fls. 12–13v.

he acted with questionable judgment in insisting on a contract that was doomed to fail – the land worn out and its terms beyond Bernardina's ability to meet. He would have seen necessity in his actions, though: Bernardina and her children were free people now and should be made to shoulder the responsibilities of their new role. I think he saw this family of freed slaves, elevated to slaveowner status themselves, as an affront to the ordering of society as he knew it should be. They were one more sign of his world slipping away. Land leased to them at Sant'Ana at least would keep them productive, and securely under his watch. Yet, for them, the impossibly high rent jeopardized whatever livelihood they might have counted on; paradoxically, Werneck's dealings threatened to leave them no place at all. In the end, in a conflict of wills, the independence Inácia intended for her former slaves and Werneck's sense of order reached an impasse.

Epilogue

Dona Inácia presents a picture of female respectability in a slave-owning regime. Devout, unmarried, and childless, she was aunt and godmother to a long list of nieces, nephews, and godchildren, both rich and poor. Her sister provides an unexpected contrast as the unmarried mother to a natural son, a notable gender switch with the men in her class who fathered illegitimate children, sometimes with their slave women. Just as surprising, no lasting scandal impaired her son's public success in local politics or as a landowner.

Inácia well represented her generation in being illiterate despite the privileges of family wealth and social position. Illiteracy imposed limitations, and Inácia depended her entire adult life on male kin, first father, then brother-in-law, and then nephew, to manage her business affairs. In her narrow, locally focused life, she seems to have grown ever more reliant on the presence of one family of slaves, whom she wished to free without ever relinquishing them.

In a reversal of her own dependent status, she unexpectedly assumed the patriarch's role toward her slaves, providing for those she considered her special dependents. And she knew this about freeing slaves: It was not enough to grant freedom or even to provide the official piece of paper as proof. In this society so thoroughly permeated by the presence of slaves, former slaves needed slaves of their own if they were to make viable new lives. To the daughters she gave slaves as gifts, and to Bernardina the services of two slaves for two years. And for the younger son, she instructed that he was to be trained at some skill by which to earn a wage and the chance, it was implied, eventually to purchase a slave or two of his own. There were degrees of freedom: from those who lived with the promise of future freedom to those who slowly over years purchased their own freedom to those, like Bernardina and her family, who were meant to be given a start in a free life.

The workings of Inácia's will expose the human connections that bound two families, one prestigious and powerful, the other obscure; one owner, the other owned; and the differing vulnerabilities of each. Inácia died at a time of serious worry about the coffee economy that had sustained the first family and enslaved the second. The slave family members remain shadowy figures, their voices barely heard in the record as we have it, except when the two brothers successfully protested the gifts made to their sisters and the oldest brother sold the debt owed him to collect his wages – saavy maneuvering by young men who lacked easy access to lawyers and legal procedure. Bernardina remains silent, yet she was central in Inácia's affections and attention, the reason in the first place for the will and all it set in motion. Through his almost daily letters we know most about Werneck, yet even so I must cautiously piece together the context from which to suggest probable motivations.

Narrated stories are dangerous because we want, and are led to expect, resolution, a removal of ambiguity. And legal cases, such as the ones used here, strive for resolution: property distributed according to precise instructions, an acceptable end to an unwanted marriage, things neatly finished off. These stories leave us without reassuring outcomes, not only because the endings remain unknown to us or because the presumed endings can only have provoked further tension, but because the motivations and understandings we most want recalled, which we believe will lift the screen of uncertainty, are beyond the reach of these sources to retrieve.

They are nonetheless worth telling because they make of slavery and of patriarchy not abstract systems of labor or power in which individuals blur into mere types, as though enslaved persons stopped being persons because they also became laboring property, or women and men behaved as predictably as puppets, but because they show, instead, identifiable persons in lived relationships, grounded in the particularities of time, place, and situation. Their stories reveal how personal, enduring, and complex the ties could be, and how unfamiliar, unexpected outcomes have the power to shift perceptions, if only slightly.

INÁCIA'S WILL, 1857

[fl. 1] In the name of the Father, Son, and Holy Spirit, Holy and Indivisible Trinity in whose faith I was born, have lived, and by the grace of God expect to die, this is my Will and statement of last wishes to be followed after my death, which I make being ill but getting about and in perfectly sound mind, fearing death which is certain, especially at an advanced age such as mine.[1] I am Roman Apostolic Catholic, following in every respect the religion of our Lord Jesus Christ in whose holy belief I will die with the divine protection of this same Lord and his Very Holy Mother, my intercessor.

I am the legitimate daughter of Sargeant Major Ignacio de Souza Wernek and Dona Francisca das Chagas, both deceased. I was born in and baptized at the Cathedral of Rio de Janeiro. I was always single and never had any children and, therefore, having no forced heirs, may dispose of my goods as I wish. I hereby name as my executor in the first place my *compadre* Baron of Paty do Alferes and, in his absence, my nephew Doctor Francisco d'Assis e Almeida, and, should he also be absent, my compadre Joaquim Pinheiro de Souza each of whom I have [fl. 1v] fully authorized to administer my goods and estate and who should be [accepted] by their oaths without deposit or security. I set the period of one year for the [presentation] of accounts in court.

I declare that I am a parishioner and sister of Our Lady of the Conception of Paty do Alferes in whose cemetery I shall be buried, my funeral being carried out without pomp and at the discretion of my executor,

---

[1] Testamento, Ignacia Delfina Wernek, Paty do Alferes, 1857, Centro de Documentação Histórica, Universidade Severino Sombra, Vassouras, Rio de Janeiro, Caixa 241.

the expenses for which will be acknowledged in court upon their mere presentation. I leave as alms for this my sisterhood, at Our Lady of the Conception, one doubloon in coin, aside from the annual pledges that I may owe. My executor will order said two *capellas de missas*[2] for my soul, one for my parents, another for my relatives, and another for the souls in Purgatory; and furthermore, for my soul, all the masses with the body present that can be said by the eighth day.

I declare that the goods that I now possess are the slaves Caetano, Thereza, Maria Roza, Luiz, Antonio Monjollo, Antonio Congo, José, Pedro, Simão, Joanna, and the outstanding debts of Manoel Francisco de Azevedo. I declare that my slave Bernardina already has her letter of manumission and as such is a freed woman, only with the onus and obligation of serving me as long as I live, which I did to remunerate her for the good services she [fl. 2] rendered me. Her six, rather, five children, to wit, Roza, João, José, Maria, and Manoel, I had baptized as free and born free and they have ever since been reputed free, which I here solemnly declare in order to remove any error that may exist in the records of the Church, and I will do the same in charters and certificates that I will give them. To the said Bernardina I leave my slaves Antonio Congo and Theresa who will serve her for two years and then will be freed. To Maria, daughter of the same Bernardina, I have already given money [for her] to buy a slave whom she [now] owns called Ignez. I leave freedom to my slave Maria Roza and at my death, my executor will issue her a charter of freedom.

I leave to my nephew, godson, and compadre Joaquim Pinheiro de Souza, the legacy of three hundred *mil-réis*,[3] net, free of the ten percent inheritance tax; to his wife Dona Maria Francisca, fifty mil-réis, and to his daughter, my goddaughter Francisca, another fifty mil-réis. I leave to the four daughters of my brother José de Souza Wernek the legacy of fifty mil-réis each and to the daughter of Roza, wife of Aurelio d'Alves Moreira, called Francisca, also fifty mil-réis. I leave to my poor godsons and goddaughters [fl. 2v] six mil-réis and four hundred *réis* each. To my sister Izabel my gold necklace and sixty mil-réis in money. I leave to José, son of Roza, wife of José Ignacio Cardozo, one hundred mil-réis. I leave

---

[2] Each *capella* consisted of 50 masses.
[3] In 1857, one *mil-réis* (1,000 *réis*) was worth 52 cents. At this conversion rate, 300 mil-réis, or 300,000 reis, was the equivalent of $156; see Julian Smith Duncan, *Public and Private Operation of the Railways in Brazil* (New York: Columbia University Press, 1932), p. 183.

to my goddaughter Francisca, wife of José Luiz dos Santos Wernek, my gold bracelets and forty mil-réis and to her daughter Maria José, my goddaughter, my gold chain and forty mil-réis. I leave to my godson Francisco, son of Luiz Corrêa de Mattos, the legacy of twenty mil-réis. I leave to my niece Maria, daughter of my sister Joaquina Theodora, the legacy of one hundred mil-réis. I leave to my goddaughter Candida, daughter of my compadre José da Rocha, the amount of fifty mil-réis. I leave to my niece Francisca, daughter of my sister Joaquina Theodora fifty mil-réis. I leave to my goddaughter Ignacia, daughter of Felicio Augusto de Lacerda, the legacy of one hundred mil-réis. I leave to my godson José Soares da Silva, son of Francisco Soares, thirty mil-réis.

I declare that the freed woman Roza, daughter of Bernardina and wife of José Ignacio Cardoso, has already received from me the slave Helena.

I declare that José Cirilo dos Passos has [fl. 3] served me as overseer since the sixteenth of January, eighteen fifty-five, at fifteen mil-réis per month, and that my executor will settle accounts with him for the time he may serve me.

I declare that I leave to Americo, son of Roza, ten mil-réis.

Of the remainder of my goods (after the above dispositions and legacies are complied with), I institute as my heirs in equal parts the freed woman Bernardina and all her children named above. Of these heirs all who are of age will receive their shares and legacies immediately; the minors, however, their shares of goods that belong to them, whether by inheritance or by legacy, will remain until their majority in the guardianship of my first executor (and in his absence, the second or third) whom I name as their tutor, and I wish him so appointed and retained until the end. In this capacity my executor will take care of the said minors, will maintain them, will have them taught some trade or skill for which they have more aptitude, will punish them when they deserve it, and will administer their property in the best way he knows, applying the income to those ends and the extra, if there is any, [fl. 3v] to the principal or to the purchase of real property.

Thus I have finished and concluded my Will and disposition of my last wishes, which I wish to have all due effect, and which I ordered written by Francisco Corrêa de Figueiredo, I only dictating it, and not knowing how to read nor write I asked Luiz Henriques to sign. Fazenda Sant'Anna, eleventh of May, eighteen hundred and fifty-seven.

At the request of the testatrix D. Ignacia Delfina Wernek,
Luiz Henriques.

Approval

May all who see this public instrument of approval of the Last Will and Testament know that in the Year of Our Lord Jesus Christ eighteen hundred and fifty-seven on the eleventh of May, at this Fazenda Sant'Anna, Parish of Paty do Alferes and [in] houses belonging to the Illustrious Baron of Paty do Alferes, in the jurisdiction of the town of Vassouras, where I the below named and designated notary public, was called and came, and appearing before me the said Testatrix, getting about but [fl. 4] somewhat ill and in her sound mind according to my judgment by the good and correct words with which she answered the customary questions, which I swear, as well as that she is the same person as she is well known to the five witnesses named and signed below, in the presence of whom was given to me two folios of paper and on them written five and a half pages ending on the back where I began this statement, she saying that it was her Will, that not knowing how to write she had had it written by Francisco Corrêa de Figueiredo and that she had only dictated it and that for the same reason it had been signed on her behalf by Luiz Henriques and that after written and signed, being read to her she found it in every way according to what she had dictated and thus it is firm and valid and [she] wishes it certified, imploring the Justices of His Imperial Majesty to enforce it according to the manner specified in it, and declares to me, Notary, that I certify it with all the solemnity of the Law. And then I, Notary, examining the said Will and not finding any blots, additions between the lines, or sources of doubt, and seeing that in truth it had been written by me Francisco Corrêa de Figueiredo and signed at the request of the Testatrix by Luiz Henriques, [fl. 4v] certified it, numbered it, signed it with my official signature (which says "Figueiredo,") as much as the law permits me and I can certify it. And, at the request of the Testatrix I signed it because she knows not how either to read or write. Luiz Henriques who also signed as a witness along with the others who were present at this act who are Pedro José Avelino, Serafim do Santo, Francisco Caetano dos Santos, and João Gomes das Chaves, all more than fourteen years old and free persons, residents in this Parish, who sign before me, Notary Francisco Corrêa de Figueiredo who wrote it and signed it in [illegible].

In witness of the truth. [the authenticated signature of]
Francisco Corrêa de Figueiredo

[signed]   At the request of the Testatrix D. Ignacia Delfina,
Luiz Henriques
Pedro José Avelino
Serafim do Santo
Francisco Caetano dos Santos
João Gomes Chaves

I certify that I opened this solemn Will with which Senhora D. Ignacia Delfina Vernek has just died in order to see her funeral dispositions and, if necessary, I swear it in *fide Parochi*. Paty do Alferes, 31 January 1858.

[signed]   Canon Vicar Manoel Felizardo Nogueira.

Comply and register,   Seen, Tax Collector's Office
Vassouras, 11 February 1858   12 February 1858
[signed] Gama e Mello   [signed] Siqueira Alagoz

[fl. 5] I swear I summoned the Most Excellent Baron of Paty do Alferes, to say whether or not he accepted the charges of the Testatrix and he, having been fully informed [of the responsibilities], responded affirmatively. Vassouras, 20 February 1858

The Notary
[signed]   Francisco Corrêa de Figuereido

STATEMENT OF APPROVAL

On the twentieth of February, eighteen hundred and fifty-eight, in this city of Vassouras, Doctor Francisco de Assis e Almeida came to my notary office [fl. 5v], in his capacity as holder of power of attorney for the Most Excellent Baron of Paty do Alferes, and said in the name of his constituent he accepted the duties of executorship, and the said constituent obligated himself by his person and his goods to fulfill the testamentary dispostions of the deceased Dona Ignacia Delfina Wernek. So said and accepted, he made this statement and signed it. I Francisco Corrêa de Figuereido wrote it.

[signed]   Francisco d'Assis e Almeida

[fl. 6] On the eleventh of February, eighteen hundred and fifty-eight in this city of Vassouras in my Notary Register on the part of Doctor

Municipal Judge Bellarmino Peregrino da Gama e Mello, I was given this Will, open with the authorizations signed on the back, of which I make this record. I Francisco Corrêa de Figueiredo wrote it.

[fl. 7] [signature]   Baron of Paty do Alferes, Grande do Imperio, etc.,
etc., etc.

By this my power of attorney, I constitute as my attorney, in the town of Vassouras, Senhor Dr. Francisco de Assis e Almeida that he should act for me as if I were present in handling the probate of my deceased aunt D. Ignacia Delfina Vernek, to take for me the oath of executor, and follow all the requirements of this case, being able to delegate to one or more attorneys as seems to him appropriate and necessary.

Monte Alegre, Paty do Alferes, 6 February 1858
[signed]   Baron of Paty do Alferes

[covering envelope, file no.] 37

Last Will and Testament of Senhora D. Ignacia Delfina Vernek, approved, numbered, sewn, sealed, and authenticated according to the law at this fazenda of Sant'Anna, 11 May 1857, by me

Notary
[signed]   Francisco Corrêa de Figuereido

FRANCISCA'S WILL, 1849

[fl. 1] In the name of God, amen. I, Francisca Lauriana das Chagas, finding myself in poor health, but of sound mind and understanding, and fearing death, make my Last Will and Testament in the following manner.[1] I am Roman Catholic Apostolic, born and baptized in the Parish of Our Lady of the Conception in Paty do Alferes. I am the legitimate daughter of Sergeant Major Ignacio de Souza Wernek and his wife Dona Francisca das Chagas, both deceased. I declare that I was always single, and in this state I had a son, who is alive, and who is called Felicio Augusto de Lacerda, whom I recognize as my natural son, and as such he is qualified [to be my heir]. And after my dispositions are complied with, I institute him as the legitimate heir of the remainder of all my goods, and it is my last wish that he should be so considered both in law as well as outside it. I nominate as my Executors, in the first place, my natural son Felicio Augusto de Lacerda, in the second place, my brother José de Souza Wernek, and third, my nephew José Pinheiro de Souza Wernek, who, one in the absence of the other in the order in which they are named, will take charge of my property with free and general administration of it, and for this I take them as trustworthy, and so they will not be obliged to present a guarantee.

I declare that I am a parishioner of the Parish of Our Lady of the Conception in Paty do Alferes, in which cemetery I order my executor to bury my body. I leave all other funeral arrangements to his discretion. [fl. 1v] It is my wish that the accounts that my executor

---

[1] Testamento, Francisca Lauriana das Chagas, Vassouras, 1849, Centro de Documentação Histórica, Universidade Severino Sombra, Vassouras, Rio de Janeiro, Caixa 241.

presents for such expenses be attended to in the appropriate court on his oath.

I leave two *capellas de missas*² for my soul, another for the souls of my parents and relatives, another for the souls of all those persons with whom I had relations of friendship, and another for the souls in purgatory. My executor will order all masses to be said with the body present, within seven days [after death]. He will give to all the poor who gather on the day on which my body is buried 640 *réis*³ each.

I declare that the goods that I possess are: some lands fronting on the river Sant'Anna, and bordering on one side with [land belonging to] Francisco Peixoto de Lacerda Brum and with [that of] Felicio Augusto de Lacerda, and at the back with the surveyed boundary of Francisco Peixoto de Lacerda Wernek, and on the other side with the same Wernek and with the Canon Manoel Felizardo Nogueira. I also possess a portion of slaves and other goods that are obvious, and which my executor knows well.

I leave to my niece Maria, daughter of João José Alves, 200 mil-réis, my gold necklace, my half table-setting of china, or what china exists. I have already given her during my life 600 mil-réis. I leave to my godsons and goddaughters who are relatives 50 mil-réis each; and to those who are not relatives, 20 mil-réis each. I leave to my sisters, who survive me, 100 mil-réis each. [fl. 2] I leave to my nephew Manoel, son of my brother José de Souza Wernek, the amount of 40 mil-réis. I leave to my executor in remuneration of services, which he has provided me, 200 mil-réis and one year in which to render accounts.

I leave to all my slave women four mil-réis each; my executor will give them [the money], if possible, on the day of my burial. I leave to my goddaughter Marianna, daughter of Felicio Augusto de Lacerda, my slave woman Vicencia. I leave to Maria Benta six mil-réis. I leave to Maria Ferreira six mil-réis. I leave to Maxima, daughter of Francisco Soares, four mil-réis. I leave to my *commadre* Francisca, wife of Dionisio Soares, six mil-réis. I leave to the daughters of the deceased Luzia four mil-réis each. I leave to Francisca, daughter of the deceased João Baptista, four

---

² Each *capella* consisted of 50 masses.

³ In 1857, one *mil-réis* was worth 52 cents. At this conversion rate, 640 *réis* was the equivalent of 33 cents; 50 mil-réis was the equivalent of $26. See Julian Smith Duncan, *Public and Private Operation of the Railways in Brazil* (New York: Columbia University Press, 1932), p. 183.

mil-réis. I leave to the daughters of my goddaughter, Innocencia, two mil-réis each. I leave to the creole [Brazilian-born black] Francisca, my goddaughter and commadre, four mil-réis. I leave to Aurelia, daughter of Maximiana, six mil-réis. I leave to my nieces, daughters of Roza and of Joaquina, and to Anna, sister of Chiquinha, and to Candidinha and Terezinha, daughters of José de Souza Wernek, 30 mil-réis each.

I leave to my niece Maria Francisca, daughter of my sister Maria do Carmo, my large ring and a remembrance ring with hands intertwined. I leave my remembrance ring of [precious] stones to my commadre Mariazinha, wife of Joaquim Pinheiro de Souza. I leave to Bernardina ten mil-réis, and in [fl. 2v] case she dies before me, they will be paid to her children. I leave my better clothes to be divided by my executor among my sisters and relatives, and the rest [of my clothes] to the poor. I leave to Faustina, wife of João Antonio, six mil-réis.

When my legacies have been complied with, I leave, as I have already said, as my heir my natural son Felicio Augusto de Lacerda.

In this way I conclude my last will and testament and disposition of my last wishes. I ask that the Justices of this Empire should enforce it as these are my last wishes. And being true I asked Doctor Luiz Gomes de Souza Telles to make the present will; and not knowing how to read or write I asked the same Doctor Telles to sign it for me.

Fazenda São José, 20 December 1849.

At the request of Dona Francisca Lauriana das Chagas, who asked that I make this will and, not knowing how to read or write, that I should sign for her.

[signature of] D^{or} Luiz Gomes de Souza Telles

Approval

May all who see this approval of the Last Will and Testament know that in the year of the birth of Our Lord Jesus Christ of one thousand eight hundred forty-nine, on the twentieth of December, at the fazenda known as São José, in the residence of Francisco Peixoto de Lacerda Brum, in the jurisdiction of the Town of Vassouras, [fl. 3] where I the notary, summoned by the Testatrix Dona Francisca Lauriana das Chagas, came, and being here she appeared before me, up and about, in health, and in sound mind and understanding as seemed to me according to the correctness of the words with which she responded to my customary questions, and, by her, in the presence of five witnesses named and signed below, were given to me these two sheets of paper, and on them written on three and a half pages ending on the back where I began this Approval, telling me it was her Will and, that not knowing how to read or write, she had asked Doctor Luiz Gomes de Souza Telles to write it for her, and to sign it for her; and having it read to her, she found everything to be as she dictated; she implores the Justices of His Imperial Majesty to enforce it and have it enforced, and that I, Notary, should accept it. Not finding any alteration, writing between the lines, blot, or anything else that would cast doubt, I approved, numbered, and sealed it with my seal which says "Figueiredo" as much as the Law permits me I can certify it. The same Dr. Luiz Gomes de Souza Telles signed for her for the above mentioned reason before the five witnesses: Father Custodio Gomes Carneiro, Manoel Correa de Mattos, Francisco Peixoto de Lacerda Brum, Jozé Narcizo de Lima, Florentino Jozé do Nascimento, all are of age and free persons. I João Correa de Figueiredo, Notary, wrote and signed in [illegible]. In witness of the truth.

> [signed]   João Correa de Figueiredo
> At the request of the Testatrix = Dr. Luiz Gomes
>   de Souza Telles
> Padre Custodio Gomes Carneiro
> Manoel Correa de Mattos
> Francisco Peixoto de Lacerda Brum
> José Narcizo de Lima
> Florentino Joze do Nascimento

[fl. 3v] I certify that I opened this solemn Will, with which Dona Francisca Laurinana das Chagas has just died, in order to see her funeral dispositions, and I swear it *in fide Parochi*. Paty do Alferes, 24 February 1854.

> [signed]   Canon Vicar Manoel Felizardo Nogueira

> Comply and register, Vassouras, 6 March 1854
> [signed] Farias

Seen, Tax Collector's Office   Fl. 14 480 réis
       7 March 1854   Paid four hundred and eighty réis
       Agent Bomfim Magon   Vassouras, 7 March 1854
                                 [signed] Magon

STATEMENT OF ACCEPTANCE

On 7 March 1854 in this town of Vassouras Felicio Augusto de Lacerda came to my Notary Office and said that he of his free will accepted the duties set out above by the testatrix, and obligated himself by his person and his goods to fulfill the testamentary provisions [and to present accounts][4] in the specified time, or when ordered by the court to do so. And having thus obligated himself, he made this statement and signed it. I João Correa de Figueiredo wrote it.

[signed] Felicio Augusto de Lacerda Figueiredo

[separate, covering envelope, File no.] 22 Last Will and Testament of Dona Francisca Lauriana das Chagas, approved, numbered, authenticated, sewn, closed and sealed by me, Notary

João Correa de Figueiredo

Complied

---

4 It is noted in the will that "these words were added between the lines."

BIBLIOGRAPHY

ARCHIVES

Arquivo da Cúria Metropolitana, Salvador
Arquivo da Santa Casa da Misericórdia, Salvador
Arquivo do Estado de São Paulo, São Paulo
Arquivo do Forum de Paraibuna, Paraibuna
Arquivo do Instituto Histórico e Geográfico Brasileiro, Rio de Janeiro
Arquivo Nacional, Rio de Janeiro
   Seção de Arquivos Particulares, Werneck Family Papers
   Seção do Poder Executivo
   Seção do Poder Judiciário
Arquivo Público do Estado da Bahia, Salvador
   Seção Judiciária
Biblioteca Nacional, Rio de Janeiro, Seção de Manuscritos
Centro de Documentação Histórica, Universidade Severino Sombra, Vassouras

OTHER SOURCES

Alencastro, Luiz Felipe de, ed. *Império: A corte e a modernidade nacional.* Vol. 2 of *História da vida privada no Brasil.* Ed. Fernando A. Novais. São Paulo: Companhia das Letras, 1997.

Almanak administrativo, mercantil e industrial da corte e provincia do Rio de Janeiro. Rio de Janeiro, 1849–1852, 1856–1868, 1871.

Almeida, Candido Mendes de, comp. and ed. *Codigo Philippino; ou Ordenações e leis do reino de Portugal, recopilados por mandado d'el-rey D. Philippe I. 14 ed. segundo a primeira de 1603 e a nona de Coimbra de 1824. Addicionada com diversas notas . . .* Rio de Janeiro: Typ. do Instituto Philomathico, 1870.

Antonil, André João. *Cultura e opulência do Brasil.* 1711. Reprint, São Paulo: Melhoramentos, 1976.

Anuário Genealógico Brazileiro 1 (1939), 4 (1941).

Barickman, B. J. *A Bahian Counterpoint: Sugar, Tobacco, Cassava, and Slavery in the Recôncavo, 1780–1860.* Stanford: Stanford University Press, 1998.

———. " 'A Bit of Land, which They Call Roça': Slave Provision Grounds in the Bahian Recôncovo, 1780–1860." *Hispanic American Historical Review* 74, no. 4 (November 1994): 649–687.

Barman, Roderick J. *Brazil: The Forging of a Nation, 1798–1852.* Stanford: Stanford University Press, 1988.

Bethell, Leslie. *The Abolition of the Brazilian Slave Trade: Britain, Brazil and the Slave Trade Question, 1807–1869.* Cambridge: Cambridge University Press, 1970.

Blake, Augusto Victorino Alves Sacramento. *Diccionario bibliographico brazileiro.* 7 vols. 1900. Reprint, Rio de Janeiro: Conselho Federal de Cultura, 1970.

Bliss, Kathryn. *Colonial Habits: Convents and the Spiritual Economy of Cuzco, Peru.* Durham: Duke University Press, 1999.

Braga, Greenleigh H. Faria, *De Vassouras: História, fatos, e gente.* Rio de Janeiro: Ultra-Set, 1978.

———, comp. and ed. *Vassouras de ontem.* Vassouras: Irmandade da Santa Casa de Misericórdia da cidade de Vassouras, 1975.

Brazil. Congresso. Câmara dos Deputados. *Anais.*

Brazil. Laws, statutes, etc. *Coleção das Leis do Brasil.*

Brazil pittoresco: album de vistas, panoramas, paisagens, monumentos, costumes, etc., com os retratos de Sua Magestade Imperador Don [sic] Pedro II et [sic] da Familia Imperial, photographiados por Victor Frond, lithographiados pelos primeiros artistas de Paris . . . e acompanhados de tres volumes . . . sobre a historia, as instituições, as cidades, as fazendas, a cultura, a colonização, etc., do Brazil, por Charles Ribeyrolles. Paris: Lemercier, 1861.

Burnard, Trevor. " 'Do Thou in Gentle Phibia Smile': Scenes from an Interracial Marriage, Jamaica, 1754–1786." Paper presented at the Race and Slavery Seminar, Department of History, University of Texas at Austin, Spring 1997.

Castro, Hebe Maria Mattos de. *Ao sul da história: Lavradores pobres na crise do trabalho escravo.* São Paulo: Brasiliense, 1987.

———. *Das cores do silêncio: Os significados da liberdade do sudeste escravista, Brasil século XIX.* Rio de Janeiro: Arquivo Nacional, 1995.

———. "Laços de família e direitos no final da escravidão." In *História da vida privada no Brasil,* ed. Fernando A. Novais. vol. 2, *Império: A corte e a modernidade nacional,* ed. Luiz Felipe de Alencastro. São Paulo: Companhia das Letras, 1997.

Castro, Jeanne Berrance de. *A milícia cidadã: A Guarda Nacional de 1831 a 1850.* São Paulo: Companhia Editora Nacional, 1977.

Catharino, Ernesto José Coelho Rodrigues. *Eufrásia Teixeira Leite: Fragmentos de uma existência, 1850–1930.* Rio de Janeiro: Edição do Autor, 1992.

Chalhoub, Sidney. *Visões da liberdade: Uma história das últimas décadas da escravidão na corte*. São Paulo: Companhia das Letras, 1990.

Childs, Matt D., "'A Peculiar Sight, and Very Fit for a Photograph': Master-Slave Rituals of Power at a Gold Mine in Nineteenth-Century Brazil." *History Workshop Journal* 53 (Spring 2002), forthcoming.

Codigo commercial do Imperio do Brazil. Annotated by Salustiano Orlando de Araujo Costa. 4th ed. Rio de Janeiro: Laemmert, 1886.

Conrad, Robert. *The Destruction of Brazilian Slavery, 1850–1888*. Berkeley: University of California Press, 1972.

Costa, Emília Viotti da. "Brazil: The Age of Reform, 1870–1889." In *The Cambridge History of Latin America*. vol. 5: C. *1870 to 1930*, ed. Leslie Bethell. Cambridge: Cambridge University Press, 1986.

———. *The Brazilian Empire: Myths and Histories*. Chicago: University of Chicago Press, 1985.

d'Araujo, Manoel do Monte Rodrigues. *Elementos de direito ecclesiastico em relação á disciplina geral da igreja e com applicação aos usos da igreja do Brasil*. 3 vols. Rio de Janeiro: Livraria de Antonio Gonçalves Guimarães, 1857–1859.

Davis, David Brion. *The Problem of Slavery in Western Culture*. Ithaca: Cornell University Press, 1966.

Dean, Warren. *Rio Claro: A Brazilian Plantation System, 1820–1920*. Stanford: Stanford University Press, 1976.

Diccionario da lingua portugueza. Comp. Antonio de Moraes Silva. 2 vols. 8th ed. Rio de Janeiro: Editoria-Empreza Litteraria Fluminense, 1889–1891.

Duncan, Julian Smith. *Public and Private Operation of the Railways in Brazil*. New York: Columbia University Press, 1932.

Faria, Sheila de Castro. *A colônia em movimento: Fortuna e família no cotidiano colonial*. Rio de Janeiro: Nova Fronteira, 1998.

Fernandes, Florestan. *The Negro in Brazilian Society*. Trans. Jacqueline D. Skiles, A. Brunel, and Arthur Rothwell. New York: Columbia University Press, 1969.

Ferrez, Gilberto, ed. *The Brazil of Eduard Hildebrandt*. Rio de Janeiro: Distribuidora Record, 1991.

Ferrez, Gilberto. *Photography in Brazil, 1840–1900*. Trans. Stella de Sá Rego. Albuquerque: University of New Mexico Press, 1984.

Ferrez, Gilberto, and Weston J. Naef. *Pioneer Photographers of Brazil, 1840–1920*. New York: Center for Inter-American Relations, 1976.

Florentino, Manolo, and José Roberto Góes. *A paz das senzalas: Famílias escravas e tráfico, Rio de Janeiro, c.1790–c.1850*. Rio de Janeiro: Civilização Brasileira, 1997.

Flory, Thomas. *Judge and Jury in Imperial Brazil, 1808–1871: Social Control and Political Stability in the New State*. Austin: University of Texas Press, 1981.

Franco, Maria Sylvia de Carvalho. *Homens livres na ordem escravocrata*. São Paulo: Ática, 1976.

Gomes, Flávio dos Santos. *Histórias de quilombolas: Mocambos e comunidade de senzalas no Rio de Janeiro, século XIX.* Rio de Janeiro: Arquivo Nacional, 1995.

Graham, Richard. *Britain and the Onset of Modernization in Brazil, 1850–1914.* Cambridge: Cambridge University Press, 1968.

———. *Patronage and Politics in Nineteenth-Century Brazil.* Stanford: Stanford University Press, 1990.

———. "Slave Families on a Rural Estate in Colonial Brazil." *Journal of Social History* 9:3 (Spring 1976): 382–402.

Gudeman, Stephen, and Stuart B. Schwartz. "Cleansing Original Sin: Godparenthood and the Baptism of Slaves in Eighteenth-Century Bahia." In *Kinship Ideology and Practice in Latin American,* ed. Raymond T. Smith. Chapel Hill: University of North Carolina Press, 1984.

Higgins, Kathleen J. *"Licentious Liberty" in a Brazilian Gold-Mining Region: Slavery, Gender, and Social Control in Eighteenth-Century Sabará, Minas Gerais.* University Park: Pennsylvania State University Press, 1999.

Hünefeldt, Christine. *Paying the Price of Freedom: Family and Labor among Lima's Slaves, 1800–1854.* Berkeley: University of California Press, 1994.

Instrucções para a Commissão Permanente nomeada pelos fazendeiros do municipio de Vassouras. Rio de Janeiro: Typ. Episcopal de Guimarães e Cia., 1854.

Insurreição negra e justiça, Paty do Alferes, 1838. Transcribed by João Luiz Pinaud, Carlos Otavio de Andrade, Salete Neme, Maria Cândida Gomes de Souza, and Jeannette Garcia. Rio de Janeiro: Ed. Expressão e Cultura-Exped Ltda. e Ordem dos Advogados do Brasil, 1987.

Johnson, Elizabeth. "Slavery and the Benedictine Order in Late Colonial São Paulo." Master's thesis, University of Texas at Austin, 1996.

Karasch, Mary C. *Slave Life in Rio de Janeiro, 1808–1850.* Princeton: Princeton University Press, 1987.

Koster, Henry. *Travels in Brazil.* 2 vols. Philadelphia: M. Carey and Son, 1817.

Laërne, C. F. van Delden. *Brazil and Java: Report on the Coffee-Culture in America, Asia, and Africa.* London: W. H. Allen, 1885.

Lara, Silvia Hunold. *Campos da violência: Escravos e senhores na Capitania do Rio de Janeiro, 1750–1808.* Rio de Janeiro: Paz e Terra, 1988.

Lauderdale Graham, Sandra. "A cultura do patriarcado rural às vésperas do império." Paper presented at the Colóquio Internacional, "De Cabral a Pedro I," Fundação Calouste Gulbenkian, Lisbon, Portugal, 29–31 March 2000.

———. *House and Street: The Domestic World of Servants and Masters in Nineteenth-Century Rio de Janeiro.* Cambridge: Cambridge University Press, 1988.

———. "Slavery's Impasse: Slave Prostitutes, Small-Time Mistresses, and the Brazilian Law of 1871." *Comparative Studies in Society and History* 33, no. 4 (October 1991): 369–394.

Lee, Monika Kittiya. "The Ungrateful Art of Correspondence: A Love Affair." Honors thesis, University of Texas at Austin, 1995.

Lewin, Linda. "Natural and Spurious Children in Brazilian Inheritance Law from Colony to Empire: A Methodological Essay." *The Americas* 48, no. 3 (January 1992): 351–396.

Machado, Maria Helena. *Crime e escravidão: Trabalho, luta e resistência nas lavouras paulistas, 1830–1888.* São Paulo: Brasiliense, 1987.

———. *O plano e o pânico: Os movimentos sociais na década da abolição.* Rio de Janeiro: Editora Universidade Federal do Rio de Janeiro; São Paulo: Editora da Universidade de São Paulo, 1994.

Malheiro, Agostinho Marques Perdigão. *A escravidão no Brasil: Ensaio histórico-jurídico-social.* 3 parts in 1 vol. Rio de Janeiro: Typ. Nacional, 1866–1867.

———. *A escravidão no Brasil: Ensaio histórico-jurídico-social.* 3 parts in 2 vols. 1866–1867. Reprint. Petrópolis: Vozes, 1976.

Maloiy, G. M. O., et al. "Energetic Cost of Carrying Loads: Have African Women Discovered an Economic Way?" *Nature* 319 (February 1986): 668–669.

Marcílio, Maria Luiza. *A cidade de São Paulo: Povoamento e população, 1750–1850.* São Paulo: Pioneira, 1974.

Mattoso, Katia M. de Queirós. *Bahia: A cidade do Salvador e seu mercado no século XIX.* São Paulo: Hucitec, 1978.

———. *Bahia, século XIX: Uma província no império.* Rio de Janeiro: Nova Fronteira, 1992.

McCann, Bryan. "Slavery Negotiated: Mediators on the Middle Ground, the Paraíba Valley, Brazil, 1835–1888." Master's thesis, University of New Mexico at Albuquerque, 1994.

Merwick, Donna. *Death of a Notary: Conquest and Change in Colonial New York.* Ithaca: Cornell University Press, 1999.

Mesquita, Eni de. "O papel do agregado na região de Itú – 1780–1830." *Coleção Museu Paulista* 6 (1977): 13–121.

Metcalf, Alida C. *Family and Frontier in Colonial Brazil: Santana de Parnaíba, 1580–1822.* Berkeley: University of California Press, 1992.

Muldrew, Craig. *The Economy of Obligation: The Culture of Credit and Social Relations in Early Modern England.* New York: St. Martin's Press, 1998.

Müller, Daniel Pedro. *Ensaio d'um quadro estatístico da província de São Paulo: Ordenado pelas leis provincias de 11 de abril de 1836 e 10 de março de 1837.* 1838. Reprint, São Paulo: Governo do Estado de São Paulo, 1978.

Nabuco, Joaquim. *Cartas a amigos.* Ed. Carolina Nabuco. São Paulo: Instituto Progresso Editorial, 1949.

Nader, Helen. *Liberty in Absolutist Spain: The Habsburg Sale of Towns, 1516–1700.* Baltimore: Johns Hopkins University Press, 1990.

Naro, Nancy Priscilla Smith. "Customary Rightholders and Legal Claimants to Land in Rio de Janeiro, Brazil, 1870–1890." *The Americas* 48, no. 4 (April 1992): 485–517.

Nazzari, Muriel. "Transition toward Slavery: Changing Practices regarding Indians in Seventeenth-Century São Paulo." *The Americas* 49, no. 2 (October 1991): 131–155.

Nishida, Mieko. "Manumission and Ethnicity in Urban Slavery: Salvador, Brazil, 1808–1888." *Hispanic American Historical Review* 73, no. 3 (August 1993): 361–391.

Pereira, José Saturnino da Costa. *Diccionario topographico do Imperio do Brasil.* Rio de Janeiro: Typ. P. Gueffier, 1834.

Phillips, Roderick. *Putting Asunder: A History of Divorce in Western Society.* Cambridge: Cambridge University Press, 1988.

Pondé, Francisco de Paula e Azevedo. "A fazenda do barão de Pati do Alferes." *Revista do Instituto Histórico e Geográfico Brasileiro* 327 (April–June 1980): 83–155.

Porto, M. J. de Campos. *Repertorio de legislação ecclesiastica desde 1500 até 1874.* Rio de Janeiro: Garnier, 1875.

A Provincia de São Paulo. São Paulo, 1888.

Ramos, Belisário Vieira. *Livro da família Werneck.* Rio de Janeiro: Cia. Carioca de Artes Gráficas, 1941.

Reis, João José. *A morte é uma festa: Ritos fúnebres e revolta popular no Brasil do século XIX.* São Paulo: Companhia das Letras, 1991.

———. "Escravos e coiteiros no quilombo do Oitizeiro, Bahia, 1806." In *Liberdade por um fio: História dos quilombos no Brasil.* Ed. João José Reis and Flávio dos Santos Gomes. São Paulo: Companhia das Letras, 1996.

———. *Slave Rebellion in Brazil: The Muslim Uprising of 1835 in Bahia.* Trans. Arthur Brakel. Baltimore: Johns Hopkins University Press, 1993.

Reis, João José Reis, and Flávio dos Santos Gomes, eds. *Liberdade por um fio: História dos quilombos no Brasil.* São Paulo: Companhia das Letras, 1996.

Russell-Wood, A. J. R. *The Black Man in Slavery and Freedom in Colonial Brazil.* London: Macmillan Press and St. Antony's College, Oxford, 1982.

———. *Fidalgos and Philanthropists: The Santa Casa da Misericórdia of Bahia, 1550–1755.* Berkeley: University of California Press, 1968.

Salles, José Roberto da Cunha. *Fôro penal: Theoria e pratica do processo criminal brazileiro.* Rio de Janeiro: Garnier, 1882.

Santos, Noronha. "Anotações a Introdução das 'Memórias.'" In Luiz Gonçalves dos Santos (Padre Perereca). *Memórias para servir à história do Reino do Brasil.* 2 vols. 1825. Reprint. Belo Horizonte: Editora Itatiaia, 1981.

São Paulo (state). Arquivo do Estado de São Paulo. *Repertório das sesmarias concedidas pelos Capitães Generais da Capitania de São Paulo desde 1721 até 1821.* São Paulo: Tip. do Globo, 1944. Reprint, São Paulo: Secretaria de Estado da Cultura, 1994.

Schwartz, Stuart B. "The Manumission of Slaves in Colonial Brazil: Bahia, 1684–1745." *Hispanic American Historical Review* 54, no. 4 (November 1974): 603–635.

———. *Slaves, Peasants, Rebels: Reconsidering Brazilian Slavery*. Urbana: University of Illinois Press, 1992.

———. *Sugar Plantations in the Formation of Brazilian Society: Bahia, 1550–1835*. Cambridge: Cambridge University Press, 1985.

Las siete partidas. Trans. Samuel Parsons Scott. Chicago: Commerce Clearing House, 1931.

Silva, Eduardo. *Barões e escravidão: Três gerações de fazendeiros e a crise da estrutura escravista*. Rio de Janeiro: Nova Fronteira, 1984.

Silva, Joaquim Norberto de Souza. "Memória histórica e documentada das aldêas de indios da província do Rio de Janeiro." *Revista do Instituto Histórico e Geográfico Brasileiro*. "Parte documentada." 17 (1854): 498–499.

Siqueira, Alexandre Joaquim de. "Memória histórica do município de Vassouras, 1852." In Greenleigh H. Faria Braga, comp., *Vassouras de ontem*. Rio de Janeiro: Cia. Brasileira de Artes Gráficas, 1975.

Slenes, Robert W. "Black Homes, White Homilies: Perceptions of the Slave Family and of Slave Women in Nineteenth-Century Brazil." In *More Than Chattel: Black Women and Slavery in the Americas*, ed. David Barry Gaspar and Darlene Clark Hine. Bloomington: Indiana University Press, 1996.

———. "The Demography and Economics of Brazilian Slavery: 1850–1888." Ph.D. diss., Stanford University, 1976.

———. "Escravidão e família: Padrões de casamento e estabilidade familiar numa comunidade escrava (Campinas, século XIX)." *Estudos Econômicos* 17, no. 2 (May–August 1987): 217–227.

———. *Na senzala, uma flor: Esperanças e recordações na formação da família escrava, Brasil sudeste, século XIX*. Rio de Janeiro: Nova Fronteira, 1999.

———. "Senhores e subalternos no oeste paulista." In *História da vida privada no Brasil*, ed. Fernando A. Novais, vol. 2: *Império: A corte e a modernidade nacional*, ed. Luiz Felipe de Alencastro. São Paulo: Companhia das Letras, 1997.

Slenes, Robert W., Carlos Vogt, and Peter Fry. "Histórias do Cafundó." In Carlos Vogt and Peter Fry, with the collaboration of Robert W. Slenes. *Cafundó: A África no Brasil – Linguagem e sociedade*. Campinas: Editora da Unicamp; São Paulo: Companhia das Letras, 1996.

Soares, Sebastião Ferreira. *Notas estatísticas sobre a produção agrícola e carestia dos gêneros alimentícios no Império do Brasil*. 1860. Reprint, Rio de Janeiro: IPEA/INPES, 1977.

Soeiro, Susan. "The Social and Economic Role of the Convent: Women and Nuns in Colonial Bahia, 1677–1800." *Hispanic American Historical Review* 54, no. 2 (May 1974): 209–232.

Souza, José Antônio Soares de. "O efêmero quilombo do Pati do Alferes em 1838." *Revista do Instituto Histórico e Geográfico Brasileiro* 295 (April–June 1972): 33–69.

———. "Vassouras e suas residências urbanas." *Revista do Instituto Histórico e Geográfico Brasileiro* 290 (January/March 1971): 22–65.

Stein, Stanley J. *Vassouras: A Brazilian Coffee County, 1850–1900*. Cambridge: Harvard University Press, 1957.

Stulzer, Aurélio. *Notas para a história da vila de Pati do Alferes*. Rio de Janeiro: Lito-Tipo Guanabara, 1944.

Sweigart, Joseph E. *Coffee Factorage and the Emergence of a Brazilian Capital Market, 1850–1888*. New York: Garland Publishing, 1987.

Taunay, Affonso d'Escragnolle. *Pequena história do café no Brasil (1727–1937)*. Rio de Janeiro: Departamento Nacional do Café, 1945.

Taunay, C. A. *Manual do agricultor brazileiro, obra indispensavel a todo o senhor de engenho, fazendeiro e lavrador*. 2nd ed. Rio de Janeiro, 1839.

Tollenare, L[ouis] F[rançois] de. *Notas dominicais, tomadas durante uma viagem em Portugal e no Brasil em 1816, 1817 e 1818*. Salvador, Bahia: Editora Progresso, 1956.

Vernek, Francisco Peixoto de Lacerda. *Memoria sobre a fundação de huma fazenda na provincia do Rio de Janeiro, sua administração e épocas em que se devem fazer as plantações, suas colheitas, etc., etc.* Rio de Janeiro: Laemmert, 1847.

Vide, Sebastião Monteiro da. *Constituições primeiras do Arcebispado da Bahia. Feitas e ordenadas pelo . . . 5º Arcebispo do dito Arcebispado do Conselho de Sua Magestade: Propostas e aceitas em o synodo diocesano que o dito Senhor celebrou em 12 de junho do anno de 1707. Impressas em Lisboa no anno de 1719 e em Coimbra em 1720. . . .* São Paulo: Typ. "2 de Dezembro," 1853.

Vogt, Carlos, and Peter Fry, with the collaboration of Robert W. Slenes. *Cafundó: A África no Brasil – Linguagem e sociedade*. Campinas: Editora da Unicamp; São Paulo: Companhia das Letras, 1996.

Werneck, Francisco Klörs. *História e genealogia fluminense*. Rio de Janeiro: Edição do Autor, 1947.

Werneck, Luiz Peixoto de Lacerda. "Breves considerações sobre a posição atual da lavoura de café," *Almanak Laemmert*, Rio de Janeiro, 1855.

_____. *Idéias sobre colonização, precedidas de uma sucinta exposição dos princípios que regem a população*. Rio de Janeiro: Laemmert, 1855.

Wood, Michael. *The Magician's Doubts: Nabokov and the Risks of Fiction*. London: Chatto and Windus, 1994.

Zaluar, Augusto Emílio. *Peregrinação pela província de São Paulo, 1860–1861*. Belo Horizonte: Itatiaia, 1975.